Mastering Magic Cards

An Introduction to the Art of Masterful Deck Construction

George Baxter
and
Larry W. Smith, Ph.D.

Wordware Publishing, Inc.

Library of Congress Cataloging-in-Publication Data

Baxter, George, 1972-
    Mastering magic cards : an introduction to the art of masterful deck
construction / George Baxter and Larry W. Smith.
     p. cm.
    Includes index.
    ISBN 1-55622-457-5
    1. Card tricks.   2. Conjuring--Equipment and supplies.
    I. Smith, Larry W.   II. Title.
    GV1549.B36   1995
    795.4'38--dc20   95-1307
                                                 CIP

1506 Capital Avenue
Plano, Texas 75074

Printed in the United States of America

ISBN1-55622-457-5

10 9 8 7 6 5 4 3 2

9501

All inquiries for volume purchases of this book should be addressed to
Wordware Publishing, Inc., at the above address. Telephone inquiries may be
made by calling:

(214) 423-0090

Acknowledgements

Many thanks go to Charles Wolfe whose tireless editing efforts and superior knowledge of the game helped make this book what it is.

We would like to thank Wizards of the Coast for their gracious cooperation and general help.

I would like to thank my mother, Wynne Baxter, for providing the support and encouragement to complete the book at times when it seemed impossible to continue. I don't know what I would do without her.

Thanks to Corey Segall and Matt Scoggins for their personal contributions.

Thanks to Robert Utley for his last-minute editing.

Thanks to Squadron 8 class of '95 for their patience.

Last but not least, thanks to the Texas A&M Commons crew for their assistance and commentary.

As always, my wife Priscilla Smith has been there for me, especially in writing this book. She is wonderful beyond words.

This book is dedicated to both our families.

Contents

Foreword

by Richard Garfield,
creator of Magic Cards

I never expected Magic to get the following it has. I used to calculate the success of my games by how much time other people spent on them. With Magic, I created a time black hole, it seems.

The variety of effects are amazing—friendships formed, stores saved, children learning to read and reason. There are bad things too: stores robbed and people getting too involved with the game. I believe the game has brought vastly more good than bad, however.

I have a dream that game-playing become as legitimate and influential a pastime as movie-watching. It seems it should be, as it is more socially involved, and it generates more creativity on the part of the participants. I really think game-playing is a key ingredient in a mentally fit society.

It is flattering to see people interested enough in Magic to be writing books on it. I thank George Baxter and Larry Smith for helping to legitimize game-playing as a hobby.

Section 1

About This Book

Introduction

WARNING: *The lands of Dominia are not a safe place to visit. Few people leave unscathed, and none leave without a huge collection of cards. Enter at your own risk, but be aware that once you have played, it is unlikely that you'll ever quit.*

Foolish mortal, you have opted to read further. More than likely you have already bought and played Magic cards, are irrevocably addicted, and your fate is already sealed. You are more than likely incredibly hooked on the game and see no possibility of redemption. So be it! If you must be addicted and feel an uncontrollable need to play, it is best that you play effectively, and that is what this book is all about. If you have never played and are just interested in the subject or are thinking about starting, this book can teach you everything about Magic strategy, from the most basic axioms known to nearly everyone who plays to some of the most complex and intricate ideas known. This book can serve to make a good player better or to help a beginner become just as good with simply a little time and effort.

The tactics and strategy of Magic are constantly changing as new cards are created and people think of new card combinations. Magic is popular because regardless of what everyone thinks is the best deck, there is always a better one, and sooner or later someone will construct it. In order to effectively keep up with tournament players, who are generally the vanguard of Magic strategy, you must have an understanding of the underlying principles and theories.

This book's purpose is to make you aware of what you need to know to be an effective Magic player. It is designed to help you learn how to be a quality player, regardless of what new cards are introduced and what new rules are invented. The driving ideas behind this book deal with creativity and intelligent game play, which are the essentials of good Magic playing. Intelligent thought is the essence of Magic, and that is what this book is meant to induce.

Mastering Magic Cards also makes an excellent reference book, with a complete list of all known cards in Appendix H, what they do, their rarity, and what the authors think about them. This section is useful to anyone who plays. It lets you learn if there is a card you should be trying to trade for, and whether you should think about a particular card a little longer before you toss it away as useless. Thus, the book serves as a encyclopedia of information for any type of Magic player, since it includes everything from the history of how *Magic: The Gathering*™ came into being to how to play and win tournament games.

Although the book is comprehensive, it is important that you read the rule book first. A rudimentary understanding of the game is essential in order to begin understanding the intricacies of Magic. However, you don't need to have played more than a game or two to be able to follow the ideas developed herein. If you have read the rule book, then read on, and hopefully by the end, you will be a high-level, quality, tournament-ready player, ready to destroy your opponents. And don't worry about that warning at the beginning of the introduction; if you've read the rule book, it's already too late!

History

Magic: The Gathering™, or Magic Cards, was first released in August 1993 by creator, Richard Garfield, a professor of combinatorial mathematics at Whitman College in Walla Walla, Washington. Magic is a fantasy game, played with beautifully hand-painted $2\frac{1}{2}$-by-$3\frac{1}{2}$-inch trading cards. The game requires all of the strategy of chess, the trading savvy of baseball cards, and the deception of poker. It is a game worthy of your intellect!

Magic, one of the newest additions to the strategic world of games, has three major advantages over its predecessors. First, it is easy to learn but difficult to master. Most strategic games require a long learning period, whereas the basic rules of Magic can be learned in under an hour. However becoming an effective player takes considerable experience and analysis. The second advantage is that a game of Magic is normally played in a relatively short period of time. Although the lengths of games are widely variable, generally games can be easily played in under half an hour. Finally, and perhaps most importantly, Magic infuses the element of trading into the game so that the concepts are not static for anyone and are constantly changing and evolving.

The game was casually introduced with very conservative expectations, only to be overwhelmed by an unexpected, yet welcomed, response of enthusiasm. The game has literally captured the imaginations of thousands and taken on a life of its own. Although the object of Magic is deceptively simple, "to beat your opponent with your carefully constructed deck of cards," the game itself is as complex as one wishes to make it. People of all ages can enjoy the game, as it can be played at any degree of difficulty. Some people simply shuffle all their cards together and play, and some people spend weeks honing their thousands of cards down to a sixty-card deck.

Magic is patterned after the game of *Cosmic Encounter* published by Eon Products and later marketed by Mayfair Games. Like Magic, Cosmic Encounter contains an almost limitless variety of alien interactions (or game combinations). Fascinated by how marbles were played in elementary school and the game of Strat-o-matic™ Baseball, Richard Garfield created the game of Magic by combining aspects of all of these. The prototype of Magic consisted of 120 cards that were split randomly between two players. The object of the game was to ante a card and play (duel) until you were too bored to continue. Games could last hours or minutes. At the end of the game, both players counted the number of cards they had and the player with the most won. This was the birth of Magic.

The next stage of the game introduced decks that were independent of each other. Players would still ante cards for play but the winner would keep the cards. This allowed players who were at a lower level of investment to play with others who could afford superior cards. Most of the time, those who had better cards would win more often but lose more valuable cards when they lost. The contents of an individual player's deck were unknown before the duel took place, thereby not allowing the better players to relax and take things for granted. Consequently, the game took on a new level of appearance and infinite possibilities.

The second state was unsurprisingly not the final version. The final version allowed the introduction of new types of cards and new complexities. This version was fully illustrated with color pictures. The pictures were both of a serious and humorous nature, thereby adding to the appeal of the game. For example, Captain Kirk was depicted on the Righteousness card.

Now that a central part of Magic was formed, the key to victory was the construction of winning decks and the effective playing of them. Early playtesters constructed the most effective decks that they could muster. They made everything they could, from small creature swarm decks to land destruction decks.

Finally, the creators feared that the game might become stale and lack cohesion, and that the ability of the game system to hold together without falling in chaos would be seriously compromised. To solve this problem, the world of "Dominia" was conceived, which is an "infinite system of planes through which wizards travel in search of resources to fuel their magic." This added the aspect of role playing to the game. Players could develop themes for their decks that were fun, such as the Elf or Giant deck. Players were also able to construct decks that reflected their own personalities.

Players in the game of Magic tend to swing through cycles of playing to win, playing for fun, collecting and trading, and back again. They find it enjoyable to make an excellent trade with someone, complete a set of cards, or design a colorful fun deck; however there is no comparable feeling to winning a tournament. To be the best at that moment in time. To taste the sweet wine of victory. But no matter how you choose to play the game, you will always be playing against a vast number of people who purchase a vast number of cards, and there is always someone out there who is putting together the next great deck. Just think how many people there are in this country and other continents around the world. The numbers are staggering, and the percentage of them who are playing Magic is growing at a very rapid rate.

One final item deserves mentioning. It is hard to invent a general purpose game that can be played by all age groups and offers the participants an adequate level of challenge. Take the game of chess, for example, with its simple but elegant moves. Although there are not an infinite number of move combinations, there are enough different types of moves to make the game challenging enough for all levels of expertise. The new game of Magic offers its players an almost limitless playing field composed of fantasy terms and mathematical combinations, which can remain exciting as long as people remain creative.

Now that Magic has progressed with time, it is not uncommon for players to come into contact with cards they have never seen before. Eventually, the game will evolve to a point where the pool of cards in existence is so large it will be too difficult to be familiar with all of them. After the printing of the Fallen Empires, there exist over 1,000 cards, and nearly no one can claim to own all of them. Many of the veteran addicts are familiar with each and every one and can recite their name, abilities, casting cost, and color with no reference to aid them; however, whether they will be able to keep up with the growing pool of cards remains to be seen.

With each passing day, more and more people are lured toward the challenge that Magic provides. Wizards of the Coast™ prints more and more cards with each new limited release. Considering how pervasive the game is in society, it is difficult to believe that the game has come so far in the span of only a year.

Magic continues to grow and is quickly becoming recognized as one of the most elaborate strategy games in history. The development of the Convocation International Rating System has helped to legitimize Magic as an intellectual contest of the mind on par with chess. As each player strives to become better than his competitors, he seeks to create a deck that will defeat any opponent. While it is unlikely that any such deck will soon surface, it is our hope, that, with the addition of this book, we will begin the grand debate of just how to construct the ultimate deck.

Section 2

Getting Started with Magic Cards

Introduction

In the previous section we introduced you to a brief history of *Magic: The Gathering*™ and how today's version evolved over time. In this section we will show you how to play a simple introductory game of Magic, where to purchase cards, and demonstrate the process of constructing winning decks. This section will give you a general overview of most of the processes involved in playing Magic.

In order that you will fully understand the concepts that are presented in this book, you should be familiar with two sources of information. The first is the rule book that accompanies each starter deck entitled *Magic: The Gathering,*™ *A Fantasy Trading Card Game by Richard Garfield*. This pamphlet is similar to a rule book and describes all the basic aspects of the game. The second source is a more detailed account of the game entitled *The Magic: The Gathering*™ *Pocket Players' Guide*. It is not as important that you read the *Pocket Players' Guide*, because it mainly contains clarifications of the rules presented in the rule book; however it is always a good idea to read and own a copy of the *Pocket Players' Guide* because it can resolve arguments during play, and very few people will fully understand the rules after just reading the rule book.

Where to Purchase Cards

Magic cards are available at most hobby and game stores. They can be purchased in a wide variety of packages called Starter Decks, Boosters, etc. There are several different series of Magic cards, most of which are limited editions that are out of print. If you are a beginner, you should at least purchase a starter pack consisting of 60 cards, enough cards to play in a tournament. (They cost about $7.95 as of the printing of this book.) Here is a typical starter deck from the Deckmaster™ series showing the attributes (which we will explain later) of each card, name, type, color, mana cost for card type, and other mana and power/toughness:

Colors	BLU	Blue
	BLK	Black
	R	Red
	G	Green
	W	White

Card Characteristics of a Typical Starter Deck

Name of Card	Card Type	Color	Casting Cost		Power/ Toughness	Rarity
			Type [1]	Other [2]		
Circle of Protection: White	Enchantment	White	W	1	-	Common
Circle of Protection: Red	Enchantment	White	W	1	-	Common
Circle of Protection: Blue	Enchantment	White	W	1	-	Common
Creature Bond	Enchant Creature	Blue	BLU	1	-	Common
Dark Ritual	Interrupt	Black	BLK	-	-	Common
Dwarven Warriors	Summon Dwarves	Red	R	2	1/1	Common
Energy Flux	Enchantment	Blue	BLU	2	-	Uncommon
Fire Elemental	Summon Elemental	Red	2 R	3	5/4	Uncommon
Fireball	Sorcery	Red	R	-	-	Common
Firebreathing	Enchant Creature	Red	R	-	-	Common
Forest	Land	Colorless	-	-	-	Common
Forest	Land	Colorless	-	-	-	Common
Forest	Land	Colorless	-	-	-	Common
Forest	Land	Colorless	-	-	-	Common
Glasses of Urza	Artifact	Artifact	-	1	-	Uncommon
Grizzly Bear	Summons Bears	Green	G	1	2/2	Common
Guardian Angel	Instant	White	W	-	-	Common
Healing Salve	Instant	White	W	-	-	Common

Name of Card	Card Type	Color	Casting Cost		Power/ Toughness	Rarity
			Type [1]	Other [2]		
Holy Armor	Enchant Creature	White	W	-	-	Common
Holy Strength	Enchant Creature	White	W	-	-	Common
Ironroot Treefolk	Summon Treefolk	Green	G	4	3/5	Common
Island	Land	Colorless	-	-	-	Common
Island	Land	Colorless	-	-	-	Common
Island	Land	Colorless	-	-	-	Common
Island	Land	Colorless	-	-	-	Common
Mana Vault	Artifact	Artifact	-	1	-	Rare
Merfolk of the Pearl Trident	Summon Merfolk	Blue	BLU	-	1/1	Common
Mesa Pegasus	Summon Pegasus	White	W	1	1/1	Common
Mons's Goblin Raiders	Summon Goblins	Red	R	-	1/1	Common
Mountain	Land	Colorless	-	-	-	Common
Mountain	Land	Colorless	-	-	-	Common
Mountain	Land	Colorless	-	-	-	Common
Mountain	Land	Colorless	-	-	-	Common
Mountain	Land	Colorless	-	-	-	Common
Paralyze	Enchant Creature	Black	BLK	-	-	Common
Pestilence	Enchantment	Black	2 BLK	2	-	Common
Phantasmal Forces	Summon Phantasm	Blue	BLU	3	4/1	Uncommon
Plague Rats	Summon Rats	Black	BLK	2	*/*	Common
Plains	Land	Colorless	-	-	-	Common
Plains	Land	Colorless	-	-	-	Common
Plains	Land	Colorless	-	-	-	Common
Plains	Land	Colorless	-	-	-	Common
Reconstruction	Sorcery	Blue	BLU	1	-	Common
Reverse Polarity	Instant	White	2 W	-	-	Uncommon
Royal Assassin	Summon Assassin	Black	2 BLK	1	1/1	Rare
Scathe Zombies	Summon Zombies	Black	BLK	2	2/2	Common

Name of Card	Card Type	Color	Casting Cost		Power/ Toughness	Rarity
			Type [1]	Other [2]		
Sol Ring	Artifact	Artifact	-	1	-	Uncommon
Spell Blast	Interrupt	Blue	BLU	-	-	Common
Stream of Life	Sorcery	Green	G	-	-	Common
Swamp	Land	Colorless	-	-	-	Common
Swamp	Land	Colorless	-	-	-	Common
Swamp	Land	Colorless	-	-	-	Common
Swamp	Land	Colorless	-	-	-	Common
Terror	Instant	Black	BLK	1	-	Common
Tranquility	Sorcery	Green	G	2	-	Common
Tunnel	Instant	Red	R	-	-	Uncommon
Uthden Troll	Summon Troll	Red	R	2	2/2	Uncommon
Wall of Fire	Summon Wall	Red	2 R	1	0/5	Uncommon
Wall of Water	Summon Wall	Blue	2 BLU	1	0/5	Uncommon
Wild Growth	Enchant Land	Green	G	-	-	Common

1 - Mana of color   2 - Mana of other type (colorless)

Each deck contains a different sampling of cards so you can purchase several starter packs or a different combination of other packs. As you can see in this starter deck, there is a good sampling of unique cards with a few duplicates, four Forests, four Islands, five Mountains, four Plains, and four Swamps. If your objective is to collect as many cards as possible, then you can obtain your cards by playing others for cards or purchasing decks from various sources. Appendix C contains a list of sources for buying Magic cards.

Basic Rules for Early Deck Construction

The key to becoming a successful Magic player is the ability to construct winning decks that contain an effective mix of cards. This is the process called *deck construction*. As you progress in the game, you will learn that good deck construction is the majority of the effort involved in winning at Magic. The rest of the skill in Magic is properly playing your deck once you have created it, and this skill, once learned, applies to most any deck. Thus, deck construction is probably the most important and most difficult skill to learn in order to be an effective Magic player.

A good rule for most beginning players to keep in mind is to limit the amount of trading of cards to almost nothing while you are not sure of relative card values. We recommend that you only trade common cards for the first month of play. This allows you to increase the quality of your decks without accidentally harming the quality of your master collection. A list of commonality of all the cards through the Fallen Empires limited series is provided in Appendix H. Use this as a reference in most of your trades to make sure you are at least trading equivalent rarities of cards. At the same time, not all rare cards are valued the same, and it is a good idea to have some experience with the cards before trading heavily. The reason for this approach is that it will give you enough time to determine the value of many cards, thereby allowing you to avoid those clever sharks who will try to separate you from your best cards. This will also give you enough time to decide which colors you enjoy playing the most and what type of playing style you feel most comfortable with.

With a minimal investment, you should be able to construct a reasonable playing deck. We recommend that you purchase at least one starter deck and around five booster packs to start your collection. Today's total cost for this is approximately $20. Starter decks normally contain two rare cards and several uncommon cards. You only get one rare card in a booster pack; however, the ratio of rare cards in a booster pack is higher for the price you pay, so they tend to be a better overall buy. Starter decks are essential because they contain a copy of the game rules, which you will undoubtedly need even if you already . know how to play.

Once you have purchased your cards, arrange them into separate stacks containing spells of each of the different colors, colorless spells, and lands. In a normal starter deck, you should have approximately 35% lands of varying color in proportion to the colors you play with. For example, if you construct a deck which uses thirty green cards and ten white, you would use roughly fifteen forests and five plains. A good strategy for your beginning games is to play with two colors at a time, in order to begin learning the basics of the colors and how they interact. Also, to begin, you should generally follow the 33% rule, in which your cards consist of 33% creatures, 33% land, and 33% other cards. Red and green tends to be the best combination to start with because it provides many creatures and straightforward game play. It is also a very commonly used color combination because the two colors function very well together and can therefore provide a good deal of insight into how the colors mesh together.

The first decks you construct should be relatively simple and easy to play. This does not mean you should not put any thought into them; instead it means that you should probably stick with creature-based decks and other easy-to-play decks to begin with. Simple creature decks should provide a good base to work from before you move on to decks that are more difficult to master and will still help you learn basic tactics and deck construction techniques. After you construct your initial deck, you will learn through experience which will allow you to play more sophisticated combinations and create more intricate decks.

In general, who you play against will also determine the rate at which your skill progresses. The better your opponents are, the faster you will progress, since you will see new ideas and more complex combinations. However, this is not usually a great deal of fun because you will probably lose more since you are dealing with players who will have better deck construction and gameplay. If you play against people your own skill level, you will probably win more, but you will not learn as fast. Thus, it is a good idea to try to play against better opponents, at least every once in a while, in order to improve your skill level.

Notes on Deck Construction

Deck construction is the essence and art of Magic. In order to win consistently, you will have to learn how to construct decks that will give you the capability to win. While it may seem that someone might be able to construct a deck that would always win, this is not the case, at least not under convocation rules. Regardless of how good a deck is, a player with the ability to construct an exceptional deck should also be able to construct a deck to beat it. This, of course, does not mean that this deck would be able to beat any other deck, but there is no such thing as an indestructible deck.

Because of this, deck construction is both an art and a science. It is a matter of bonding creative ideas with numerical analysis in order to build something that is both surprising and effective. Some decks that were at one time consistent tournament winners are now nothing but derelict antiques because they came into common use and stopped being surprising. For this reason, it is imperative that anyone who wants to win at Magic understand the principles of good deck construction.

Guidelines

The following are some basic guidelines that apply to nearly any Magic deck. They involve the most elementary components of deck construction, and as such are not meant to be a comprehensive analysis. More in-depth coverage will be offered in the sections to follow on basic and advanced deck construction.

60-card Rule

If it can be avoided, you should almost never play with more than 60 cards in your deck. More importantly, if you are playing in a situation in which you can use fewer cards, you generally should. For example, if you are playing in a non-sanctioned tournament in which they allow you to use 40 cards, you should use 40. This is because the fewer cards you have, the greater control you have over the randomness of the deck. Since convocation rules state that you can use no more than four of any type of card, this means the more cards you have in your deck, the less likely the chance that you will draw any specific card. This becomes a particular problem when dealing with the cards which are limited to one per deck, such as the Black Lotus. Thus, using the minimum number of cards allowed under the rules you are playing by helps control the uncertainty of your deck.

Mana Rule

Another basic rule that should be kept in mind is that, in general, your deck should use roughly 33% mana-producing land or zero casting cost artifacts which produce mana. This rule is far from absolute but is a good guideline to play by in order to have enough mana to cast your spells, and to simultaneously avoid having too much mana and not enough spells to cast with it. The exact amount of mana in your deck will vary depending upon several factors:

A. How many colors you are playing with. The more colors you have, the more mana-producing land you will need to play with. This is due to the fact that you want to avoid not having mana of the proper color in your hand, and the more colors you have, the more different types of land you will need to ensure that you will have the appropriate mana to match the spells in your hand.

B. How the colors are weighted; that is, what the percentages are of each color. This is important, because it is imperative that your color-producing mana be balanced with the amount of cards that use it. Otherwise you are likely to find yourself without enough mana to cast important spells.

C. What the casting costs are of each card. This is another important consideration. If most of your cards require only one or two colored mana, you will be able to work with a smaller percentage, because you will need fewer lands in play. However, if your spells all cost several colored mana or involve "X" in their casting cost, you will probably need to use a higher land percentage.

D. How versatile your mana is. Are you using mixed lands, cities of brass, sanding stones, fellwar stones, or celestial prisms? The inclusion of these types of cards allows you to play with a lower percentage of land, because each land you play gives you more options of what to do with it.

A Note to the Beginner

In some cases, you can use as little as 27% lands. Small creature decks rarely need more than this amount to function well because they rarely need more than one or two lands to cast about 85% of their spells. On the other hand, when a player is using multiple colors and cards with expensive casting costs, it is best to be a little more conservative and perhaps play with up to 40% lands. Mixed lands usually provide an easier route to generating a deck because of their added versatility, and when you begin trading, it is a good idea to keep an eye out for them. The only difficulty with relying only on mixed lands is that they can be converted to basic mountains with the Dark card Blood Moon, and this can leave you in serious trouble.

When you first begin playing Magic, you should seek out others who play as well. The more new ideas you encounter with players, the faster your own knowledge of Magic will grow. As you play more experienced players, you will benefit from the time they have had to learn the secrets of the game and to create more effective winning decks. You will generally lose to them, but at the same time, with every defeat, your understanding will grow.

Draw Rule

If you have the ability to draw more cards than your opponent, you will be provided with more options. Each time you draw a card, you are given another possibility, and the more possibilities you have, the greater your chances of having a decisive option. Also, extra drawing of cards is a good counter for the natural depletion that occurs in the course of a game. In general, the player who is drawing more cards will generally glean a telling advantage in most games.

A Starter's Game of Magic

Now that you have learned a little about the art of constructing winning decks, we will examine the process of using five booster packs and a starter deck to create an effective winning deck. We will discuss elementary rules for constructing a deck and some philosophies for beating your opponent. This approach will allow you to begin playing immediately and to progress to your own level of comfort over time.

Don't worry if you do not understand some of the concepts discussed here; they will be explained later. This example is intended to give you a general idea of how you can make an effective deck without spending a great deal of money. You can read this now and keep it in mind as you read the rest of the book, paying close attention to how the maxims presented are applied. It might also be a good idea to look over this section again after you have finished the book in order to reinforce your understanding of these concepts. If you do not know what a card discussed here does, you can look it up in Appendix H.

To illustrate this point, I decided to go out and buy a few cards at the local gaming store. I decided that when I purchased the cards, I would try to assume the mind set of someone who was just starting the game buying their first cards, but I would apply the knowledge that I have amassed about construction and trading. We will start with the beginning purchase, one starter deck and five booster packs:

Starter Deck

Land

3 - Plains   3 - Forests
5 - Mountains   5 - Islands
6 - Swamps   1 - Plateau

Blue	Red	Green
Blue Elemental Blast	Disintegrate	Fog
Life Tap	Hurloon Minotaur	Craw Wurm
Creature Bond	Wall of Stone	Stream of Life
Spell Blast	Fireball	Grizzly Bear
Merfolk	Firebreathing	

Black	White	Artifacts
Frozen Shade	Holy Strength	Living Wall
Howl from Beyond	Swords to Plowshares	Ornithopter
Erg Raiders	Holy Armor	Iron Star
Pestilence	Mesa Pegasus	Ivory Cup
Scathe Zombies	C.O.P. Red	
Terror	C.O.P. White	

Booster Pack 2

Land

2 - Forests   1 - Swamp
1 - Island   1 - Mountain

Blue	Red	Green
Blue Elemental Blast	Lightning Bolt	Craw Wurm

Black	White	Artifacts
Drain Life	Wall of Swords	Dancing Scimitar
	Samite Healer	

Booster Pack 3

Land

1 - Island   2 - Plains
1 - Swamp   1 - Mountain

Blue	Red	Green
Energy Flux	Earthbind	Giant Spider
	Hill Giant	
	Shatter	
	Goblin Balloon Brigade	

Black
Lord of the Pit
Weakness

White
C.O.P. Green

Booster Pack 4

Land
1-Plains   1-Island
1-Forest

Blue
Control Magic
Prodigal Sorcerer

Red
Atog

Green
Llanowar Elves
Scrib Sprites
Wild Growth
Instill Energy

Black
Unholy Strength
Drudge Skeletons

White
Black Ward

Artifacts
Dingus Egg

Booster Pack 5

Land
1 - Forest   1 - Island
1 - Mountain   1 - Swamp

Blue
Psychic Venom
Unsummon
Flight

Red
Stone Rain
Gray Ogre
Orcish Artilary

Green
Lure
War Mammoth
Wall of Wood
Elvish Archer

White
Death Ward

As a first step, I like to assemble the cards into separate piles according to color and then count the total mana I possess for each color. If there is not enough mana for a particular color, then I might see if someone would want to trade a land for a land. Most players should have an ample supply of land cards to trade, and many would be happy to give them away, or at worst sell them to you at a low cost.

Creatures   **Land**
Red: 6   Mountains: 10
Blue: 3   Islands: 9
Green: 10   Forest: 8
White: 3   Plains: 6
Black: 7   Swamp: 9

Cards with a high standalone playing value are:

Green   **Black**   **Blue**
2 - Craw Wurm   1 - Drudge Skeleton   1 - Spell Blast
1 - Llanowar Elf   1 - Lord of the Pit   1 - Prodigal Sorcerer
1 - Scrib Sprite   1 - Unholy Strength   1 - Control Magic
1 - Giant Spider   1 - Terror   ──────────────
1 - Stream of Life   1 - Dark Ritual   Total = 3
1 - Lure   ──────────────
1 - Elvish Archer   Total = 5

──────────────
Total = 8

Red   **White**   **Artifacts**
1 - Fireball   1 - Swords to Plowshares   1 - Dancing Scimitar
1 - Disintegrate   1 - Samite Healer   1 - Living Wall
1 - Kird Ape   1 - Wall of Swords   ──────────────
1 - Goblin Balloon Brigade   ──────────────   Total = 3
──────────────   Total = 3
Total = 4

While constructing an early deck, you should take into account the rules for early deck construction outlined earlier in this section. The first of these rules is the "33% rule." The deck should have roughly one third mana, one third Creatures, and one third Interrupts, Enchantments, Sorceries, Artifacts, and Instants. As you progress in the game, you will probably deviate from this rule, but as a beginner, one should probably stick to the basics, as I will here.

The second rule that you should get into the habit of following is the 60-card rule, mentioned previously in the guidelines for play. For beginning players, this rule is not terribly important since a starting player will most likely not possess a large number of restricted cards. However, almost everyone plays by convocation rules, and since you can only play with four of any one card, it is a good idea to play with sixty cards anyway. If you desire to play in tournaments, then you should definitely get used to playing with the 60-card format.

In your early decks, it is best to work with a creature orientation. This means that you should take a look at what colors will provide the largest number of creatures. In the above cards, red, green, and black provide the largest number of creatures, so I went ahead and chose these colors for the example.

It is usually best to use a variety of creature sizes in your decks. Many beginners make the mistake of attempting to build decks that contain only the largest of creatures. This is not a good winning strategy unless your deck is geared to generate these large creatures quickly, as you will probably suffer early in the game. Decks such as this, with fast large creatures, rely upon a good deal of fast mana, which is hard for beginners to acquire. If the deck is not constructed to produce these large creatures quickly, then these creatures will sit in your hand for the first five to eight turns while you are being overrun by small and medium-sized creatures. On the other hand, you should try to avoid the small horde decks unless you can find some way to avoid being overpowered by larger creatures in the later stages of the game. As a general rule, you should construct your deck such that you can get out small support creatures to block and inflict damage early in the contest until medium and large creatures can take charge and inflict enough damage to kill your opponent.

When constructing an early deck, you should keep in mind that you might be required to remove an opponent's artifacts, enchantments, or creatures to secure a victory. Some cards are better than others for each of these types of removal, but one has to work with what the color provides. For example, the Disenchant is probably the most versatile card in the game for removing artifacts and enchantments. However, if you are not playing with white you cannot use Disenchant; you might have to make do with a Tranquility or a Shatter.

Now that you have a general idea of what a first deck should contain, let's put it all together. A good way to construct decks is to organize them in terms of three blocks, each containing five card pockets with each pocket containing four cards each. This will help you to look at what percentage of the deck consists of creatures, what percentage is mana producing, and what percentage is sorcery, enchantments, instants, and interrupts. Each block is 33% of the deck, which will help you to visualize the necessary mana distribution.

Block 1

	Casting Cost	Power/Tough	Special
Pocket 1: Large Creatures			
Craw Wurm	GG4	6/4	
Craw Wurm	GG4	6/4	
Lord of the Pit	BkBkBk4	3/5	T F1 *
Ironroot Treefolk	G4	3/5	
Pocket 2: Medium/Small Creatures			
Erg Raiders	BK1	2/3	**
Frozen Shade	BK2	0/1 (S+1/+1)	***
Frozen Shade	BK2	0/1 (S+1/+1)	***
Kird Ape	R	1/1 (2/3)	
Pocket 3: Small Creatures			
Llanowar Elf	G	1/1	t/+1g
Grizzly Bear	G1	2/2	
Nether Shadow	BB	1/1	
Scrib Sprites	G	1/1	F1
Pocket 4: Small Creatures			
Goblin Balloon Brigade	R	1/1	
Dwarven Warriors	R2	1/1	****
Scathe Zombies	B2	2/2	
Gray Ogre	R2	2/2	
Pocket 5: Defensive Creatures			
Drudge Skeleton	B1	1/1	Regen
Living Wall	4	0/6	Regen
Giant Spider	G3	2/4	*****
Dancing Scimitar	4	1/5	F1

Legend:

T - Trample, F1 - Flying, Regen - Regeneration, t/1g - Tap to add one green mana

*   Controller must sacrifice one creature a round to Lord of the Pit or suffer 7 points of damage.

**   Erg Raiders must attack each round or their controller suffers 2 points of damage.

***   The Nether Shadow may attack on the turn it is summoned and comes directly into play from the graveyard if there are three creatures above it in the graveyard stack.

****   Dwarven Warriors may tap to make a creature unblockable if that creature has power less than two.

***** Giant Spider may block flying creatures.

The next block of cards in the deck contains all of the non-creature cards. It is best to think of this block as containing cards that enhance your creatures, deal damage to your opponent, provide fast mana, and allow you to draw cards or remove your opponent's troublesome artifacts, enchantments, creatures, and lands. In the case of our deck, we would probably deal with artifact removal by adding the Shatter card. For damage spells and creature removal, the Lightning Bolt, Fireball, and Disintegrate cards might be adequate since they may also be used to reduce an opponent's life points. The Terror is also a good card to play for creature removal since it buries any non-black creature for just two mana. Tranquility will help fight against enchantments. Stream of Life will replenish lost life and help keep you alive longer. Giant Growth, Unholy Strength, Lure, and Howl From Beyond provide excellent creature enhancers.

Block 2

Pocket 1: Direct Damage
Fireball
Disintegrate
Lightning Bolt
Drain Life

Pocket 2: Removal
Terror
Tranquility
Shatter
Stone Rain

Pocket 3: Creature Amps
Unholy Strength
Lure
Howl From Beyond
Giant Growth

Pocket 4: Fast Mana/Other
Wild Growth
Dark Ritual
Pestilence
Red Elemental Blast

Pocket 5: Land/Creature
Elvish Archer
Mountain
Mountain
Mountain

The next block consists only of land cards. I was limited in my choice of lands because of the number of certain types of cards. In this case, I have more mountains than are probably necessary. I added lands in pocket 5 of block 2 because I felt it necessary to increase the number of lands I used because of the number of colors I was using and the expense of the casting cost of certain cards.

Block 3

Pocket 1: Land
Swamp
Swamp
Swamp
Swamp

Pocket 2: Land
Swamp
Swamp
Swamp
Swamp

Pocket 3: Land
Forest
Forest
Forest
Forest

Pocket 4: Land
Forest
Forest
Forest
Forest

Pocket 5: Land
Mountain
Mountain
Mountain
Swamp

Because this deck consists of three colors, we must stretch the 33% rule a little, since there must be a higher ratio of lands. If you have the proper number of cards, it would probably be best to cut your deck down to only two colors. You might also consider trading some cards to improve the winning characteristics of the deck. In order to improve the quality of my deck, I made the following trades:

Trade 1: Gave Hurloon Minotaur for Terror

Reason: Hurloon Minotaurs have an expensive casting cost, making them ineffective in my deck, and Terror is a cheaper and more powerful card.

This trade was advantageous for me as far as card value is concerned.

Trade 2: Holy Strength and Resurrection for Thicket Basilisk

Reason: Both Holy Strength and Resurrection are white cards and do not possess the trading value or standalone value of the Basilisk. The Basilisk slides well into the deck as a defensive creature and combined with the Lure can be a devastating weapon. This trade resulted in a wise profitable value as well.

Trade 3: Swords to Plowshares for Sol Ring

Reason: The Swords to Plowshares is a white card which is useless in my deck and the Sol Ring provides fast mana. This was an even trade.

Trade 4: White Knight and Wall of Swords for Timber Wolf

Reason: Once again, the White Knight and the Wall of Swords are both white, which I will not play with. Though they are uncommon and appear to be better than the 1/1 Banding Wolf, the Wolf is the only green creature available in the revised edition cards that possesses banding and it is a rare card. This was an even trade.

Trade 5: Drain Life for a Llanowar Elf

Reason: Although Drain Life is an excellent card, it requires too many swamps in order to be effective. I needed the fast mana, and the Llanowar Elf provides considerably more than the Drain Life. This was more or less an even trade.

Trade 6: Samite Healer for Drudge Skeleton

Reason: A Drudge Skeleton is much more useful in this deck for several reasons. Obviously, the Samite Healer is white and therefore useless for this deck. Also, a Drudge Skeleton offers excellent and cheap defense and thus complements my deck exquisitely. This was an even trade.

Trade 7: Hill Giant for Dark Ritual

Reason: A Hill Giant was not important for my deck at this point, and I am attempting to phase red out of my deck. Dark Ritual is an extraordinary card providing fast mana, and as such, made an excellent addition to my deck. This trade was somewhat in my favor, since very few people use Hill Giants.

Trade 8: Dingus Egg for Disrupting Scepter and two Dark Rituals

Reason: The Disrupting Scepter offered me the ability to destroy an opponent's hand, and the Dark Rituals offer good, fast mana. The Dingus Egg really had no place in my deck. This trade was not in my favor value-wise, however.

Trade 9: Orcish Artillery for Dark Heart of the Woods and Scavenger Folk

Reason: The Orcish Artillery is good card but too expensive for the deck and is usually most effective when played in a red-white deck.

Both the Scavenger Folk and Dark Heart of the Woods are from the Dark expansion set, adding to their future value, and therefore of beneficial trade value. The Dark Heart of the Woods provides excellent life-giving capacity. The Scavenger Folk have the versatility of being cheap 1/1 creatures and being able to destroy artifacts, which is difficult for both black and green to do. I believe that this trade was to my advantage.

Trade 10: Control Magic for Demonic Tutor

Reason: The Control Magic is a good card, but since it is blue I will not use it. The Demonic Tutor is cheap and a very effective card in that it is limited to one under convocation rules. Basically, the Demonic Tutor provides the caster with any other card in their deck he wants. This was an even trade or possibly slightly in my favor.

Trade 11: Weakness for a Llanowar Elf

Reason: Again, the fast mana of the Llanowar Elf is more important than the Weakness. This trade was also in my favor.

Trade 12: Instill Energy for a Juggernaut

Reason: There is little advantage to using the Instill Energy in this particular deck, but the Juggernaut is a relatively fast, cheap creature that can inflict a large amount of damage. This was a somewhat advantageous trade for me.

Trade 13: Aladdin's Lamp for a Hypnotic Specter

Reason: This was probably the most annoying trade that I made. No one would take my Aladdin's Lamp for anything even though it is a rare card. The reason is because the Lamp costs ten mana to cast. Most people do not realistically believe that they could really cast it. Finally, one of my friends traded me a Hypnotic Specter for it after I begged him and everyone else in the room to make the trade. The Specter is a nice uncommon card because it is relatively cheap, flies, and removes a card at random from an opponent's hand if it damages them. Afterwards, he ripped up the lamp to symbolize an end to my pleading. In the end, I think I could have found someone to trade for my Aladdin's Lamp and gotten a better deal, but very few people actually want an Aladdin's Lamp. Therefore, I consider this trade to be pretty much even, despite the fact that I gave a rare card for an uncommon card.

Trade 14: Psychic Venom for Craw Wurm

Reason: Psychic Venom is blue and the Craw Wurm is a cheap 6/4 creature that fits well into my deck. This trade was slightly in my favor.

Trade 15: Crystal Rod for Scavenger Folk

Reason: I did not need the Crystal Rod, and the Scavenger Folk are cheap creatures and provide artifact removal. Since they are Dark cards, they will probably increase in value, which made this a good trade.

Trade 16: Iron Star for two Scavenger Folk

Reason: The Iron Star is not very effective in my deck because I have very few red spells to use it with. The Scavenger Folk are good for reasons explained above. This trade was in my favor.

Trade 17: Nether Shadow for Living Artifact

Reason: The Nether Shadow is good, but I do not think that it is as good as the Living Artifact, which makes it very difficult to kill. The Nether Shadow is better in mass numbers, which I cannot achieve with my current cards. This trade was also to my advantage, for the most part.

Trade 18: Plateau for Wheel of Fortune

Reason: The Plateau is nice and should not be underrated, but in my deck I play my cards rather quickly, so I think the Wheel of Fortune is well worth giving up a Red White Mixed land that does not help my deck. This was probably a disadvantageous trade for me value-wise; however, Wheel of Fortune cards are not easy to come by, and it is an excellent addition to the structure of my deck.

Trade 19: Plague Rat and Scathe Zombie for two Dark Rituals

Reason: This was a good trade because it enabled my deck to provide a greater amount of fast mana, thereby allowing it to generate much more quickly. The two cards I gave up are not very useful in my deck. In fact, under convocation rules neither is particularly good, since you can only use four of them in a deck.

After these trades have taken place, the deck can be reshaped by reducing the red and increasing black and green. The deck was also made more creature-intensive with a good deal of fast mana and a lower land ratio. The fast mana comes from the Llanowar Elves and the Dark Ritual cards. The Llanowar Elves are particularly powerful because they act as both creatures and as a source of mana. The resulting newer deck has more ways to cope with dangerous artifacts with the addition of the Scavenger Folk, who can act as both creatures and tools for artifact destruction.

Block 1

Pocket 1: Large Creatures
Craw Wurm
Craw Wurm
Craw Wurm
Lord of the Pit

Pocket 2: Mid-sized Creatures
Frozen Shade
Frozen Shade
Hypnotic Specter
Grizzly Bear

Pocket 3: Small Creatures
Timber Wolves
Llanowar Elves
Llanowar Elves
Llanowar Elves

Pocket 4: Small Creatures
Scrib Sprites
Scavenger Folk
Scavenger Folk
Scavenger Folk

Pocket 5: Defensive Creatures
Drudge Skeleton
Drudge Skeleton
Giant Spider
Basilisk

Block 2

Pocket 1: Artifacts/Artifact Creatures
Juggernaut
Living Wall
Disrupting Scepter
Sol Ring

Pocket 2: Deck Manipulation/Life
Accumulation
Living Artifact
Dark Heart of the Woods
Wheel of Fortune
Demonic Tutor

Pocket 3: Creature Removal
Pestilance
Terror
Terror
Fireball

Pocket 4: Fast Mana
Dark Ritual
Dark Ritual
Dark Ritual
Dark Ritual

Pocket 5: Creature Enhancement
Giant Growth
Howl from Beyond
Lure
Unholy Strength

Block 3

Pocket 1: Land/Creature
Elvish Archer
Swamp
Swamp
Swamp

Pocket 2: Land
Swamp
Swamp
Swamp
Swamp

Pocket 3: Land
Mountain
Mountain
Mountain
Swamp

Pocket 4: Land
Forest
Forest
Forest
Forest

Pocket 5: Land
Forest
Forest
Forest
Forest

This deck is extremely versatile, as it contains all of the elements of hand destruction, artifact removal, and creature removal. It also provides the controller with a high, fast mana capacity along with extensive creature capacity. All in all, the deck is fairly well rounded, although it lacks any means to remove enchantments. Tranquility could be added to the deck, but this could be just as harmful as good, since it removes *all* enchantments in the game.

Section 3

Strengths and Weaknesses of the Five Colors

In this section, we will discuss the relative advantages and disadvantages of the individual colors of Magic—white, blue, black, red, and green—with respect to color evaluation and deck construction. The player should be aware that the information presented here is not absolute and is simply a discussion of the relative strengths. The function and general conventions of the use of each color will also be considered. In light of all this information, remember that the disadvantages of each color can be overcome. Advantages are not cast in concrete and can be squandered by unwise use of them.

How Colors Are Used

In Magic, colors are used to indicate the color of mana for a spell that is cast. Each card has a color, whether it be white, blue, black, red, green, or colorless.

Black 💀

Color of Death

The nights in Dominia are full of power, as shadows and black magic traverse their way across the fetid swamps and bogs. Among the dark spirits of the night are the magicians who choose to ally themselves with the accursed power of death. These wizards trade most of their humanity for the power that stems from the bogs and swamps and offers them might that few dream of. The magic of death is often a double-edged sword, however, malevolent to its wielder as well as its victim. Few people summon the awesome might of the Lord of the Pit without being ready to sacrifice their very worldly existence to wield its incredible power, if only for just a few moments. The black magician hunts in the night for his purest enemies, the practitioners of green and white magic.

Weapons of Darkness

There are several advantages inherent to the black magician which allow him many benefits during a duel. One of the primary advantages of black is speed. A black necromancer wields the sacrifice, particularly the Dark Ritual cards. These cards give black an often telling speed advantage, as the necromancer will seldom want for black mana. Black also has a great many regenerating creatures such as the Walking Dead, Drudge Skeletons, and Will-O-The-Wisps. These cards give black a defense that is difficult to overcome with normal creatures.

For example, a black magician can often draw in the first turn a Dark Ritual which will allow him to spend three black mana. Using this, he can summon a Will-O-The-Wisp, Drudge Skeleton, or other regenerating creatures, which will allow him to thwart creature attacks until such a time as he can develop other schemes. Thus, speed and regeneration work together to create a defense.

Black is also blessed with several very powerful enchantments, such as Pestilence or the Abyss. Both of these cards allow the black player to keep the game relatively clear of unwanted creatures and once again allow black to move forward with its plans of darkness. In addition, black is gifted with probably the greatest potential for land destruction. The Demonic Hordes, Blight, and Sinkhole cards make it nearly impossible for your opponent to proceed with his plans due to the lack of mana which black so easily enforces on its opponents.

Another weapon for black is the ability to thwart its opponent with the hand elimination. The Hypnotic Specter, the Hymn to Tourach, and the Mind Twist can collectively keep your opponent desperate for cards and thus desperate for additional options. Black also possesses some of the most powerful large creatures in the game, such as the Yogmoth Demon and the Lord of the Pit. Although these creatures have their individual drawbacks, once they have had a chance to attack, they present a mighty force for the opponent to deal with. Overall, black is not a color to be ignored or taken lightly.

The Price of Evil

As you may have foreseen, there are some disadvantages of black. No magician can deal too closely with the dark and expect to come away totally unscathed. Black may bite the hand that wields it. The Lord of the Pit, for example, expects an offering of flesh and blood in return for its services and will take it, one way or another, as will the Juzam Djinn. Black is also distinctly lacking in its ability to deal with enchantments. Plainly put, black has practically no defense against an opponent's enchantments and is wide open to punishment by them. Artifacts also present a grave difficulty in that black's response to these are direly limited. The Antiquities Limited Edition offers a few cards to deal with this difficulty such as The Gate to Phyrexia, Phyrexian Gremlins, and Artifact Possession, but these cards are a thin defense against a weapon that most decks use in some form or another.

Black is also perilously vulnerable to spells like Cleanse or Karma. These cards can cause a player who relies heavily on black to suffer immensely. This deficiency is worsened by the fact that black has few methods to regain life and thus damage taken is often permanent. In spite of these drawbacks, black is still an excellent color and offers many advantages to the shrewd player.

White

Path of the Righteous

Across the plains of Dominia, the forces of preservation and life work their magic to heal and protect the weak and helpless. The sun shines ever so brightly across the flatlands which provide a home to the righteous workers of the will of their deities, hoping to spread the light of their faith to the rest of the world. The mage who draws power from these plains is imbued with the ability to work these same wonders, the arts of self-defense and rejuvenation. The white magician specializes in spells mainly of a defensive nature and is bound to creatures of virtue. He draws power from the plains of Dominia and uses his power, presumably, to pursue the conscientious path. White magic, although harmless at first glance, often conceals behind this facade weapons of war that are formidable and necessary, since white is directly opposed to the two most aggressive colors, red and black.

The Rewards of Virtue

When dealing with defense, no color is superior to white. The white card selection hosts a plethora of methods by which it can defend against nearly any type of assault imaginable. One of the primary weapons in this bristling porcupine of defense is white's intrinsic ability to remove nearly any offensive opposing cards from play. The Disenchant card allows the removal of both enchantments and artifacts, thus eliminating two of the greatest dangers of the game. Swords to Plowshares allows the removal of a creature, thus allowing nearly any affront to the purity of white to be removed from the game. The sole exception is a land card, in which white's ability to react is very limited. The main option for white to pursue in this case is that of the Armageddon, which destroys both players' land and is thus not an optimal solution.

Classical white is primarily a defensive weapon. However, the addition of new cards in the limited editions has allowed a great deal of flexibility for white and thus provided great offensive power. Although the majority of white's creatures are small, they often possess beneficial powers, such as banding, first strike, and trample. In fact, after the addition of the new limited edition cards, white is teeming with banding and first striking creatures, allowing a great deal of offensive as well as defensive power. This power, for example, is manifested in the Benalish Hero, the Mesa Pegasus, the War Elephant, the Tundra Wolf, and the Pikeman. Additionally, white has the Serra Angel, one of the most effective large creatures of the game. These cards add greatly to any deck's flexibility and aggressive alignment. Therefore, due in part to the addition of several limited edition cards, white possesses a great deal of flexibility and versatility.

Cost of Purity

Although white is often an indispensable part of a well-balanced deck, there are several major disadvantages to its playing power. One major problem is the fact that white's development time is extremely slow in many cases. White often requires several cards together to be effective, and although once it gets going it is quite devastating, it may take quite a while to develop. Many decks that you will face will not offer you any leeway to overcome this type of difficulty. This is by no means an insurmountable problem, especially when white is combined with another color.

Another deficiency of white is its inability to deal direct damage. White has no damage-dealing spells like those of Drain Life or Hurricane. White is primarily a defensive color and is often dramatically lacking when it is attacking. White is very seldom used to stand alone and generally relies on other colors to mount an effective attack.

Green

Teeming Life

As the towering oaks climb their way slowly to the eternal sun, in the heart of the forest wildlife scatters about, pursuing its daily tasks. Amidst all this stands a type of Druid, the green magician. Magicians practicing the green arts derive their powers from the forest and from the life surging around them. They funnel this power into harnessing the forces of nature, the flora, the fauna, and the weather, and forge them into weapons for their own use. Green is a color of life, and the primary weapon of the green magician is life itself in the form of the creatures which he can summon to serve him. All creatures of the forest are eager to obey masters of the arts of life. The power of green is generally used against its opposing colors, blue and black.

The Will of the Woods

The green magician possesses many advantages that make green an excellent color for use in many decks. Green's primary advantage is its quickness. Green can generate creatures very quickly and thus is ideally suited for small creature or "horde" decks. The Minions of Gaea are quick to flock to the aid of the powerful sorcerer. In general, if a deck relies greatly on creatures, green is a good color to use.

Green's array of enchantments is a dominating weapon and source of power. The Living Artifact, Regeneration, and Venom offer the green magician a powerful force to wield, and when used in conjunction with a Verduran Enchantress, then offer an often winning advantage. Green is a good color to use in a deck if you plan on playing with many enchantments, as it essentially dominates this field.

Classical green was almost completely impotent against an opponent's artifacts; however, the addition of the Antiquities and the Dark limited editions allows green some limited ability to deal with artifacts. Crumble is a generally unsatisfactory solution to an enemy's artifact, since artifacts are usually expensive and the Crumble card adds a casting cost to the artifact controller's life. The Scavenger Folk, however, which was added to the Dark edition, offers an excellent opportunity for artifact destruction and releases green from its shackles when dealing with artifacts.

Green has the ability to remove enchantments through the use of Tranquility but has few other methods to do so. This offers some flexibility but is often not the best solution.

The Giant Growth card offers green an excellent surprise advantage and can often force your opponent into unexpected sacrifices. In addition, green has the Stream of Life spell, which offers an inexpensive way to regenerate life, an ability lacking in many colors.

Life Is Not Always Fair

Green has several disadvantages that often make it necessary to play in conjunction with another color. Green lacks the ability to deal damage directly to an opponent or enemy creature; this makes it very difficult to overcome powerful enemy creatures. Green also lacks large flying creatures, which, in addition to the lack of direct damage spells, often spells catastrophe when an opponent plays a Lord of the Pit or other large flying creature.

One of the most serious deficiencies of green is that the Tranquility spell, its only form of enchantment defense, destroys all enchantments in play. This includes the enchantments under the caster's control. The innate difficulty with this is that much of green's strength comes from its excellent enchantments, which will be destroyed if Tranquility is played. Therefore, as with most other colors, green is more often than not complemented with another color.

Red

Mars' Children

On the battlefield atop the rocky crag, cleared of the gray smoke of fire and wrath, the ground was bathed with the crimson hue of shed blood. This is the essence of the red magician's power. Wherever red power is wielded, chaos, fire, war, and destruction soon follow. Magicians who practice red magic are seldom in need of followers, as they are surrounded by droves of goblins and kobolds. They draw their power from the mountains and fetter it to their own ends. Those ends are always and forever destruction. Red is a color of obvious and immediate power and its use is perhaps the easiest to master. Red is the traditional enemy of both blue and white.

The Power of the Flame

Red is the essence of destruction and provides the most powerful damage dealing spells in the game. Disintegrate, Fireball, Lightning Bolt, Chain Lightning, and Pyrotechnics, just to name a few, offer a devastating array of damage-dealing spells. No other color's weapons of assault come close to the chaos and havoc of red. A wizard who practices red magic will have little trouble dealing death and damage to an opponent. This offers red a great deal of versatility when dealing with an enemy who relies mainly on creatures. All of red's damage-dealing spells can be directed at either the opponent or the opponent's creatures. This provides not only a means to win the game but a way to keep the dangerous hordes of enemy creatures from your doorstep.

The red magician has some of the most powerful creatures in the game. The Shivan Dragon and the Rock Hydra can provide a powerful punch to accompany the already devastating effects of the direct damage spells. This combination makes red an excellent addition to any "fast deck." In addition, red offers easy artifact destruction in the Shatter and Shatterstorm cards, which can be overwhelming to an opponent who relies too heavily on artifacts. Red is also strong in land removal capability, since the Stone Rain card is the only basic land destruction card that exists in the revised edition. Although simple to use, red offers some of the most effective weapons of destruction in the game.

Payment in Blood

The major deficiency of the color red is its nearly complete inability to deal with opposing enchantments. Red can neither counter nor remove opposing enchantments and has no real way to decrease their efficacy. The Conversion enchantment of the white card makes red nearly useless. If a red player can scrounge some red mana from a Ruby Mox, Black Lotus, or Sunglasses of Urza, there will still be no method for removing the conversion from play. The other main difficulty for red is in its focus on destructive capabilities. It neglects any method to regain lost life in the same way that black does. Hence, the red practitioner will generally kill or be killed very quickly.

Blue   ◐

The Magic of the Mind

The blue magician is a master of deceit, illusion, trickery, and deception. He is also the controller of the elemental powers of air and water. His association with these elements puts him in constant combat with his traditional enemies: green, the color of the forest, and red, the color of earth and fire. To deal with these enemies, the blue magician draws his power from the oceans of Dominia and funnels this power to spells that generally deal with tricks of the mind and countering an opponent's spells. Blue mages are often seemingly calm and unobtrusive until an enemy moves against them. They then move with all of the power and fury of a raging sea in the midst of a hurricane.

The Mind Is the Ultimate Weapon

In many ways, blue is one of the most effective colors of the game and should never be overlooked when constructing a deck. Many experienced players rely heavily on blue because novice players generally do not appreciate its value and are not equipped to deal with the powerful array of weapons it offers. Blue's primary attraction for long-term players is its counter ability. The Counterspell, Power Sink, and Mana Drain offer some of the most devastating weapons in the entire game. A counterspell can keep any card from entering the game except for a land when the spell is cast. Blue is also equipped with the unique ability to copy or steal artifacts and creatures, and if your opponent is playing blue, you can never feel entirely certain of your position in the game. No matter what weapon you use, you may soon find it backlashing against you, as the blue player finds it possible to use his opponent's strategies against him. Blue has several powerful flying creatures, and with the addition of the Dark and Legends expansion sets, blue has gained a fairly good fast mana capability. The result of all this is that it is important to try and master blue. Although it is not an easy task, it is generally well worth the effort.

Fallacies and Slips of the Mind

One of the major shortcomings of blue is that it is very slow. This poses a problem when reacting to fast creature decks in many cases, and generally other colors are needed to deal with any opposing "fast" decks. Blue is also sadly lacking in its abilities to deal with enemy enchantments and artifacts. Blue has no real assets to deal with artifacts and enchantments once they are on the table, and this can lead to some serious weaknesses. In addition, blue has no particularly effective land destruction capability, which is another small detriment. As a whole, blue is a very effective color, however, and if you are having trouble learning to play it effectively, do not get discouraged. In the end your effort will be well worth the time.

Combinations of Colors

One of the most important points to remember in deck construction and general analysis of the colors of Magic, is that single-color decks are seldom the most effective decks. Almost all the colors are weak in at least one respect, and as such are vulnerable to decks that prey on that weakness. The addition of one or two other colors generally strengthens the overall strength of the deck manifold. As with all tautologies in this book, this is simply a generalization and not an immovable axiom. There is certainly no reason why a single color deck could not be effective if the creator puts enough time and imagination into it. For example, fast decks can be composed of all one color, since the intention is to do away with the opponent before he can develop his own deck. In this case, it is often a boon to deal with only one color, because this will increase the speed of your deck. In general, however, it is important to remember that most of the truly effective decks do not rely solely upon one color. When you mix colors together, you subtract their weaknesses and sum their strengths. This is why it is often a good idea to find colors whose strengths and weaknesses are the exact opposite. The result should be a fairly effective combination.

Section 4

Proper Playing Techniques

Introduction

In order to win in Magic, you will need to be aware of many important playing techniques. An inexperienced player using an experienced player's deck would almost certainly not play as well as if he used his own deck, because without knowing how to properly play the more complex elements of Magic, he would consistently lose to someone who plays with an inferior deck but knows his cards.

Magic is not just a game of deck construction. If it were, it could simply be simulated on a computer after each deck was made. Although deck construction is a key element to winning Magic games, is useless without proper playing technique. No deck will win consistently unless it is properly played.

The most important aspect for a player to remember is to really "know your deck." You must be aware of what cards are in your deck, why, and when they should be played. If you know your deck, you can then reasonably predict the chance of certain cards showing up in your deck at different points in the game, and you can make more informed choices and prepare for the cards you expect or hope to see. Deck awareness is also essential in order to understand what tricks the deck is capable of. You may waste an Instill Energy on a Llanowar Elf, when one turn later you may have been able to play it on a Gaea's Leige, if you are not familiar with the deck. Therefore, it is unwise to play with someone else's deck, unless you are very familiar with it. Also, it is for this reason that when constructing a deck, you should pay close attention to exactly what elements the deck has. The more familiar you are with a deck, the better your chances of winning.

One of the most important axioms of good Magic play is never to play cards too early and never to hesitate to play them at the appropriate time. Playing a card at the proper time implies that it is achieving its maximum effectiveness. You and your opponent will have roughly the same number of cards to work with in the course of a game, so if your cards are individually more effective than his, your deck will cumulatively be more effective and you should be victorious. Also you must always analyze the situation around you and try to act upon it at the appropriate times. Don't worry about how Gloom has spoiled your Circles of Protection; start thinking about the implications of the cards you have remaining and how you can twist his intentions to meet your own needs. Maybe you included a Sleight of Mind in your deck in order to make sure you had circles of the right color. If you Sleight the Gloom to affect black cards, you have hoisted your opponent by his own petard. Quick thinking and forethought are two of the most essential skills of a good player, and you should generally try to utilize as much thought as possible during both deck construction and playing a game. Effective thinking is one of the most important elements of winning games of Magic.

The Use of Fast Effects

One of the most important elements of the game to master is fast effects. They are one of the most complex and simultaneously necessary card types in the entire game. Proper use of them will greatly increase the effectiveness of your deck, and ineffective use will almost certainly doom you to failure. They are not the simplest cards to learn or understand, but they are essential to good game play and deck construction. Additionally, a great many cards fall under this category, and thus if you do not know how to use them properly, the true power of many cards will be lost to you.

The fast effects vary for each of the colors in the game. Although some general paradigms apply, it is instructive to examine them separately. Green has some of the simpler fast effects at this time, so it makes a good introduction to the concepts necessary to play fast effects to their maximum effectiveness. Green has no interrupts outside of the Lifelace and avoid fate, so green's fast effects are obviously made up mostly of instants. Some of the more interesting and useful of these include such cards as Giant Growth, Fog, and Berserk. These cards seem simple, but players can make a plethora of errors when dealing with them. A player can easily make the mistake of playing any of these cards too soon in the game, thus decreasing his or her overall effectiveness. If Fog is played early in the game, it might prevent only a minimal amount of damage; however, if it is saved until your opponent has acquired enough creatures to impose large amounts of damage, Fog could be just the right surprise to snatch victory from the jaws of defeat. This problem is evident in many players' use of the Giant Growth. Some players use this card to inflict an extra three points of damage early on while they have a creature advantage. This is often foolish because the card could be more effectively used to kill an enemy creature or to prevent fatal damage to one of yours. Giant Growth, like all fast effects, can be used at any time during the game, and there should be no hurry in using them. For example if you play a Giant Growth on your attacking Kird Ape during the second turn of the game, you inflict three extra damage points. If you save it until your opponent lightning-bolts your Kird Ape and cast it on him then, you keep your Kird Ape alive for extra turns, in which it will be able to inflict two points of damage (assuming you have forests in play). If it hits your opponent twice, it will be more efficient to use the Giant Growth this way.

There are some other green cards that require a bit of skill in order to play them as well. There is the Stream of Life, which should be played later in the game when you possess enough mana to make it useful. The Living Artifact card should be played in multiples if possible, as its effects are multiplied this way. When it is played this way, it should be played on the opponent's artifacts and not on your own. This makes it more difficult for your opponent to attempt to rid himself of the enchantments by destroying the artifact, since he will have to destroy his own artifact to do so.

Red is another fairly straightforward color, and some of the same rules for the color green also apply to red. The Lightning Bolt, for example, can often be misused in the same way as Giant Growth. Some players make the mistake of using these spells too early in the game. The desire of course is to inflict damage early, but generally this will not be the best use of the card. You have the option to play it any time you have a spare red mana, and thus it does you no real harm to hold on to it and watch for a more useful opportunity in which to use it. This rule also applies to the spell Blood Lust. Fireballs and Disintegrates, however, are not the same story as the Stream of Life. This card only results in the addition of life, which is limited solely to a player target, but these massive damage spells are also good for destroying creatures. In many instances, it is more beneficial to destroy a creature than damage your opponent. For example, if your opponent has a Juggernaut in play, you are better off disintegrating the Juggernaut than doing more damage to your opponent, unless the damage will kill him. Otherwise, the Juggernaut is almost sure to do more damage to you if you cannot block it.

The use of instants is nearly the same for each of the other colors as well. For white there is the Healing Salve, Divine Offering, Alabaster Potion, and the Disenchant. The color blue has the Unsummon and the Twiddle. Black has the Terror. The point of all this is that it is usually best to save your instants. A general rule to follow is to try to play your cards to their greatest effectiveness at all times. This is the essence of winning; your cards are more effective than your opponent's. The developed skill of this strategy is in identifying when you should play the instant card to win the game. You might ask yourself the following question, "If I play this card now, will it have a serious effect on the outcome of the game?" If you have more than one of these instants available, then it may be wiser to play one card in order to gain a temporary advantage, since you have another of the same card to fall back on should a situation arise later on in the game that requires its use.

There are similar tactical difficulties playing the color blue. Blue is probably the most difficult color to play and requires the most practice. The counterspell makes blue perhaps the most powerful color of all, and probably the most difficult. Blue is a reactionary color, and you should ask yourself the same questions as you do when playing instants. For example, if you only have one counterspell in hand, it is probably unwise to use it in order to counter a Benalish Hero, especially if your deck has some easy way to do away with the Hero. Until you have another counter to fall back on you should save it for something particularly threatening. Another important point to remember when playing blue is that you should always have mana available to react to the actions of your opponent. Don't use all your mana to play a Water Elemental during your turn because your opponent may play something that is an absolute nightmare for you and you will have no mana left to counter it. In general, unless you have something of imperative importance in your hand, it is best to save blue mana to counter a spell. If you do not have a counterspell to play, but you do not need two of your mana for something else you are doing, it is a good idea to intentionally save two blue mana. This will make your opponent think twice before playing something important, because he is expecting you to counter it.

In summary, be careful when playing a card. Don't play a card just to play one. Similarly, you should try to avoid playing with an empty hand. As a general rule, you should always entertain an opponent with thoughts of that one powerful card that you are holding back. This is especially important when playing with blue, as you never know when your opponent's last card is a counterspell or something less useful.

Strategy and Mathematics

The game of Magic has some interesting parallels with the field of game theory originally developed by a mathematician. Although games that require more than two persons appear to be more complicated, a two-person duel can offer just as much thrill and challenge as long as the rules of play are comprehensive enough. When you come to the table to play an opponent, you should always assume two basic things:

1. You have an intelligent player.
2. You have a strategy so complete that it cannot be upset by your opponent.

As J.D. Williams states in his book, *The Compleat Strategyst*:

> "You have an opponent who, you must assume, is intelligent and trying to undo you. If you choose a course of action which appears favorable, he may discover your plans and set a trap which capitalizes on the particular choice you have made."

He further states:

> *"A strategy is a plan so complete that it cannot be upset by enemy action or Nature;* for everything that the enemy or Nature may choose to do, together with a set of possible actions for yourself, is just part of the description of the strategy."

A sensible object of a player is to gain as much as possible from the contest as he/she can in the face of a skillful opponent who is pursuing an antithetical goal. Just as successful strategies of many other games revolve around numbers and combinations of events, Magic relies on a conflict in which there are two sets of opposing interests. Each player has a theoretically finite number of strategies, developed over time, from which a single player may choose one. However, in Magic, the possibilities are nearly endless and therefore offer a great range to choose from. In general, however, each player wishes to follow a conservative plan that will maximize his or her average gains; that is as a player of Magic, in any given turn you seek to increase your advantage over your opponent. Mathematics has been called the "queen of sciences" and can be used as another formidable weapon against your opponent in developing winning strategies.

Playing Magic is as much a test of cerebral fitness as almost any other widely played game. Playing Magic will improve your memory, stimulate concentration, increase your overall visualization, and sharpen your mind. Magic is a form of mental competition, and you will need your mind to win a game.

Mathematically speaking, it is up to you what type of strategy you wish to use in the game of Magic. We do not recommend one approach over another but will say that any approach is probably better than no approach at all. Since there are a countless number of game combinations that you can face, some statistical system might aid you in determining how to outwit your opponent.

Probability and Statistics

A rudimentary knowledge of probability can be quite helpful in deck design. This section will outline some of the basic probability calculations that can be applied in the game of Magic. If you want to circumvent the mathematics, the final results of the analysis are summarized at the end; however, these methods can be worthwhile when designing your own decks and trying to determine whether they are well designed. The probability that event "A" will occur out of "n" possible outcomes can be expressed mathematically by the formula:

$$P(A) = \frac{\text{possible or favorable outcomes}}{\text{total outcomes}}$$

For example, the probability of choosing a single card, say the ace of spades, from a well-shuffled deck of 52 cards is:

$$P(A) = \frac{1}{52}$$

Since we only get to pick one card and no other, the result is said to be "mutually exclusive" and assumes that the probabilities are equally likely. The probability of any event "A" not happening, denoted "A'" is equal to

```
P(A') = 1 - P(A)
```

and it follows that the probability of "A" happening is

```
P(A)  = 1 - P(A')
```

This idea is essential in determining the probability of obtaining a card in your first draw. The probability of getting a card from a particular block of cards can be determined as follows. We draw eight cards for our first turn, and each card has a chance of being a card from the selected block. The probability we select *at least* one of the cards "A" from the block is one minus the probability that we draw none of the cards from the block "A'." The probability we draw a card that is not from block three as our first card is

$$P(A_1') = \frac{40}{60} \text{ (The number of cards which are not from the selected block)}$$
$$\text{(The number of cards in the deck)}$$

Now, the probability that the second card we draw is not from the selected block becomes

$$P(A_2') = \frac{39}{59} \text{ (The number of cards which are now not from the block)}$$
$$\text{(The number of cards left in the deck)}$$

Applying this idea to each of the eight draws in a starting hand, and multiplying each individual probability together, we arrive at the result for the probability of <u>NOT</u> drawing a card from the selected block:

$$P(A') = \frac{40}{60} \times \frac{39}{59} \times \frac{38}{58} \times \frac{37}{57} \times \frac{36}{56} \times \frac{35}{55} \times \frac{34}{54} \times \frac{33}{53} = 0.0305 \text{ or } 3.1\%$$

This means that the probability of actually drawing a card from any specified block is 1 - 0.0305 or 0.9695 or roughly 97%. This calculation is useful if you are designing a deck where one complete block is land, which is usually an accepted figure. Thus, if block three is all land, you have a 97% chance of drawing at least one land in your starting eight cards.

We can calculate the probability of drawing a card from any specific pocket in exactly the same way, starting with the probability of not drawing a card from a pocket:

$$P(A') = \frac{56}{60} \times \frac{55}{59} \times \frac{54}{58} \times \frac{53}{57} \times \frac{52}{56} \times \frac{51}{55} \times \frac{50}{54} \times \frac{49}{53} = 0.5551 \text{ or } 55.5\%.$$

Subtracting this value from 1 results in 44.55, roughly 45%. This means if we have one pocket (four cards) of any given card in a deck, the probability that we will draw one in our starting eight cards is approximately 45%. This is another important calculation, because current tournament rules limit most cards to four. In order to calculate the probability of getting any specific card, we will once again use the same method

$$P(A') = \frac{59}{60} \times \frac{58}{59} \times \frac{57}{58} \times \frac{56}{57} \times \frac{55}{56} \times \frac{54}{55} \times \frac{53}{54} \times \frac{52}{53} = 0.866 \text{ or } 86.7\%$$

Thus, the probability to get any specific card is about 13.3%. This is applicable if you are playing with a limited card like a Wheel of Fortune or Mind Twist.

You can apply these same methods to calculate the probability of any card you put in your deck. You may notice that the numbers on the top of each fraction, the numerator, range from (60-N) to (53-N), where N is the number of cards in the deck. The denominator is always 60 to 53, thus you can easily calculate the probability of having at least one of any card in your first eight cards.

If you are interested in the odds of getting a certain card in your first "X" cards, you can simply extend the equation "X" times, so that there are "X" fractions multiplied together.

The above is, of course, only a theoretical conclusion. Your ability to win the lottery or a large jackpot in a slot machine is also theoretical. We could perform an empirical experiment a number of times and see how often a particular card is chosen. After the experiment, we might discover that any card is equally likely to be drawn, or we might find that certain cards are drawn more often than others. The results depend upon the individual and how the deck is shuffled. An appropriate analogy would be asking yourself if you would win more games of Blackjack if the dealer is playing with a single deck of cards versus multiple decks. The answer probably lies in the way in which the deck or decks are shuffled. These variables are hard to express analytically and therefore constitute the primary reason why the art of prediction is unpredictable at best. This is what makes most games such as Magic interesting and fun to play. If you are a person who feels lucky, then you probably are just as lucky as you feel.

Playing Etiquette

In general, Magic playing can be divided into two types: tournament play and friendly play. There are important distinctions between these two types of duels. This section deals with those aspects which you should generally avoid in friendly games, because the point of friendly games is to have fun and develop new ideas. Therefore, when you play your friends, you do not have to play cutthroat Magic. Instead, you should use the opportunity to try something new, develop new ideas for tournament play, or practice using new cards. There are certain cards and certain ways of playing that one should not employ unless sitting behind bulletproof glass, because they are not fun and not conducive to good friendly play. When you play with your friends, experiment to your heart's content and expand your ideas; don't simply try to make ridiculously powerful decks to destroy your friends every time you get the opportunity.

This is not to say you shouldn't play to win, or that you should not try to make effective decks. The point is that certain cards and certain actions are not fun or worthwhile in friendly play. There are certain cards that will cause most players to groan when they see their opponent play them. These cards are of obvious value and are used considerably in tournament decks. However, they are not good cards to help you think of new ideas. As such, you should avoid playing them, except in tournaments or when developing tournament decks.

The first such card that comes to mind is the Chaos Orb. This card is one of the most effective cards in the game. If you are skilled at dropping it, which most people can become skilled at fairly quickly, it provides the elements of enchantment, creature, artifact, and land destruction all at once. The most repugnant fact is that it does all this for a cost of three colorless mana. The result is that some experienced players go to extremes and carry magnetic boards or tape with them to tournaments and stick their cards to the walls. This is a fine solution for tournament play, and I recommend it highly, as the Chaos Orb is possibly the most degenerate card in the game. However, this option is not acceptable for friendly play, and any good sportsman should leave it out of a friendly competition deck.

The Black Vise is another card which should be avoided if at all possible. This card is necessary in the world of Magic as a way to defeat counter decks and therefore is very useful. It is, however, ruthlessly effective, and incredibly obvious. Almost any player will immediately recognize the value of a Black Vise. Once again, this prevents the manifestation of new ideas for deck construction and should be avoided in friendly play. Along the same lines, the Ivory Tower presents an even worse situation than the Black Vise. The Tower gives you life for every card you have in your hand above four. The use of this card can lead to disgusting situations in which players just hold their hands and build up more life than realistically possible to remove in the course of a few hours. When combined with a Library of Leng, this problem becomes even more intense and aggravating. As such, we recommend these cards be avoided if at all possible in the interests of creativity and fun.

The type of deck you construct can also be a source of tension and problems in friendly games on several fronts. First of all, if you are an experienced player and playing with beginners, it might be fun to try and make a less powerful deck to make the game more interesting. Simply knocking around players who haven't had the benefit of a great deal of exposure is not fun for your opponent and does not build your skill of the game. At the same time, if you play worthless decks, your opponent will not learn anything, and the whole game will be a waste of time. Counter decks are also generally not fun decks for friendly play, particularly decks based almost solely around counter cards. With four Power Sinks, four Counterspells, four Spell Blasts, four Mana Drains, and any number of the more specific counterspells, you can deny your opponent the ability to do almost anything. However, this will not be a fun experience for him or you and will be completely without skill-building merit. Although these decks might get you fifth place in a tournament, ignore them for friendly play.

Finally, the way in which you play the game is important. Always be courteous to your opponent or you might just regret it in the future. During non-tournament play, you should make it a point to allow an opponent to take back actions if he changes his mind before you have reacted. In general, most players will even allow this in tournament play, as anyone would appreciate the same courtesy received, and you can be sure that if you don't let them take something back, you will be doomed to the same problems. For example, if your opponent asks to take something back early in the game and you do not allow it, you had better watch your own gameplay closely because you can be certain that there is no chance your opponent will let you take anything back. Simply stated, if you are not playing in a tournament or preparing for one, you should try to have fun and be imaginative. We feel this is the best recipe for strengthening your skill of the game.

Section 5

The Essentials of Good Basic Deck Construction

What Is Deck Construction?

The best way to describe what deck construction is all about is with an analogy. In both collegiate and professional sports, the process of selecting the best athletes is to form the best team possible. This process is called recruiting and is a profession within itself. College and professional sports teams spend large sums of money and countless hours on planes, interviews, etc., trying to select the best available new talent and trading existing talent into their respective organizations. And what is the purpose of it all? To win as many games as possible during the regular playing season to be able to play in a championship game such as the Superbowl or the World Series.

Constructing the best deck of Magic cards is almost like being a professional recruiter. You must think the same way. The players in Magic become "cards" (instead of individuals) and the rest is the same, except for the money, of course. The most fundamental objective of constructing a deck of Magic cards is to win games against your opponents—not too different than selecting the best available talent for your football team to win games during the regular playing season. All in all, both endeavors describe a process and strategy of how to outmaneuver your opponent for the sole purpose of winning and bringing more money into the organization! In the case of professional sports, an additional incentive of financial survival is highly desirable.

What's in a Deck?

The first and probably most important rule of effective deck construction is to have a "theme" for your deck. A theme is the characteristic strategy of a deck. There are an infinite number of themes possible with Magic, because of the incredible number of combinations available with over one thousand cards. You must choose a theme that feels comfortable to you at your playing level and remember to keep the theme consistent during construction of the deck. To construct the most effective decks, you should have prior knowledge of the guidelines that you and your friends have set or you have obtained by playing in a tournament.

Most tournaments require that all decks are subject to "convocation restrictions." These restrictions form the basis for a normal game. The first rule is that you may not have more than *four* cards of any one type in your deck with the exception of the five basic land types: swamps, forests, mountains, plains, and islands. A second rule is that some cards are restricted to only one per deck. The following is a list of these cards:

Ali from Cairo	Mirror Universe
Ancestral Recall	Mishra's Workshop
Berserk	Mox Pearl
Black Lotus	Mox Emerald
Braingeyser	Mox Ruby
Candelabra of Towers	Mox Sapphire
Channel	Mox Jet
Copy Artifact	Recall
Demonic Tutor	Regrowth
Feldon's Cane	Sol Ring
Ivory Tower	Timetwister
Library of Alexandria	Time Walk
Maze of Ith	Wheel of Fortune
Mind Twist	

As new cards are produced, this and other restrictive lists are constantly being updated. There are also many cards that are either involved in ante play or have too many paradoxes inherent in them. The cards listed next are banned from convocation decks:

Bronze Tablet   Jeweled Bird
Contract from Below   Shahrazard
Dark Pact   Tempest Efreet
Demonic Attorney   Time Vault
Divine Intervention

Most tournament decks are usually allowed a fifteen-card sideboard from which you can swap cards in between games. This board must always contain fifteen cards, regardless of how many cards you swap, and thus your deck size cannot change between games.

There are several major characteristics of different card decks. An individual card deck can be rated according to various categories. Some categories are:

1. **Counter Ability**: The "counter ability" of a deck is the most effective measure of its ability to stop an opposing player from utilizing his or her deck to the fullest capacity. All counters are played as interrupts, and one must usually stop an action while it is being cast. This is an ineffective counter to special land cards and also will tie up mana because it is a reaction to the opposing player's spell.

2. **Fast Mana Capability (Speed Mana)**: Speed mana includes cards that speed up the development of a deck by increasing the amount of mana that a player has early in the game. This is an important aspect because you can only play one land per turn. In some cases, it might mean the difference in casting a large creature like a vampire on a second turn instead of a subsequent turn such as the fifth. The classic examples of speed mana are the Moxes, the Lotus and the Sol Ring. Each of these cards is very powerful and desirable to have in your arsenal since all, except the Sol Ring, are out of print.

3. **Damage Capacity**: This factor is a very broad category, as it includes everything in your deck that can inflict damage on your opponent. Most of the time, this refers to creatures and direct damage spells. In some deck configurations, it is difficult to discern the damage capacity because only certain combinations of cards will inflict damage.

4. **Creature Removal**: This category is the ability of a card or deck to remove creatures from play. This ability overlaps with damage capacity in the sense that in many cards, such as Lightning Bolts, the ability to do damage to both creatures and the opposing player is present.

5. **Creature Defense Capacity**: This category is the ability of a card or deck to defend against creatures of all types.

6. **Offensive Creature Capacity**: This category is the ability of a deck to utilize creatures of all types for damaging the opponent.

7. **Mana Capacity**: This category is the percentage of mana contained in a deck.

8. **Damage Spell Percentage**: This category applies strictly to the percentage of damage dealing instants or sorcery a deck possesses.

9. **Enchantment Removal Capacity**: This category is the ability of a deck to remove enchantments from play.

10. **Artifact Removal Capacity**: This category is the ability of a deck to remove artifacts from play.

11. **Card Drawing Capacity**: This category pertains to the ability a deck has to draw more cards than those drawn during the draw phase.

12. **Life Giving Capacity**: This category is the ability of a card or deck to add to your total life points.

13. **Intelligence**: This category pertains to a deck's ability to obtain information about an opponent's unseen cards.

14. **Land Destruction Capacity**: This category pertains to the ability to eliminate the opponent's lands.

15. **Hand Destruction Capacity**: This category involves a deck's ability to reduce the number of cards an opponent has in his hand.

Each of these factors and others you may think of should be considered when constructing your deck. The best way to effectively use a deck is to recognize its inherent weaknesses. Once these weaknesses are identified, they may be overcome. Each of the above factors should be weighed within each of your tournament decks. The best combinations to look for are those that provide you with the highest percentage of as many of the above characteristics as possible. This can be accomplished through the use of versatile cards. For example, the Mishra's Factories from the Antiquities is both a land and a creature. This would fill two different categories, mana capacity and creature capacity. Another example is the Disenchant, which removes both enchantments and artifacts, once again filling two different categories. When constructing decks for tournament play, keep your eyes open for as many versatile cards as you can find.

Deck Theme

Under convocation restrictions, the size of decks must be at least 60 cards with no more than four of any given type of card. Because of the four-card restriction, a player cannot be dependent upon any single card. This is primarily due to the probability that drawing one of the four cards in the first hand of eight is only roughly 45%. With these relatively high odds, the four-card rule makes it difficult for anyone to consistently draw one card each game. Even if the one card comes into play, there is always the possibility that it will be countered with another card. In other words, it is not a good idea to rely on only one card within a deck.

The most effective decks are those that have cards that can be effective on their own without relying on help from other cards and are also able to function well as combinations in the deck. For example, let's examine a deck constructed from common and uncommon cards which function powerfully as individuals yet also perform well together:

The Cheap Mooch Deck

Block One	Block Two	Block Three
Pocket 1	**Pocket 1**	**Pocket 1**
Clone	Control Magic	Island
Clone	Control Magic	Island
Clone	Control Magic	Island
Clone	Control Magic	Island
Pocket 2	**Pocket 2**	**Pocket 2**
Air Elemental	Psychic Venom	Island
Air Elemental	Psychic Venom	Island
Air Elemental	Psychic Venom	Island
Air Elemental	Psychic Venom	Island

Pocket 3	Pocket 3	Pocket 3
Juggernaut	Glasses of Urza	Island
Juggernaut	Sol Ring	Island
Juggernaut	Basalt Monolith	Island
Juggernaut	Basalt Monolith	Island
Pocket 4	**Pocket 4**	**Pocket 4**
Serra Angel	C.O.P. Red	Plains
Glasses of Urza	C.O.P. Red	Plains
Steal Artifact	C.O.P. Red	Plains
Steal Artifact	C.O.P. Red	Plains
Pocket 5	**Pocket 5**	**Pocket 5**
Disenchant	Island	Plains
Disenchant	Island	Plains
Disenchant	Island	Plains
Disenchant	Island	Plains

Sideboard: 15 C.O.P. of mixed colors

Deck Versatility

The above deck configuration is a good example of a versatile deck and should function well against your opponent's deck environment. In the first place, the deck was made to react to a number of your opponent's actions. For instance, if an opponent plays a deck containing black creatures and cards to benefit them, then the Mooch deck must steal those creatures and copy them using the other deck's enhancements against itself. For protection, the deck relies upon circles of protection. If the player of this deck has no idea of the opponent's colors, then during a "convocation match," the circles may be switched out of the sideboard after the first duel.

Card Economy

One of the most basic elements of deck design commonly overlooked by starting players is the idea that cards are only good with respect to what they cost you to use. That is, a card which does a good thing but is horrendously expensive is not a good card unless your deck has some way to circumvent it. For example, the Kird Ape, a common card, costs one red mana to cast and gives you a 1/1 creature, which becomes a 2/3 creature if you have forests in play. This is exceptional, because you will almost never see a 2/3 creature for one mana without some nasty side effect. At the same time, Elder Dragon Legends, which have wonderful powers, are almost useless in tournament play because they cost incredible amounts of mana from different colors. This means that unless you have some clever way to make all this mana available, you will be dead long before you ever get to use these cards. In other words, a card is only good if you get it for a good price, in terms of mana and side effects.

Another important element of card economy is the idea of maximum card effectiveness. In order to beat your opponent, your cards must be more effective than his or hers. This is usually manifest in the ability to destroy your opponent's cards. If one of your cards lets you destroy many of your opponent's cards, than you are getting an effective deal. For example, the Mind Twist is an incredibly effective card because it can allow you to destroy your opponent's hand. This means you could theoretically kill seven or more of your opponent's cards with one card. This is good card economy. At first, the counter cards may seem to violate this and thus not seem economic. However, the act of countering an opponent's cards does not simply destroy one opposing card, it also interferes with your opponent's plans and probably makes some cards in his or her hand useless. Thus another maxim for effective deck construction is to try and make each card in your deck more efficient than cards in your opponent's deck. This is easier said than done!

Surprise Value

Another important idea in deck construction is to try and do that which has not been commonly seen. Most people will include cards in their decks to counter most basic deck themes. Generally, players will include cards to counter burn decks, counter decks, land destruction, and all of these basic themes. It is for this reason that you should be constantly attempting to facilitate your own ideas for decks and not simply play the decks presented in this or any other book. Although many of them are effective, they are generally considered by players who are creating their own decks and thus will often be ineffective.

Sample Decks

The following several chapters will illuminate some of these rules by example. These decks are included as ideas as to the elements of basic theme and card economy. Using these decks will probably help you learn some of the basic ideas of deck construction; however, it is not a good idea to simply try and use them to beat your friends. In order to become a better player, you should try to improve on these decks or create your own from your own ideas. The final sections of this book will deal with how to make even more effective decks and the thought processes involved in this act.

Section 6

Burn Decks

The Brute Force Approach

The idea behind the burn deck is a very simple one, that is to quickly reduce your opponent's life to zero using direct damage spells. These decks are sometimes effective in their simplicity, and a well-constructed one can often beat other tournament-quality decks. One of the major advantages of burn decks is that they do not require many combinations of effective cards. Basically, all you need are mana and damage spells; however, this uncreative mixture will not net you a quality deck. Most high-caliber decks will develop some form of defense well before a burn deck will put them out of the game. The result is that in order to create a truly effective burn deck, other elements must be infused into the deck mix. Certain combinations can often be devastating, especially if your opponent is not prepared to deal with a well-balanced burn deck. It is for this reason that when you are constructing any deck, it should be capable of effectively dealing with a burn deck.

A burn deck almost implicitly requires the use of red cards, since red has the most direct damage spells of any color. Fireball, Disintegrate, Lightning Bolt, Chain Lightning, and Pyrotechnics are the most obvious examples of ways to directly inflict damage on your opponent. These cards are excellent in and of themselves but are not the final word in damage dealing, and their exclusive use will result in an ineffective deck. First of all, the other colors offer cards which can be as effective or more effective than these. The green spell Hurricane, for example, is very useful because it provides a means to do away with all enemy flying creatures. The Hurricane does damage to *all* flying creatures, thereby eliminating many problems at once, which adds to the efficiency of the deck. Spells like the Hurricane and Earthquake are excellent because they allow their caster to reserve their direct damage spells, such as Disintegrate or Drain Life, for later use instead of using them on opposing creatures. This is very beneficial because you can use your direct damage spells to knock your opponent out of the game after he or she has taken considerable damage from the Hurricane or Earthquake.

Black is often a desirable color in a burn deck because it includes the Drain Life, which has a healing element to it, once again offering two effects with one card. Additionally, black offers Pestilence, an excellent card that allows its caster to remove multiple creatures from play. Blue offers the Psionic Blast, which is an instant and thus versatile. White does not offer any obvious direct damage spells but should not, by any means, be ruled out of a burn deck.

Several shortcomings are inherent in a burn deck. One of the most problematic is its inability to deal with fast creature decks, particularly horde decks. Lightning Bolts generally will not be enough to deal with a great number of enemy creatures, or to deal with large ones. In order to combat this problem, several options are available. As previously mentioned, the Hurricane offers an excellent way to remove enemy flying creatures. Additionally, the Earthquake is an optimal solution, as it will do damage to all non-flying creatures, and also is red and does not require the addition of another color. Pestilence is often a good addition since it can remain in play if added together with regenerating creatures. The major difficulty with using Pestilence is that it requires a good deal of black mana to be very effective. One of the optimal solutions to the problem of creature decks is the Abyss, a black legend card, which will quickly eliminate all non-artifact creatures on the table by destroying one each turn.

White provides one of the best solutions to the malady of small creature decks with the cards Balance or Wrath of God. These cards are both excellent because they are able to resolve several problems at once. It is important to keep in mind that strong tournament decks are able to consistently eliminate multiple opposing cards with minimal card cost. Both the Wrath of God and Balance have the power to act in this manner. The Wrath of God will simply bury all creatures in play. Since burn decks do not typically use creatures, the Wrath of God is excellent, since it hurts your opponent by killing his creatures without any negative results for you. Balance is not quite as easy to master as the Wrath of God. Balance, as its name suggests, balances the number of creatures, cards in hand, and lands in play for both players. This card can be difficult to play if your burn deck is heavily laden with land or requires that you hold multiple cards such as Fireballs in your hand. Though Balance is difficult to use in a burn deck, once its difficulties have been overcome, it will provide its controller with a remedy not only to creature decks but also to land destruction and hand destruction.

There are other simpler and more reliable ways of dealing with the creature threat. This method is simply the use of regenerating creatures, such as the Will-O-The-Wisp. It essentially deals with one of the opposing creatures for a very low cost and will usually have long-term benefits. A Shivan Dragon cannot hurt you if you have a wisp in play to block it. Thus, the hurdle of dealing with fast creature decks can be overcome with a little ingenuity and creativity. However, one must become somewhat of an economist when trying to overcome this menace. It is best to limit the number of anti-creature cards to a point where they are easily sideboarded out against a creatureless deck, or else you will be left with many useless cards in your deck.

The other major deficiency of a burn deck is that anyone playing one will burn through his or her hand and be left without cards early in the game. A burn deck player will need some way to replenish his hand or will suffer from this deficit within a few turns. Damage spells will generally leave your hand very quickly in an effort to deal with enemy creatures and inflict damage, so it is necessary to find some type of remedy for this type of card deficiency. To compensate, there are several cards which can be included in a burn deck. The Wheel of Fortune is an excellent solution because it is red, and it allows you to draw a whole new hand. However, it is limited in tournament play and thus will not be an incredible boon. The Timetwister, Ancestral Recall, and Braingeyser offer another good solution if you are including blue in your deck, but most of these cards are out of print and difficult to acquire. The Howling Mine is probably the easiest solution because it is readily available and will add many cards to your hand, but it has the disadvantage of allowing your opponent the very same benefits, which is often times more useful for him because he derives the benefit without having to play the Howling Mine himself.

The main reason that very few tournament players use these kinds of decks is that they are relatively easy to overcome, and the more imaginative players will construct decks that beat them without much trouble. The red circle of protection generally is a tragedy for these decks, and counterspell decks will stop them cold. In general, these are good decks for beginning players, but as you become more advanced, you should move on to something more complicated and effective. This does not mean that a powerful burn deck cannot be constructed. A wily player can develop one of these decks into a devastating weapon, or at least include some elements of the burn deck in other decks that can inflict equal or more damage.

How to Beat Burn Decks

To early players, burn decks will often seem to be the end-all of all decks. Before convocation rules, everyone spoke about decks of all Lightning Bolts and Mountains in which you should theoretically knock your opponent out in the fourth round. But under current convocation rules, these decks are illegal and are not particularly effective. When the damage spells in a burn deck are augmented by a well-thought-out array of support cards, the results can be quite intimidating and often very effective. However, there are several intrinsic deficiencies that make these decks relatively easy to beat.

The first and most obvious solution is a Circle of Protection: Red. This card will eliminate the damage inflicted by most direct spells, Fireball, Disintegrate, Lightning Bolt, etc. Since the majority of these cards are red, a C.O.P.: Red in a deck or sideboard can almost always stop a burn deck dead in its tracks. This solution is not versatile in general and is more applicable in situations where the C.O.P. serves another purpose. For example, if you are concerned about vulnerability to burn decks, the inclusion of several Circles of Protection can eliminate this danger. This deck is even more effective if combined with cards like Orcish Artillery, Earthquake, or Power Surge. This way you can prevent damage from enemy spells or your own. This further means that the circle is useful even if you are not being pelted and destroyed by enemy damage spells, thereby more fully utilizing the circle's potential.

Counterspells and more particularly Blue Elemental Blasts offer a cheap and reliable solution to the burn deck. Blue Elemental Blasts allow most all of your opponent's work to go for naught at a cost of one blue mana, and thus are exceptional cards when you playing against a burn deck. In addition, the more general counterspells offer the opportunity to eliminate other sources of damage, such as Drain

Life. Thus, Counterspells offer an easy opportunity to overcome the burn deck.

Another simple solution is land destruction, which can present a serious problem to a burn deck player. If you are playing against an opponent who wants nothing more than to Fireball you for fifteen points of damage, do not hesitate to make short work of your opponent's lands. They cannot launch their direct damage assault without the aid of a significant amount of mana. To this end, land destruction offers a very feasible solution to this problem.

A Sample Burn Deck

This deck is essentially designed to typify the elements of the burn deck and is fairly cheap for a beginning player to assemble. To this end, we did not include any cards that are out of print or particularly hard to get, except perhaps the Fork. The white cards are not pervasive, and it is not a good idea to use so few of one color of a card. At the same time, they are very useful in overcoming any specific problems that may be causing the deck trouble. In general, this deck can be modified in several different ways to make it more effective. However, this would entail the difficult acquisition of cards that are out of print. Still, with sufficient creativity, nearly any type of deck can be effective.

When playing this deck, there are a few things to remember. First, the age-old adage to hold your Lightning Bolts should always be kept in mind. A Lightning Bolt is an instant and should be kept until it is needed. Using it on the first turn to do three points of damage to your opponent may seem humorous at the time but will not seem so funny when your opponent pulls out a Juggernaut and leaves you high and dry. Hurricanes should be used mainly to remove flying creatures and not so much to cause damage, since they will also do damage to you as well. The Disenchants should be saved for particularly troublesome artifacts or enchantments, since you only have two, and you should always save your Forks for surprise value. In general, this is not a particularly fun deck to play since it is not very aesthetic and offers very few options in order to be clever. It can provide a foundation to make a more interesting deck, however, when you have a few of the more difficult cards to acquire.

Deck Name: The Flame Thrower

Block One	Block Two	Block Three
Pocket 1 **Desc: Instant Damage**	**Pocket 1** **Desc: White Removal**	**Pocket 1** **Desc: Land**
Lightning Bolt	Balance	Forest
Lightning Bolt	Balance	Forest
Lightning Bolt	Disenchant	Forest
Lightning Bolt	Disenchant	Mountain
Pocket 2 **Desc: Chain Lightning**	**Pocket 2** **Desc: Artifact Combo**	**Pocket 2** **Desc: Land**
Chain Lightning	Howling Mine	Mountain
Chain Lightning	Howling Mine	Mountain
Chain Lightning	Black Vise	Mountain
Chain Lightning	Black Vise	Mountain
Pocket 3 **Desc: X Damage Spells**	**Pocket 3** **Desc: Artifact Mana/Life Gen.**	**Pocket 3** **Desc: Land**
Fireball	Sol Ring	Mountain
Fireball	Basalt Monolith	Mountain
Fireball	Basalt Monolith	Mountain
Fireball	Ivory Tower	Mountain
Pocket 4 **Desc: X Damage Spells**	**Pocket 4** **Desc: Life Gen./Spell Enhan.**	**Pocket 4** **Desc: Land**
Disintegrate	Stream of Life	Mountain
Disintegrate	Stream of Life	Mountain
Disintegrate	Fork	Mountain
Disintegrate	Fork	Plains
Pocket 5 **Desc: X Blanket Damage**	**Pocket 5** **Desc: Card Drawing/Land**	**Pocket 5** **Desc: Land**
Hurricane	Jayemdae Tome	Plains
Hurricane	Wheel of Fortune	Plains
Earthquake	Forest	Plains
Earthquake	Forest	Plains

Sideboard:

Disenchant	Earthquake	Forest
Disenchant	Tranquility	Plains
Hurricane	Tranquility	Plains
Hurricane	Tranquility	Mountain
Earthquake	Tranquility	Mountain

Section 7

Land Destruction and Asphyxiation Decks

Secrets of Land Destruction

An overtly obvious method to beat your opponent is to reduce or destroy his or her ability to cast spells. If you can destroy your opponent's ability to cast spells, then your opponent cannot establish defenses. If he cannot defend himself, then he has lost. One way to inhibit your opponent's ability to move forward with his plans is by limiting his ability to generate mana, since almost every spell requires it. Land destruction decks are less common than they used to be due to the fact that much of the land destruction capability has been cut. Black lost the Sinkhole, and green lost the Ice Storm, two particularly effective land destruction cards. This can occur whenever the base set of cards is revised. Green's Ice Storm and Black's Sinkhole were both removed from the base set leaving only red's Stone Rain as a land destruction card. Black's land destruction capability was later enhanced with the introduction of the Blight in the Legends limited edition. Unfortunately, this card did not come close to making up for the loss of the Sinkhole.

Effective land destruction decks should provide enough land destruction potential as to eliminate as many lands as you think an opponent might play. This means that the deck normally has about 33% mana destruction spells or lands. In other words, you need to have the same probability of getting a land destruction card as your opponent has of getting land.

These decks are not easy to construct because they usually rely on multiple colors, and the majority of the cards necessary to construct them are difficult to acquire since many of them are out of print. A good base color to use in land destruction decks is the color green.

Because of the multicolor nature of land destruction decks, the green creatures Birds of Paradise can help overcome the difficulties associated with trying to provide such a variety of colored mana. In fact, a Birds of Paradise is almost indispensable in this deck.

Another tactic used to provide color is the employment of mixed lands. Mixed lands are a nice addition to these decks, but there is difficulty when facing an opponent who uses the Blood Moon card, which turns all special lands into mountains. If you have the Birds of Paradise, Blood Moon is not quite as threatening but it does provide a logical reason to add Tranquility to a sideboard. Mixed lands are virtually indispensable to a land destruction deck, and with the addition of Birds of Paradise, the cost of creating such a deck becomes quite expensive.

Another difficulty that land destruction decks face is the problem of artifact mana. Sometimes a set of Moxes and a Sol Ring can provide just enough mana in a deck to overcome the possibility of land destruction. It is for this reason that most good land destruction decks contain cards for artifact destruction such as Shatter or Crumble. Crumble is particularly useful because of its cheap casting cost and because most mana producing artifacts have a very low, if any, casting cost, making the gain of life minimal. This is an exceptional card in this situation because Crumble only takes one green mana to cast, and since you need so many colors to make a land destruction deck effective, it is imperative that your spells be inexpensive. Thus, in general, Crumble is almost always an excellent addition to a land destruction deck.

Land destruction decks often have problems in dealing with small creature horde decks because of the small creature's low casting cost and speed. There are a few ways around this and you should almost always have some way to deal with this problem, due to the fact that small creature decks are very common. One solution to this problem is the use of the Paralyze card. Paralyze is inexpensive and, if employed in a land destruction deck, is devastating. Since you are simultaneously destroying your opponent's lands, it will be nearly impossible for him to untap his creature. It is particularly effective because it is black, and black is almost always pervasive in a land destruction deck. Another route to defeating small creature decks is to use Lightning Bolts, which are fairly versatile cards. Both of these anti-creature spells also help to exterminate mana-producing creatures, which can be another method for your opponent to circumvent your land destruction. Finally, a few Will-O-The-Wisps are also nice to use in these decks because they will hold off the horde until other means of removal are available. They are also only one mana, which is necessary in order to keep multiple colors from becoming problematic too quickly.

The final major difficulty of land destruction decks is their inability to deal damage effectively. They are usually swamped with cards trying to eliminate enemy lands, artifact mana, and small creatures. That is why it is good to concentrate the majority of a good land destruction deck's damage-dealing capacity into a few cards. Three to five large creatures or damage spells may be effective, especially creatures, because they stay on the table and do not require additional expenditures. Another possibility is to use Black Vices, Ankh of Mishra, and Dingus Eggs. These artifacts work well with land destruction, and the combination of all or some of them greatly improves these decks.

After the production of Legends and the introduction of Equinox, land destruction was damaged. The first way around this card is the use of the Strip Mine, which cannot be stopped by an Equinox because it is not a spell. The Blight is also an effective solution, because in order to use the Equinox, you must tap the land, in which case the Blight destroys it. Of course you can always Disenchant the Equinox, which will remove the problem altogether. However, Disenchant is a very good card and should not be squandered lightly.

How to Beat Land Destruction

The simplest way to overcome land destruction is to use speed. If the cards in your deck do not require significant mana to cast, then it will not make any difference if your opponent destroys your land. For example, if the majority of your damage is dealt by small creatures with casting costs of one, you will be able to cast them with a land which you play in your turn, and your opponent cannot destroy it without allowing you to tap it for mana. Artifact mana is also a good way to get around the problems of land destruction.

Counterspells also provide an effective solution to a land destruction deck. If you can counter enough of your opponent's land destruction spells to allow enough mana to develop to some degree, you should be able to beat the land destruction deck, because once your deck is developed, the land destruction deck will be somewhat lacking.

Also, it is a good idea to put some cards like Equinox or Consecrate Land in your sideboard if you are going to be playing in a tournament. Land destruction decks can be very problematic, and it is a good idea to be prepared for them.

Playing Land Destruction

In playing this land destruction deck, there are a few things to keep in mind. This deck is actually very straightforward to play. In general, you should concentrate on destroying your opponent's lands until he or she seems to be sufficiently subdued, and until you have accumulated enough mana. At this point, you should cast a large creature and use it to inflict a great deal of damage. You should avoid putting out your creatures until you are sure that your opponent is relatively powerless because you have a limited number of creatures in your deck. If they are destroyed, you have very few methods of inflicting damage on your opponent. Therefore, it is important that you do not launch you creature assault too early in the game or you will suffer in the long run.

Deck Name: The Asphyxiator

Block One	Block Two	Block Three
Pocket 1 **Desc: Birds of Paradise**	**Pocket 1** **Desc: Artifact Removal**	**Pocket 1** **Desc: Artifact Mana**
Birds of Paradise	Shatter	Black Lotus
Birds of Paradise	Shatter	Sol Ring
Birds of Paradise	Crumble	Mox Emerald
Birds of Paradise	Crumble	Mox Jet
Pocket 2 **Desc: Creature Defense**	**Pocket 2** **Desc: Restricted Cards**	**Pocket 2** **Desc: Artifact Mana/Card Drawing**
Will-O-The-Wisp	Time Walk	Mox Pearl
Will-O-The-Wisp	Ancestral Recall	Mox Ruby
Will-O-The-Wisp	Demonic Tutor	Mox Sapphire
Will-O-The-Wisp	Regrowth	Library of Alexandria

Pocket 3 Desc: Large Creatures	Pocket 3 Desc: Land Destruction Black	Pocket 3 Desc: Mixed Land Black/Green
Shivan Dragon	Sinkhole	Bayou
Shivan Dragon	Sinkhole	Bayou
Demonic Hordes	Sinkhole	Bayou
Demonic Hordes	Sinkhole	Bayou
Pocket 4 **Desc: Land Kill**	**Pocket 4** **Desc: Land Destruction Red**	**Pocket 4** **Desc: Mixed Land Red/Green**
Strip Mine	Stone Rain	Taiga
Strip Mine	Stone Rain	Taiga
Strip Mine	Stone Rain	Taiga
Strip Mine	Stone Rain	Taiga
Pocket 5 **Desc: Land Creature**	**Pocket 5** **Desc: Land Destruction Green**	**Pocket 5** **Desc: Mixed Land Black/Red**
Mishra's Factory	Ice Storm	Badlands
Mishra's Factory	Ice Storm	Badlands
Mishra's Factory	Ice Storm	Badlands
Mishra's Factory	Ice Storm	Badlands

Sideboard:

Paralyze	Tranquility
Paralyze	Lightning Bolt
Paralyze	Lightning Bolt
Shatter	Lightning Bolt
Shatter	Lightning Bolt
Crumble	Diamond Valley
Crumble	Diamond Valley
Tranquility	

Some problems with land destruction decks are that they require many colors, making them expensive to construct. For the most part, land destruction decks that are cheap and effective cannot be constructed.

Section 8

The Counter Deck

A counter deck's effectiveness is based on its ability to interrupt and arrest an opponent's actions. Because their effectiveness is based on reaction and not their own aggression, these decks fall under the slow deck theory. Good counter decks usually create an environment that renders many of the cards in the opponent's deck useless. For example, a deck might use a Pestilance which will create a hostile environment in order to make an opponent's creatures ineffective, and simultaneously counter the rest of the elements of his opponent's deck. That is, you let your opponent cast his creatures and kill them with the Pestilence, saving your counterspells for the rest of his spells. Most good counter decks are not aggressive, but instead they are simply designed to react to an opponent's moves and hopefully use their momentum against them. This type of result can be evident when an opponent "taps out" on a spell which is countered. For example, when an opponent spends all his or her mana on a Fireball and it is countered, he is completely powerless and at your mercy. Also, a Power Sink is another possibility in order to leave your opponent without any usable mana, which becomes increasingly more likely as the amount of mana your opponent uses in a spell increases. In this case, you have used your opponent's momentum against them, leaving them defenseless against whatever form of aggression you have in your deck. Those addicted to blue's ability to "Just say no" will love tormenting their opponents by halting their carefully constructed decks and stopping their key cards from being played.

There are five major deficiencies of counter decks. These include:

1. Lack of speed
2. Inability to counter fast decks
3. Inflicting damage

4. Removal of a permanent after it has slipped through counters

5. Land

Counter decks are relatively slow, as almost any deck involving blue will generally be, and the player must find some way to compensate or be overrun by an opponent. You can circumvent this speed deficiency by employing fast mana in the deck, such as the Black Lotus and Mox, but these cards are almost impossible to acquire if you are a new player, and generally some other solution will be necessary. With the introduction of the Legends, Mana Drain was added to the set along with a great many other kinds of counters, adding more versatility to the counter deck. Mana Drain is the most exceptional, however, because it has the same two blue mana casting cost of regular counter-spells and has the added ability of taking the mana from an opponent's spell and adding to the caster's pool during the main phase. This is a great advantage to the blue player if he has someplace to channel the mana and provides an optimal solution to the speed problems of blue. The only negative aspect of this solution is that the deck must somehow be able to use mana or suffer horrendous mana burn. One way to use all of the extra mana of a Mana Drain is to put all of that colorless mana into an artifact, or if you add red into a Fireball or Disintegrate. Generally, any card which has "X" in its casting cost will be beneficial for a deck using Mana Drain. Some large creatures like the Mahamoti Djinn, Juggernaut, and Shivan Dragon have a great deal of colorless mana in their casting cost and are good combinations with Mana Drain.

In a properly played counterspell deck, it is imperative that the controller never leave himself without the option of countering an opponent's card. For example, the first counter decks rely on the fact that they can keep their opponents from annoying them with the essential cards of their deck. If at any moment a counter deck is tapped out, then they are vulnerable.

One of the most problematic situations for a counterspell deck is when there are too many cards to counter. This problem comes into play against fast decks, particularly small creature fast decks. For example, it seldom seems worthwhile to counter a Benalish Hero, however, when your opponent has four of them, they become a problem. Still, countering any one of them does not make a huge difference. In addition, your opponent may be pelting you with Lightning Bolts or other low casting cost spells, and you may be unable to counter them all. One way around this problem is the use of hand destruction cards in your deck. If you can force your opponent to discard his hand, then, at worst, you will only have to counter one spell a turn. Certain cards like the Disrupting Scepter, Amnesia, and Mind Twist offer a good method to accomplish this. When the Mind Twist is combined with Mana Drain or Dark Rituals early on, it virtually puts the game in the bag for its caster.

When you pack your deck with counters, there is not room left for many damage dealing cards. This means that with a counter deck you will need to concentrate on the damage that you deal. You could use a small number of large creatures or a concentration of heavy damage spells in order to overcome this problem. Since you will have very few cards in your deck to deal damage, it is essential that each one be extremely effective or else you will have a great deal of difficulty winning the game.

In some situations, you do not have the mana to stop a spell in a series from being cast. In this case, you should have some means of card removal. Returning cards to your opponent's hand is a good way to do this because it allows you the chance to counter them again. Boomerang and Unsummon are often two good ways to have a second chance at countering something. Another good card to add is the Disenchant, which will take care of everything from artifact creatures to enchantments that are causing you problems. You can also consider adding a few direct damage spells such as Drain Life, Psionic Blast, and Fireballs in order to remove your opponent's creatures as well as to inflict damage.

The final problem is that if your opponent has particularly dangerous lands, you will be unable to hamper his or her deck as much as you would like. Land cannot be countered, and there are quite a few lands that can cause serious problems. This is particularly true with the addition of most of the limited editions. There are a few options available to deal with your opponent's special lands, land destruction, Psychic Venom and Blood Moon. Psychic Venom is a good weapon because it is blue. However, if your opponent does not have to tap the land for it to have its effect, this will do you no good. It is usually a good practice to put a few Strip Mines in your sideboard to create land destruction capability in your deck without adding another color. Additionally, Strip Mines can be used for mana.

How to Beat Counterspell Decks

Counterspell decks are a particularly difficult type of deck to deal with, because whatever solutions you find can probably be countered effectively. After the addition of Legends to the card pool, there are a massive number of counterspells available to a counterspell deck: Counterspell, Power Sink, Spells Blast, Mana Drain, Remove Soul, Force Spike, Flash Counter, etc. In order to have an effective deck in spite of this, you will need to put some thought into your deck.

Red Elemental Blasts can sometimes offer a way around a few counterspells, because you can counter the counterspell for only one red mana. Unfortunately, since you will only be able to have a total of four of them in your decks, they will probably not be enough to deal with the same effectiveness as the counterspell. Also, they are completely useless if your opponent is not playing blue, unless you have a Thoughtlace, and are therefore very inflexible.

Counterspells offer an acceptable solution; however, if your deck uses counterspells as well, you will have little room for other cards, and your deck will essentially become a counterspell deck itself. If you try to infuse other elements, you will generally lose out in the counterspell wars and be unable to carry out your plans.

Speed is a good solution to counterspells, because if you are putting many cards into play at a very fast pace, it is unlikely that your opponent will be able to counter them all. Unfortunately, if he or she saves counterspells to deal with particularly important cards in your deck, you will still suffer at your oppenent's hands.

In general, your deck's method for dealing with counterspells will vary with the type of deck it is. It will probably be necessary to think of some kind of creative solution, because counterspell decks are widely used and can be very effective without much thought on the designer's part. Your best bet is to watch for errors in your opponent's gameplay because whenever you use blue, it is not particularly difficult to make errors when using your spells.

Playing the Counter Deck

The example of a counterspell deck is much like the land destruction deck in its gameplay. You must try to counter all your opponent's important cards until you are ready to cast large creatures. However, this task is made easier by the use of Mana Drain which can give you a great deal of colorless mana which can be used in casting a Juggernaut or a Mahamoti Djinn.

The most important element of gameplay with this deck is the proper use of the counterspells. If at all possible, you should always save at least two blue mana at the end of your turn, regardless of whether or not you have a counterspell. This will make your opponent hesitate to play his or her important cards for fear that you will counter it. Obviously, you should not pass up playing a Mahamoti Djinn in order to simply psyche out your opponent, but if you don't really need the mana for anything else, you should try to keep it in order to alter your opponent's gameplay and possibly make him hesitate until you are actually ready to counter it.

Also, try to avoid wasting your Control Magics. Only use them on creatures which are particularly troublesome or you will probably find yourself out of them when you need them the most. At the same time, however, do not hesitate to use them if a creature is giving your opponent a great advantage.

Deck Name: Just Say "No"

Block One	Block Two	Block Three
Pocket 1 **Desc: Large Creatures**	**Pocket 1** **Desc: Counters/Fast Mana**	**Pocket 1** **Desc: Land**
Mahamoti Djinn	Mana Drain	Island
Mahamoti Djinn	Mana Drain	Island
Mahamoti Djinn	Mana Drain	Island
Mahamoti Djinn	Mana Drain	Island
Pocket 2 **Desc: Large Creatures**	**Pocket 2** **Desc: Counters**	**Pocket 2** **Desc: Land**
Juggernaut	Counterspell	Island
Juggernaut	Counterspell	Island
Juggernaut	Counterspell	Island
Juggernaut	Counterspell	Island

Pocket 3 Desc: Counter/Inhibitor	Pocket 3 Desc: Other	Pocket 3 Desc: Land
Power Sink	Time Elemental	Island
Power Sink	Time Elemental	Island
Icy Manipulator	Braingeyser	Island
Icy Manipulator	Time Walk	Island
Pocket 4 **Desc: Fast Mana**	**Pocket 4** **Desc: Restricted Cards**	**Pocket 4** **Desc: Land**
Lotus	Recall	Island
Mox Ruby	Ancestral Recall	Island
Mox Sapphire	Timetwister	Island
Mox Emerald	Library of Alexandria	Island
Pocket 5 **Desc: Fast Mana/intelligence**	**Pocket 5** **Desc: Creators/Creature Removal**	**Pocket 5** **Desc: Land**
Mox Jet	Control Magic	Island
Mox Pearl	Control Magic	Island
Sol Ring	Control Magic	Island
Glasses of Urza	Control Magic	Island

Sideboard:
Blue Elemental Blast
Blue Elemental Blast
Blue Elemental Blast
Blue Elemental Blast
Power Sink
Power Sink
Flash Counter
Flash Counter

Flash Counter
Psychic Purge
Psychic Purge
Psychic Purge
Psychic Purge
Psionic Blast
Psionic Blast

Section 9

Hand Destruction Decks

Another broad category of decks is hand destruction. The hand destruction deck theme has several advantages which make it a very noteworthy deck to use. Hand destruction works on the principle of attrition. Players have a limited number of cards they can obtain, and generally these numbers are similar for both players. Thus, in order for a hand destruction deck to be effective, for each card you play to destroy your opponent's hand, it must destroy also more than one or else you have yielded no result. Thus, the principle in designing a hand destruction deck is to make each hand destruction card capable of destroying several of your opponent's cards.

Hand destruction is possibly the most powerful type of deck if it develops early in the contest. If you destroy your opponent's hand early on, you have stunted his growth for the entire game and he has virtually no chance to win. This is the reason why the Mind Twist is so very effective and therefore a limited card. Three Dark Rituals, a Swamp, a Mox, and a Mind Twist on your first turn can allow you to destroy your opponent's entire hand before they even get to play. Without a hand card to play, your opponent has virtually no chance to develop any kind of defense and will be an easy victim for any assault you choose to launch. For a price of four cards, you have essentially won the game.

Most hand destruction decks are centered around the color black because it offers far and away the best hand destruction cards. The Hypnotic Specter offers a 2/2 flying creature for three mana, which is not a bad deal to begin with, but add the additional advantage of destroying a random opponent's cards and it becomes one of the best deals in the game. The Mind Twist is also an incredibly effective card, especially when combined with fast mana. The Fallen Empire's Mindstab Thrull and Hymn to Tourach added to black's already fearsome hand destruction capability. With the addition of the Dark, the

Amnesia card has given blue an excellent capability in hand destruction as well. Several of the Legends provided even more hand destruction capability. Nebuchadnezzar allows you to see your opponent's hand, which is a valuable asset in a hand destruction deck and additionally presents an opportunity to force an opponent to discard a key element to his deck. It is also advantageous because it is both blue and black and fits in well with the other colors of hand destruction. Gwendlyn Di Corci is another possible addition to hand destruction decks. She can be tapped to force an opponent to discard a card at random without having to inflict damage and is a 3/5 creature, which is somewhat difficult to kill. There are also the Dragon Legend and Nicol Bolas, but as with all Dragon Legends, he is expensive to use in a realistic tournament deck.

Though blue and black are the only colors to provide any effective colored hand destruction, there are several artifacts which are good additions to a hand destruction deck. The Disrupting Scepter is a very effective source of hand destruction, as you can destroy a card from your opponent's hand for just three mana each turn. When combined with other forms of hand destruction like the Hypnotic Specter, it can leave an opponent with very few options. The Wand of Ith offers a less satisfactory alternative because there is a fairly easy way for your opponent to keep from losing the card by simply giving up some life. The Cursed Rack can also be a devastating weapon in a hand destruction arsenal, particularly if it comes out early in the game. In general, most hand destruction decks will need to be augmented with artifacts in order to be particularly effective.

Hand destruction still faces its difficulties against certain decks. These include fast small creature decks and counter decks. Counter decks prove to be a problem if they are given the chance to develop because they can simply counter the hand destruction spells. The only way to effectively circumvent counter decks is to include a few counters in your hand destruction deck. It is not necessary to overload the deck, but you should have approximately six counters to make sure you may cast at least one significant hand destruction spell in order to keep the opposing counter deck from holding multiple counterspells. Some good counters to add to a hand destruction deck are the Mana Drain, which will provide mana for the more expensive hand destruction spells, and the Power Sink, which is best cast to tap out a counter deck when they attempt to cast something on their turn. Flash Counters can be useful because they are slightly easier to cast than counterspells and can counter them.

Small creature decks tend to be a difficulty because they naturally empty their hand and place their creatures into play without giving you much of an option to reduce their power. This is a difficulty that cannot be easily circumvented. A good way to get around the damage dealing capacity of the small creature decks is to utilize some of the black regenerating creatures that can hold off the horde of attacking creatures long enough to begin utilizing your other weapons.

Dealing damage can also be difficult for hand destruction decks, but it is by no means impossible. One can use the Rack, which does one point of damage to an opponent for each card they have below three. These are very effective in multiples because they inhibit opposing players from playing cards too quickly.

Beating Hand Destruction

There are a few cards that significantly damage the effectiveness of hand destruction decks. One particularly menacing card to a hand destruction deck is Balance, which causes both players to have an equal number of cards in their hands and an equal number of creatures and lands in play. If you have just finished devastating your opponent's hand and he plays Balance, you will quickly find yourself in the same situation.

There are a few blue cards that are exceptional for dealing with hand destruction. One such card is the Psychic Purge. When an opponent forces you to discard them, they inflict five points of damage for each one discarded.

The simplest way to deal with hand destruction is to get the cards out of your hand as quickly as possible. When playing against a hand destruction deck, it is acceptable not to hold your Lightning Bolts, because if you do, there is a good chance that you will be forced to later discard them.

Sample Hand Destruction Deck

This deck exemplifies most of the elements of good hand destruction decks and is primarily composed of readily available cards. In playing it effectively, you should try to start destroying your opponent's cards as quickly as possible. The earlier you begin destroying your opponent's cards, the more damaging the effects will be. Once they have already developed, it is not nearly as effective as when they are still trying to get their plans enacted. It is for this reason that you should shun putting out your creatures in lieu of destroying cards early in the game. Destroying your opponent's cards will have more far-reaching and devastating effects.

Deck Name: The Hypnotizer

Block One	Block Two	Block Three
Pocket 1 **Desc: Hippys**	**Pocket 1** **Desc: Hand Destruction**	**Pocket 1** **Desc: Land**
Hypnotic Specter	Mind Twist	Plains
Hypnotic Specter	Disrupting Scepter	Plains
Hypnotic Specter	Disrupting Scepter	Plains
Hypnotic Specter	Demonic Tutor	Swamp
Pocket 2 **Desc: Creature Def.**	**Pocket 2** **Desc: Racks**	**Pocket 2** **Desc: Land**
Will-O-The-Wisp	Rack	Swamp
Will-O-The-Wisp	Rack	Swamp
Drudge Skeleton	Rack	Swamp
Drudge Skeleton	Rack	Swamp
Pocket 3 **Desc: Creature Def./Off.**	**Pocket 3** **Desc: Removal**	**Pocket 3** **Desc: Land**
Drudge Skeleton	Drain Life	Swamp
Drudge Skeleton	Drain Life	Swamp
Juggernaut	Disenchant	Swamp
Juggernaut	Disenchant	Swamp
Pocket 4 **Desc: Creatine Off.**	**Pocket 4** **Desc: Enhance**	**Pocket 4** **Desc: Land**
Juggernaut	Bad Moon	Swamp
Juggernaut	Bad Moon	Swamp
Sengir Vampire	Hymn to Tourach	Swamp
Sengir Vampire	Hymn to Tourach	Swamp

Pocket 5 Desc: Fast Mana	Pocket 5 Desc: Random	Pocket 5 Desc: Land
Dark Ritual	Crystal Rod	Swamp
Dark Ritual	Glasses of Ursa	Swamp
Dark Ritual	Drain Life	Swamp
Dark Ritual	Sol Ring	Swamp

Sideboard:

Crystal Rod	Hymn to Tourach
Crystal Rod	Hymn to Tourach
Disenchant	Drain Life
Disenchant	Drain Life
Terror	Fear
Terror	Fear
Terror	Fear
Terror	

Section 10

The Fast Creature Decks

There are many strategies in Magic to achieve the most effective deck. The most common and reliable effective tournament decks are the fast decks. These decks are designed to eliminate opponents before they have a chance to develop. There are numerous ways to go about constructing this type of deck; however, most fast decks are creature decks or rely heavily upon creatures.

There are two different widely used strategies for the construction of fast creature decks. The first is the "multiple small fast creature deck" and the second is the "singular large fast creature deck." Both types of decks can be very effective and deal a large amount of damage early in the game. If a fast deck plays for longer than ten rounds, then it has probably failed in its attempts to claim a quick victory. All fast decks are designed for a quick kill and often have manifest weaknesses that will become evident if your opponent survives to exploit them.

The most common fast deck is the small creature horde deck. Horde decks are very popular for several reasons. They are very effective and relatively inexpensive to construct. If one does not possess the necessary cards for such a deck, they are relatively easy to acquire. Also, the concepts in developing the decks are some of the easiest to master. The best horde decks tend to come from white, green, and red, because of their great abilities to generate cheap fast creatures. Black is also able to put together fast creature decks because of the fast mana of the Dark Ritual. However, this is usually better used for large fast creature decks.

The horde decks do not require a large amount of mana to support them since most of their creatures cost no more than one or two mana. One can usually get away with using about 16 color mana-producing cards in this type of deck. This excludes mana-producing cards with a casting cost greater than zero since you cannot get them without with other mana. This low mana ratio will make you somewhat more vulnerable to land destruction than you would be with more lands; however, it is practically useless to have five or six lands in play when most of your creatures only require one to cast.

The white small creature deck has the advantage of having a great number of creatures with banding and first strike abilities. This makes for a rather wicked combination, especially for defensive maneuvers. White also benefits from cards such as the Army of Allah and Morale, which can create situations in which three of four 1/1 creatures can deal an incredible amount of damage. Also, white has Crusades and Jihads, which allow the small creatures to become significantly more powerful at a fairly low cost. You can double your damage output at a cost of two or three mana, and when you have a great number of creatures, the results can be deadly.

Green and red work together well in small creature decks because of their intermeshing damage capacity and fast creature generation. This mix provides such powerful cards as the Kird Ape, Scrib Sprite, Giant Growth, Blood Lust, and Lightning Bolt. Red's destructive addition of Fireballs, Disintegrates, and Dragon Whelps give the deck additional punch for later in the game if the deck is unable to score a quick victory. Green facilitates this with the addition of fast mana through Birds of Paradise and Llanowar Elves. Green also provides cheap 2/2 creatures such as the Grizzly Bear and Barbary Ape. The Dark boosted green with more versatility and fast mana by adding the Scavenger Folk and Gaea's Touch.

The large fast creature deck is usually concerned with producing enough fast mana early on to summon a creature large enough to dominate the playing area. There are many different versions of this which include such giant creatures as the Craw Wurm, Juzam Djinn, Juggernaut, and Mahamoti Djinn. The difficulty with the large fast creature decks is that they usually use a three or four card combination to summon their great beast. This puts the player at a great disadvantage if he loses his creature or the creature is rendered ineffective. As an example, consider this play sequence:

A player has a first hand with a Dark Ritual, two swamps, a Sol Ring, a Juzam Djinn, Juggernaut, Strip Mine, and Unholy Strength:

Play 1:   The player with the large fast creature deck goes first.

Step 1:   He lays a swamp.

Step 2:   He taps the swamp for a Dark Ritual adding three black mana to his pool.

Step 3:   He uses one black mana to cast Sol Ring.

Step 4:   He taps Sol Ring to add two colorless mana to his pool and then uses them and the remaining two black to cast the 5/5 Juzam Djinn.

This is an excellent first hand. The Djinn is a very cheap yet effective creature with just one drawback. The Djinn card does only one damage to its caster each round during his upkeep. This matter has little relevance if the player is able to inflict five points of damage each round. If the opposing player plays a Dark Ritual, they might play both a Will-O-The-Wisp and a Drudge Skeleton. They will then probably take five points of damage but will be able to stop all attacks from that point on, and at the same time, the first player will take one point of damage every following upkeep phase from his own Juzam Djinn.

The small creature horde deck is almost the opposite of the large fast creature deck. Where the large fast creature deck depends heavily upon having the right combination of cards on the first hand, the small fast creature deck is almost assured a workable draw. Where the large fast creature deck invests many cards in the production of one creature, the small fast creature deck distributes its risk amongst many creatures.

One of the best combinations for the small fast creature deck is known as the Kird Ape deck. Kird Apes count as 2/3 creatures if they have forest to play in. This is exceptional because of their low casting cost. Green is loaded with other fast creatures to complement the Apes. Both red and green have very effective instants to add to the damage that their small creatures can inflict. These include such instants as Blood Lust, Giant Growth, and Lightning Bolts.

As the game progresses with a small fast creature deck, mana tends to accumulate. This mana is very beneficial for large Fireballs and Disintegrates, although it is essentially useless for the remainder of cards in the deck.

How to Beat Fast Creature Decks

In order to beat fast creature decks, you can do several things. Cards which deal damage to all creatures in play or kill all creatures in play are effective against these types of decks. These include the Wrath of God, Balance, Pestilance, Earthquake, and many other types of cards.

Also, the use of regenerating creatures can buy you the time you may need in order to develop your own deck. Creatures such as the Will-O-The-Wisp and Drudge Skeleton can offer you excellent early game defense and allow you some breathing room.

A large trampling creature can be a nightmare for a small creature horde deck because it takes many small creatures to prevent its damage. For example, it would take nine 1/1 creatures in order to stop the damage from a Colossus. Thus, if the creatures cannot kill you before you can get this card out, your opponent is in a serious predicament.

Charles' Kird Ape Deck

This deck is probably one of the most effective and inexpensive decks to construct. The earliest version was developed by Charles Wolfe back in the days when we played for ante. Charles would rake us over the coals with this deck, winning some of our rare cards and occasionally losing a common or two. All in all, one of the first good decks for a tournament player to construct without having to make large investments is the Kird Ape deck.

The strategy behind the Kird Ape deck is to deploy your small creatures early in the contest and remove any opposition that they may later face with damage spells. Early on, most blockers can be removed with Lightning Bolts, and the others can later be taken care of with Fireballs and Disintegrates. These three types of cards also function as creature removal and can inflict damage on opponents. The Kird Ape deck is a small creature deck. It should be able to defeat its opponent within the first ten rounds. If it fails to do this, then it is doubtful that it will at all.

The following is a very simplified, inexpensive example of a Kird Ape deck, and if you ever play for ante, we strongly suggest it:

Deck Name: Charles' Kird Ape Deck

Block One	Block Two	Block Three
Pocket 1	**Pocket 1**	**Pocket 1**
Kird Ape	Lightning Bolt	Regrowth
Kird Ape	Lightning Bolt	Wheel of Fortune
Kird Ape	Lightning Bolt	Mountain
Kird Ape	Lightning Bolt	Mountain
Pocket 2	**Pocket 2**	**Pocket 2**
Scavenger Folk	Disintegrate	Mountain
Scavenger Folk	Disintegrate	Mountain
Scavenger Folk	Disintegrate	Mountain
Scavenger Folk	Disintegrate	Mountain
Pocket 3	**Pocket 3**	**Pocket 3**
Llanowar Elf	Fireball	Mountain
Llanowar Elf	Fireball	Mountain
Llanowar Elf	Fireball	Mountain
Llanowar Elf	Fireball	Forest
Pocket 4	**Pocket 4**	**Pocket 4**
Giant Spider	Hurricane	Forest
Giant Spider	Hurricane	Forest
Giant Spider	Tranquility	Forest
Giant Spider	Tranquility	Forest
Pocket 5	**Pocket 5**	**Pocket 5**
Grizzly Bear	Giant Growth	Forest
Grizzly Bear	Giant Growth	Forest
Grizzly Bear	Giant Growth	Forest
Grizzly Bear	Giant Growth	Forest

Sideboard:

Hurricane	Shatter
Hurricane	Shatter
Chain Lightning	Shatter
Chain Lightning	Shatter
Chain Lightning	Hurr Jackel
Chain Lightning	Hurr Jackel
Tranquility	Lifeforce
Tranquility	

Section 11

Advanced Deck Construction

Introduction

Now that you have been introduced to an array of basic decks, you should begin examining the inherent weakness which they all have in common. All of these decks have the basic problem in that they are all commonplace and expected. Most truly exceptional decks include methods to defeat all of the previously mentioned types of decks. Hence, they are generally not effective in and of themselves, just as mono-color decks are usually not effective alone. In order to have truly effective decks, you must begin to extend your creativity and imagination regarding deck construction.

Complex decks usually have a mixture of the characteristics of different basic decks. The more elaborate the mixture of basic deck characteristics in an advanced deck, the more versatile that deck tends to be. Additionally, advanced decks strive to be ready for any of these basic types of decks because the goal is to be prepared for any type of deck your opponent might throw your way. This is not currently the case with most tournament players, so if you can master these skills, you will have a significant advantage in any tournaments you choose to play in.

Most advanced decks are constructed around the slow deck theory, although this is not always the case. Advanced decks are usually constructed in a manner that allows them to slowly isolate all of an opponent's options or perform some other operation to immobilize the opponent. They work with cohesive strategies, which are a narrowing down of the ideas of basic deck themes, and an amalgamation of basic deck ideas. Generally, they try to use the most effective deck themes instead of the best cards. Advanced decks are not just a collection of powerful individual cards.

In constructing advanced decks, some cards may not be valuable but they are powerful in the deck because each card drawn has a purpose which meshes into the deck's theme. Most advanced decks seek to create an environment which inhibits their opponent's development without damaging the effectiveness of their own. For example, in the Abyss, the deck uses the Abyss card to create an environment which renders most of the opposing creatures ineffective. At the same time, it uses only artifact creatures and thus the Abyss deck has no negative ramifications toward itself. The higher the proportion of your opponent's cards that your environment renders ineffective, the more powerful your deck becomes. Thus, one of the basic goals in advanced deck construction is to render all or most of your opponent's cards ineffective.

There are several skills which a player must possess in order to create advanced, winning, original decks. The three most important of these are creativity, accounting skill, and playing skill. Creativity manifests itself in your ability to create deck ideas which have not been seen before. Accounting skill is the ability to properly balance your deck in order to gain the most effective use of the idea. Playing skill is your ability to properly use the deck once it is created. These three skills can help you to be the best Magic player you can be.

Creativity can be the most important or the least important skill a player can have. In order to win tournaments, you only need accounting and playing skills. It is not difficult to simply copy someone else's idea and improve it through use of accounting skill. For example, if you see a deck you really like, you can take the idea and use your accounting skill to improve upon the concept. Then, if you have the playing skill to use it properly, you may win consistently. Thus, creativity is not always a necessity; however, the addition of this skill allows you to create decks that have the element of surprise which comes into being only through the use of originality and creativity. If your deck is not original, you will lose the element of surprise and people will have already devised plans on how to defeat your deck. If you have a creative and new idea, you accrue an exceptional advantage. Additionally, most people will agree that it is more rewarding to create your own original deck idea and hone it to a weapon. When the ideas are all yours, all the self-award and credit is yours as well.

Creativity is probably the single most difficult skill to master; however, accounting skill can be just as difficult. Accounting skill is necessary in order to make your deck a weapon instead of an idea. You must learn this skill in order to weed out cards that don't match the theme of your deck or replace them with cards which are more effective for the same task. Generally speaking, this skill is very necessary in maximizing the versatility of your deck and each card in it. Accounting skill is extremely important if you wish to create truly effective winning decks.

Playing skill is essentially only acquired through practice. The best way to get this type of practice is to play in tournaments or simulate tournaments with a group of friends. In tournament play, you will come into contact with other players who are serious about winning as you are. These players will demonstrate interesting playing techniques, many of which you may not have seen before. The more tournaments you enter, the more quickly your playing skill will grow. You cannot become effective in Magic without good playing technique because the best deck will be useless if improperly used. The sport of playing in a tournament is the maximum contest and will offer you results from the school of hard knocks.

Deck Environment

Deck environment is essentially a card or a combination of cards which is designed to render an opponent's cards ineffective, make your cards more effective, or both. These cards are usually sorceries, artifacts, or enchantments. There are very few creatures or lands which alter the environment and the effects of instants and interrupts are generally too short-lived to create an environment.

Environmental sorcery often is very effective. Some examples of environmental sorcery include Balance, Wrath of God, Hurricane, Tranquility, and Earthquake. Sorcery is perhaps the least used form of environment because it lacks permanence. Without permanence, sorcery is rendered much less reliable than its more stable counterparts: however, the effects of sorcery on the environment can be very wide-ranging. For example, if you are attempting to create a creatureless environment, a few well-used Wraths of God can keep the board clear, causing your opponent to have wasted many of the cards in his deck, while you will generally not have included many creatures in your deck and will not suffer greatly.

Some examples of environmental artifacts are cards such as Copper Tablets, Armageddon Clocks, Nevinyrral's Disk, Ankhs of Mishra, Dingus Eggs, and Howling Mines. Each of these cards creates some kind of environment which an effective advanced deck will take advantage of. For example, you might use a Relic Barrier with a Howling Mine so that you receive the benefit and your opponent does not. Artifacts are perhaps the easiest of environmental cards to ensure being played on the first few turns. This is because they can be brought into play with the antiquities card Transmute Artifact. Transmute Artifact is not limited, so if an artifact is of great importance, up to four Transmute Artifacts can be added. For example, you are limited to one Forcefield in a local tournament deck; however, with four Transmute Artifacts, you can greatly increase your ability to get it out early in the game. The major difficulty with employing environmental artifacts is that each color has many different ways to dispose of them. There are almost as many cards to deal with artifacts as there are to deal with creatures.

Artifacts are not quite as commonly employed as their enchantment counterparts. This is due to the fact that it is relatively difficult to get rid of enchantments, and their effects on the environment can be very devastating. After the introduction of Legends and the Dark, the number of environmental enchantments almost doubled. Some prime examples of environmental enchantments are Arboria, The Abyss, Nether Void, Season of the Witch, Power Surge, Worms of the Earth, and Blood Moon.

There are only six different easy ways to eliminate enchantments and, with one exception, they all have their limiting factors. The first way to remove enchantments, and probably the most common, is the Disenchant. This is possibly the best common card available because it will remove both enchantments and artifacts, making Disenchants particularly versatile. The second most common card for enchantment removal is Tranquility. The only major difficulty with Tranquility is that it destroys all enchantments in play, including your own, and this can be particularly problematic if you are trying to alter the environment with your own enchantments. The third card that removes enchantments is the Desert Twister. This is an exceptional card because it can destroy not only any enchantment, but any card in play, making it extremely versatile. The major difficulty you encounter with the Desert Twister is its cost. The use of Laces and Elemental Blasts add another way to remove any card in play. The Laces and Elemental

Blasts are cheap, and they act at interrupt speed. The difficulty with this solution lies in the fact that you are using a two-card combination in order to only destroy one card of your opponent's. Nevinyrral's Disk will also eliminate enchantments, but it has the added disadvantage of destroying everything else but land in play. Finally, there is the Chaos Orb. This card is somewhat obnoxious because it adds a physical element to the game. Its major limitation is the fact that it is limited (only one may be in a tournament deck) and that an opponent can render it ineffective by taping his or her cards to the wall.

What to Prepare for When Constructing an Environment

When you formulate a deck environment, you should try to take into account all of the possible opposing decks that your deck may face. The first decks that should be compensated for are all of the basic decks, which include the land destruction, hand destruction, burn, small creature, and counterspell deck. After you formulate a strategy of how to beat each of the five basic decks, it is a good idea to determine the most current popular theme for decks and establish a counter for it. Many of your best chances to overcome opposing decks lie in the development of a strong sideboard. These fifteen cards are perhaps the most difficult cards to assemble. When you construct your sideboard, you should try to account for every possible contingency, including a way to remove each card type (land, artifacts, enchantments, etc.). Also, one of the major difficulties of constructing a strong sideboard is the fact that you have to be able to switch out a number of cards from your deck to your sideboard without destroying its theme and strength.

Section 12

The Abyss

There are many different environments that decks can be constructed around. These environments should limit an opponent without limiting themselves beyond any reasonable amount. A prime example of a strong environment to base a deck around is the Abyss. The Abyss is an enchantment that buries a target non-artifact creature each turn if there is one available from either player. The Abyss deck is constructed with artifact creatures, thus rendering the hazards of the environment ineffective. Most tournament decks rely on some measure of creatures. If they are non-artifact creatures, that entire category of cards can be rendered ineffective in an opponent's deck simply by using four of your sixty cards.

I looked at many different creatures when I constructed the Abyss. The ones I finally settled on were the Juggernauts, Clay Statues, and Mishra's Factories. The Juggernauts provide a concentrated medium for damage dealing. They are each large enough to kill an opponent in four turns. The greatest threat that the deck might face would be yet another deck based around artifact creatures, so the Clay Statues are added to provide a means to block opposing artifact creatures. Clay Statues are excellent for this purpose because they can regenerate and they are also excellent Juggernaut killers. The Mishra's Factories are superb in this deck. To begin with, they cannot be countered because they are land. They also provide colorless mana for other artifacts.

This version of the Abyss is extremely versatile. It possesses a high ratio of hand destruction, counter ability artifact, and creature and enchantment removal. The high percentage of mana and artifact ensures that it will develop quickly. It also has many of the more powerful restricted cards that give it an extra advantage over many decks.

Deck Name: The Abyss

Block One	Block Two	Block Three
Pocket 1	**Pocket 1**	**Pocket 1**
Juggernaut	Lightning Bolt	Volcanic Island
Juggernaut	Mind Twist	Volcanic Island
Juggernaut	Amnesia	Volcanic Island
Juggernaut	Amnesia	Volcanic Island
Pocket 2	**Pocket 2**	**Pocket 2**
Clay Statue	Disenchant	Tundra
Clay Statue	Disenchant	Tundra
Clay Statue	Disenchant	Tundra
Clay Statue	Disenchant	Tundra
Pocket 3	**Pocket 3**	**Pocket 3**
Mishra's Factory	Abyss	Underground Sea
Mishra's Factory	Abyss	Underground Sea
Mishra's Factory	Abyss	Underground Sea
Mishra's Factory	Abyss	Underground Sea
Pocket 4	**Pocket 4**	**Pocket 4**
Mana Drain	Disintegrate	Mox Sapphire
Mana Drain	Tutor	Mox Pearl
Mana Drain	Sol Ring	Mox Jet
Mana Drain	Basalt Monolith	Mox Ruby
Pocket 5	**Pocket 5**	**Pocket 5**
Power Sink	Ancestral Recall	Mox Emerald
Power Sink	Time Walk	Mishra's Workshop
Lightning Bolt	Library of Alexandria	Island
Lightning Bolt	Braingeyser	Island

Sideboard: Divine Offering   Equinox
              Divine Offering   Blue Elemental Blast
              Consecrate Land   Red Elemental Blast
              Consecrate Land   Red Elemental Blast
              Consecrate Land   Power Sink
              Consecrate Land   C.O.P. Red
              Strip Mine   C.O.P. Red
              Strip Mine

The Abyss' sideboard is constructed to deal with land destruction with the Consecrate Land and Equinox. It can deal with more artifacts with the Divine Offerings. The sideboard can be switched around to help face counterspell and burn decks with the Red Blasts and Blue Blasts. The C.O.P. Reds also help to stop the Red Burn decks because most burn decks forward a problem for the Abyss. If a burn deck has no creatures, then the Abysses can be switched out for the C.O.P. Reds and the Blue Blasts.

Section 13

The Mind Grinder

In the game of Magic, there are really only three different ways to defeat an opponent. These methods include reducing his or her life to zero, forcing him to take ten or more poison counters, or forcing the opponent to draw an entire deck. The last tactic is often referred to as "deck depletion." Employing this tactic has several advantages, the first of which is that you render all of an opponent's life-giving and damage-prevention cards useless. Another advantage is that generally an opponent will not be prepared for this kind of attack, since most games are usually won by reducing your opponent's life. Also, this allows certain cards you may wish to play that give your opponent life, such as Swords to Plowshares, and Crumble, to lose their major disadvantage. That is, when you use one of these cards, the major problem is that you give them life when you don't need to reduce their life, these cards have no bad side. Thus, the idea of deck depletion holds some major advantages over standard life reduction.

The Mind Grinder slowly grinds away an opponent's deck while he or she struggles to overcome its plethora of defenses. The idea behind it is to try to acquire enough life and simultaneously keep an opponent from harming you for as long as possible while you deplete his or her deck with your Millstones. The optimum situation for this deck to function is in a deck containing a Field of Dreams, which forces both players to turn the top card of their library face up, and a Millstone. When this occurs, you can moderate which cards an opponent receives by simply forcing him or her to discard those that threaten you. For example, if you know your opponent is desperately waiting for some white mana to cast a Disenchant in his or her hand, Field of Dreams will let you know that it is coming up and will allow you to force them to discard it with the Millstone.

One of the most essential cards in the deck is the Balance. Typically when playing the Mind Grinder, you drop your hand into play early on with several zero casting cost artifacts. After you have reduced the number of cards in your hand, you will than have the ability to Balance and force your opponent to discard some portion of his or her hand. This strengthens the counter ability of the deck, since most of what will remain in your hand will be counterspells, and forces your opponent to suffer from the same ailments you have. Balance also serves to eliminate all opposing creatures and is also a good counter for land destruction decks. The Icy Manipulators can be used to tap creatures before your Balance and then to tap lands, so that your opponent will have more difficulty developing after you Balance.

A large proportion of this deck is built to force your opponent to suffer under different environments. The Blood Moon punishes those who rely on special lands or mixed lands without greatly inconveniencing the Mind Grinder. The fact that the deck has absolutely no creatures adds to its environment, since all of your opposing player's anti-creature spells are also rendered useless.

The sideboard holds enough to counter all of the basic deck types. The counterspells can be rearranged depending on the mana distribution of an opposing deck. There are even more anti-creature cards in the sideboard for large fast creature decks. I chose to use Swords to Plowshares because it does not matter if an opponent gains life or not from its use. The Divine Offering is also included because of its added life-giving capacity if your opponent is using large artifacts. The extra Blood Moons also help against most land destruction decks because of their multicolored nature. The C.O.P. Reds are to help to combat burn decks and other red-based decks. If the Mind Grinder is not working for you, feel free to change it. It is a difficult deck to design and even more difficult to play. You may be able to make a deck that meshes with your playing style more effectively.

Deck Name: The Mind Grinder

Block One	Block Two	Block Three
Pocket 1 **Desc: Millstones**	**Pocket 1** **Desc: Icy Manipulator**	**Pocket 1** **Desc: Artifact Mana**
Millstone	Icy Manipulator	Mox Jet
Millstone	Icy Manipulator	Mox Sapphire
Millstone	Icy Manipulator	Mox Emerald
Millstone	Icy Manipulator	Mox Pearl
Pocket 2 **Desc: Fountains**	**Pocket 2** **Desc: Mana Drains**	**Pocket 2** **Desc: Land/Artifact**
Fountain of Youth	Mana Drain	Volcanic Island
Fountain of Youth	Mana Drain	Volcanic Island
Fountain of Youth	Mana Drain	Volcanic Island
Fountain of Youth	Mana Drain	Island
Pocket 3 **Desc: Crypt/ Glasses**	**Pocket 3** **Desc: Counterspells**	**Pocket 3** **Desc: Land**
Tornod's Crypt	Power Sink	Island
Tornod's Crypt	Power Sink	Island
Glasses of Urza	Spell Blast	Island
Glasses of Urza	Spell Blast	Island
Pocket 4 **Desc: Balance**	**Pocket 4** **Desc: Other**	**Pocket 4** **Desc: Land**
Balance	Disenchant	Island
Balance	Disenchant	Island
Balance	Braingeyser	Island
Balance	Ancestral Recall	Tundra
Pocket 5 **Desc: Enchantment** **Environment**	**Pocket 5** **Desc: Random Other**	**Pocket 5** **Desc: Land**
Field of Dreams	Black Lotus	Tundra
Field of Dreams	Sol Ring	Plains
Blood Moon	Wheel of Fortune	Plains
Blood Moon	Mox Ruby	Plains

Sideboard:

Blue Elemental Blast	Swords to Plowshares
Blue Elemental Blast	Spell Blast
Disenchant	Power Sink
Disenchant	Counterspell
Divine Offering	Counterspell
Blood Moon	C.O.P. Red
Blood Moon	C.O.P. Red
Swords to Plowshares	

Section 14

Matt's Thumper Deck

This deck came about primarily from the complaints people had on the usefulness of certain cards. These complaints prompted the construction of decks based on these "useless" cards. This is an example of one of them. Although it is not the most effective deck possible, it uses some interesting ideas, and decks such as this can often lead to exceptional decks with some honing. Some people do like the destructive nature of the Copper Tablet and Armageddon Clock and use them with reckless abandon. One common combination uses Armageddon Clocks with Stasis, Birds of Paradise, and Instill Energy on the birds. Sure, this may prevent opponents from paying the four mana required to remove counters, but this does nothing to ensure your own safety from the Clock. It's usually the same people who have the "take it like a man" syndrome—that mass destruction is "cool," even at their own expense. This may be fine and even funny for a while, but it gets old fast.

This deck uses both the Armageddon Clock and Copper Tablet to do damage to both or all players. However, another portion of the deck deals with damage prevention. This includes Reverse Polarity (the original non-tournament deck was packed with these), Martyrs of Korlis, and Artifact Wards. This is augmented by a lone Alabaster Potion, which at first may seem insignificant but has a variety of uses. It can keep a Martyr or a Veteran Bodyguard alive or can give you much-needed life. It almost acts as a backup Reverse Polarity in case one does not show up at an opportune time. Damage prevention also means dealing with an opponent's creatures. The Bodyguard helps with this, as well as the Transmogrants. As long as you are practically immune to sources of artifact damage, Transmogrants make opposing creatures virtually useless, not to mention the ever-increasing usage of artifact creatures in decks. Thus, the chances of your opponent having them are heightened. You can also use them on your Martyrs or Bodyguard to beef them up a bit. Disenchants are all-around useful and not only can deal with irritating opposing enchantments but can get rid of a Clock or Tablet if it gets too hairy (something that doesn't happen too often, if at all). It also works well with the Transmogrants, disenchanting an opponent's creatures. The Xenic Poltergeists were originally put in to deal with the Clocks in case they got too big to handle, like the Disenchants. Like the Disenchants, they have found other uses, such as rendering an opponent's Moxes useless. However, they don't have the well-rounded usefulness of the Disenchants, so they even could go out in place of some land and act as a nice surprise to your opponent. A 6/6 Armageddon creature isn't too bad.

Other odds and ends include an Island Sanctuary, which, at the right time, can be very useful. It acts as a finishing touch: If you have a Clock out, ticking away, with a source of damage prevention to boot, the Sanctuary negates the effects of pesky creatures lingering around to give you problems. A Guardian Beast is pretty self-explanatory: Nobody's going to mess with your artifacts when he's in play. The Animate Deads are in to retrieve any lost Martyrs, Bodyguards, or Beasts. Power doesn't really matter, their special abilities and/or toughness are the main considerations. Or as another side effect, you might want to animate a big creature of your opponent's to block or deal some damage. The Dark Rituals are in to help cast the Martyrs, since they use colorless mana in their casting cost. The earlier the Armageddon Clock gets out, the better. This doesn't give your opponent enough time to remove counters from it, and a Clock early gives him or her problems to deal with. If a Clock comes out too late, your opponent has a foundation to work from and may have ways of getting rid of the "problem." The importance of fast mana and the resulting quick start cannot be emphasized enough.

The Mishra's Factories are nice because they double as land and creatures (though not at the same time). Later in the game, they can be the final blow to your opponent, just enough to finish him or her off, since you will both be losing life very quickly. They can also provide some much-needed creature defense.

Now that the cards are explained individually, it is important to know how they work together. Even though some of that has been explained already, it is important to go over it with the deck as a whole. The idea is to get out a Clock or Tablet early enough to cause problems to your opponent, but to be able to deal with it yourself. You would probably build a foundation first of maybe a Transmogrant, Martyr, and a minimum mana base (enough to spur the deck onward). As you get a Clock and/or Tablet out as well as decent damage prevention, your opponent seems to be an annoyance and tries to disrupt your foundation, so with this deck you tend to be scraping to keep your permanents out on the table, and in the end, hopefully, you're victorious.

Keep in mind that this deck is primarily creative. Winning with an original, creative deck is very rewarding and shows the progress one has made with advanced deck construction. Once someone has reached these advanced stages, he learns to assess each card on basic usefulness, and if a good use isn't readily apparent he finds a way. Often the results are quite devastating, since so much time was put into their creation. As in the case with this deck, one can substitute C.O.P.: Artifacts for the damage prevention aspect, but how creative is that? Granted, every idea is only creative to a certain extent, but it forces you to think harder, to find different ways of doing the same thing—to build a better mousetrap. And when you succeed in designing, retooling, and eventually win with a creative deck, that is extremely rewarding and says a great deal on your advanced deck construction.

— Matt Scoggins

Deck Name: Matt's Thumper Deck

Block One	Block Two	Block Three
Pocket 1 **Desc: Clock Environment**	**Pocket 1** **Desc: Reverse Polarity**	**Pocket 1** **Desc: Fast Mana**
Armageddon Clock	Reverse Polarity	Dark Rituals
Armageddon Clock	Reverse Polarity	Dark Rituals
Armageddon Clock	Reverse Polarity	Dark Rituals
Armageddon Clock	Reverse Polarity	Dark Rituals
Pocket 2 **Desc: Tablet Environment**	**Pocket 2** **Desc: Wards**	**Pocket 2** **Desc: Fast Mana**
Copper Tablet	Artifact Ward	Mox Jet
Copper Tablet	Artifact Ward	Mox Pearl
Copper Tablet	Artifact Ward	Black Lotus
Copper Tablet	Artifact Ward	Mishra's Workshop

Pocket 3 **Desc: Ashnod's Transmogrants**	Pocket 3 **Desc: Disenchants**	Pocket 3 **Desc: Factories**
Ashnod's Transmogrant	Disenchant	Mishra's Factory
Ashnod's Transmogrant	Disenchant	Mishra's Factory
Ashnod's Transmogrant	Disenchant	Mishra's Factory
Ashnod's Transmogrant	Disenchant	Mishra's Factory
Pocket 4 **Desc: Poltergeist**	**Pocket 4** **Desc: Odds and Ends**	**Pocket 4** **Desc: Dual Land**
Xenic Poltergeist	Island Sanctuary	Scrubland
Xenic Poltergeist	Veteran Bodyguard	Scrubland
Animate Dead	Guardian Beast	Scrubland
Animate Dead	Demonic Tutor	Scrubland
Pocket 5 **Desc: Martyrs**	**Pocket 5** **Desc: Land**	**Pocket 5** **Desc: Basic Land**
Martyrs of Korlis	Swamp	Swamp
Martyrs of Korlis	Plains	Swamp
Martyrs of Korlis	Plains	Plains
Martyrs of Korlis	Plains	Plains

Sideboard:

Animate Dead	Eye for an Eye
Animate Dead	Eye for an Eye
Terror	Transmutation
Terror	Transmutation
Terror	Transmutation
Terror	Holy Light
Divine Offering	Holy Light
Divine Offering	

Section 15

Constructing Cheap Effective Decks

Cheap Advanced Decks

Since most advanced decks tend to be expensive to construct, there are some that can be constructed rather cheaply. Though expensive cards like Moxes and the Black Lotus add an advantage to most decks, these cards are not always needed to construct an advanced competitive deck. One can apply his or her imagination and find combinations that are relatively inexpensive to construct. In some cases, if you feel that your deck is incomplete unless it has the added advantage of containing expensive out-of-print cards, then you might try adding Proxies. A Proxy is a cheap card that you simply use as a stand-in for another card. These can be made visible by writing on a land or a card that you are unlikely to use with a permanent marker. If you enroll in a tournament and wish to use Proxies, simply inform the judge that you are using them. If he/she does not wish you to use Proxies, you can make the argument that you simply do not have the money to pay for the more expensive cards and that it is unfair to deny you the advantage of using them.

Although many cards that are out of print are very powerful and give their owners a competitive edge, this edge is not always a decisive one. If your opponent is less skilled at constructing decks yet has a large pool of cards to draw from, you can still manage to defeat him. The Surge Protector is an example of a rather inexpensive yet effective deck.

Deck Name: Surge Protector

Block One	Block Two	Block Three
Pocket 1	**Pocket 1**	**Pocket 1**
Power Surge	Dwarven Warriors	Mountain
Power Surge	Dwarven Warriors	Mountain
Power Surge	Dwarven Warriors	Mountain
Power Surge	Dwarven Warriors	Mountain
Pocket 2	**Pocket 2**	**Pocket 2**
C.O.P. Red	Tundra Wolves	Plains
C.O.P. Red	Tundra Wolves	Plains
C.O.P. Red	Tundra Wolves	Plains
C.O.P. Red	Tundra Wolves	Plains
Pocket 3	**Pocket 3**	**Pocket 3**
Fireball	White Knight	Mountain
Fireball	White Knight	Mountain
Fireball	Orcish Artillery	Mountain
Fireball	Orcish Artillery	Mountain
Pocket 4	**Pocket 4**	**Pocket 4**
Disintegrate	Firebreathing	Plains
Disintegrate	Firebreathing	Plains
Sunglasses of Urza	Firebreathing	Mountain
Sunglasses of Urza	Pikemen	Mountain
Pocket 5	**Pocket 5**	**Pocket 5**
Alabaster Potion	Plains	Mountain
Alabaster Potion	Plains	Mountain
Disenchant	Plains	Mountain
Disenchant	Plains	Mountain

Sideboard:

Disenchant	Lightning Bolt	Red Blast
Disenchant	Lightning Bolt	Pikemen
Firebreathing	Red Blast	Icatian Soldiers
Lightning Bolt	Red Blast	Martyr's Cry
Lightning Bolt	Red Blast	Martyr's Cry

The surge protector deck was originally constructed in response to counterspell decks. Most counterspell decks are burdened by the fact that they must leave a large amount of untapped mana. This can be easily overcome with Power Surge because for each land a player keeps untapped, he takes a point of damage. The Power Surge functions well in this environment because its controller can cast multiple X damage spells or pump any excess mana into a fire breathing creature.

The large number of first striking creatures provides the deck with creature dominance in many situations. First Strike added with Fire-breathing allows any first-striking creature a definite advantage to its non-first-striking counterparts.

The C.O.P. Red has two environmental uses in this deck. The first use is that it allows its caster to protect himself from Power Surge. The second advantage is that it can make it such that the Orcish Artillery will not deal damage to them.

This deck is rather simple to construct and can be made with cards costing under $30.

Gregory Ison, a player from Colorado, has put together another very effective advanced deck that is relatively cheap to construct. Gregory modeled his deck with an environment based around the card Manabarbs. Manabarbs causes each player to take a point of damage for each land he taps. This environment affects both players, but Gregory's deck does not suffer because of the large number of mana-producing creatures it has. The creatures act as sources of damage and provide the deck with the necessary fast mana to generate quickly.

Once there are a few Birds of Paradise and Llanowar Elves in play, the Manabarbs prove no obstacle to the casting of spells for their caster. Opponents are reluctant to use their lands when they will suffer damage from the Manabarbs. This along with the Howling Mines will cause them to hold cards, making them susceptible to Vice damage.

The deck is well-rounded with creature, artifact, and enchantment removal. The Black Vices help to cope against counterspell decks and decks with a high card-drawing capacity. The Wheel of Fortune and Howling Mines add to the deck's own drawing capacity and help to make it more difficult to get under the Vices.

Though the deck contains a large number of rare cards, there are none that are no longer in print.

Deck Name: The Quagmire

Block One	Block Two	Block Three
Pocket 1	**Pocket 1**	**Pocket 1**
Lightning Bolt	Manabarbs	Giant Growth
Lightning Bolt	Manabarbs	Giant Growth
Lightning Bolt	Manabarbs	Giant Growth
Lightning Bolt	Manabarbs	Giant Growth
Pocket 2	**Pocket 2**	**Pocket 2**
Kird Ape	Wheel of Fortune	Mountain
Kird Ape	Regrowth	Mountain
Kird Ape	Power Surge	Mountain
Kird Ape	Righteousness	Plains
Pocket 3	**Pocket 3**	**Pocket 3**
Llanowar Elves	Howling Mine	Forest
Llanowar Elves	Howling Mine	Forest
Llanowar Elves	Howling Mine	Forest
Llanowar Elves	Howling Mine	Plains
Pocket 4	**Pocket 4**	**Pocket 4**
Birds of Paradise	Black Vise	Forest
Birds of Paradise	Black Vise	Forest
Birds of Paradise	Black Vise	Plains
Birds of Paradise	Black Vise	Mountain
Pocket 5	**Pocket 5**	**Pocket 5**
Scryb Sprites	Disenchant	Swords to Plowshares
Scryb Sprites	Disenchant	Swords to Plowshares
Scryb Sprites	Disenchant	Swords to Plowshares
Sol Ring	Disenchant	Swords to Plowshares

Sideboard:	Red Blast	Tsunami
	Red Blast	Tsunami
	Red Blast	C.O.P. Red
	Red Blast	C.O.P. Red
	Karma	Lifeforce
	Swords to Plowshares	Lifeforce
	Swords to Plowshares	Lifeforce
	Flash Fires	

With added expense the deck can be improved. Some cards to consider adding to the deck, if they are available to you, are the Mox Ruby, Mox Pearl, Mox Emerald, Ancestral Recall, and Black Lotus. Most people cannot afford these cards, but their addition is not a massive advantage. Other additions which would not be as difficult to manage are mixed lands, Pendelhaven, and City of Brass. One could also consider adding cards such as Psychic Purge to the sideboard.

When played, Gregory's deck made a good showing against many more powerful decks. It ranks among some of the best decks in play. Not only is it a deck of high caliber, it is also easy on the pocketbook.

One can see that it is not that difficult to construct advanced tournament decks with limited funds. Though it helps to have access to the out-of-print "spoiler" cards, these cards are not essential to be competitive. One can survive without them, especially in decks where everything has a relatively low casting cost.

Section 16

Corey's Trading Chapter

Will you trade my a Northern Paladin for a Force of Nature? Is this a good trade? Is this a fair trade? These are just some of the questions people ask themselves when they are in the process of making a trade. This chapter is dedicated to showing you how to become a better trader. You will learn how to make good trades, improve the value of your collection, be more comfortable with trading, and feel that you have developed an effective defense against getting ripped off.

Types of Traders

We will discuss four main topics. First of all, there are two different types of traders, players, and collectors. Secondly, the attitude of traders is an important factor to consider. We categorize them into "Sharks," "Fish," and "Guppies." The third topic is the value of cards and how to "trade up." Finally, we talk about how you should approach a person you want to trade with and deliver a good pitch. We will give you the knowledge and techniques you need to know about trading and then show you how to put it all together so that you will be able to make the best trade possible out of any given situation.

It's pretty easy to distinguish a player from a collector. A player is one who does not care a great deal about the condition of the card. Usually, the card has to be in playable condition. Traders, on the other hand, rate the condition of their cards anywhere from very fine to mint. Then there is a mixture of the two: people who collect *and* play. Many of them have play cards and separate collection cards, while others use sleeves to protect them when they play. Regardless of whether you are a player or a collector, you have certain wants and desires for cards. You also have a limit for what you want to pay for a card. How to assimilate these two elements of your trading policy will be examined later in this chapter.

Attitude of Traders

There are three main types of attitude in Magic. First is the "shark." When you see these people, just remember this phrase, "They want to get the most for the least." These are the people you would be generally wasting your time on trading with. If you trade with a shark, then you will be on the losing end of the stick. Occasionally you can twist their greed to your own advantage. For example, if they want a card bad enough, they will give you an even deal or possibly an advantageous one. There are different extremes of a "shark," but even the least extreme is usually bad to trade with, especially early in your trading career. Some of them won't try to take everything they can get, but they will still try to come out ahead in the trade. If you want to shark, which is usually a bad policy, let me give you some hints. First, don't shark people you know or people that you will be frequently in contact with. The word spreads fast that a person is a shark in a local area, and soon few people will trade with you. The best thing to do if you want to shark is to shark someone who you will never see again, maybe at a convention out of town or someone who just came into town for a couple of days. Sharking an opponent shouldn't be your total attitude, regardless of whether you care about these aspects. You should switch from sharking when in appropriate situations to being on the slightly better end of the stick on most deals.

The second attitude type is the "fish." This is a broad area. Most of the traders fall into this category. People with this type of attitude run the spectrum of trading types. They can either trade even up, are on the low end of the trade, or are on the high end of the trade. Fish expect a small loss or a gain. Most of the time this is a personal loss or gain in the sense that what the value of one card is to one person is not the same value for the other person. Other times there is a true difference, such as when two cards have widely varying dollar values.

Most people playing Magic would think the Shivan is a little more useful than a Royal Assassin, and thus it essentially is more valuable. That is, the best side to be on in a trade is the side that most people will agree with you on. This is the attitude that you want to have most of the time. You get slightly better deals, and this results in upgrading your cards and making your collection more valuable. For example, let's say we trade a Nightmare for a Shivan Dragon, and then a Shivan for a Fork and a Dual Land. You are getting more rare cards that are good rares and at the same time upgrading the value of your cards. A

Fork and a Dual Land are certainly more valuable than a Nightmare. When trades like this are made repeatedly, your collection will quickly improve in quality.

The last attitude is the "guppie" attitude. These people are the ones sharks and fish feed on. Guppies are generally one of the following things:

1. They are either new to the game of Magic and have no idea about what a lot of the cards do and what they are worth.
2. They could be totally ignorant and don't care about what they get and whether or not it is fair.

If you consider yourself a guppie, then let me give you some hints. First, watch how other people trade for two or three weeks or until you think you know the value of many cards. The biggest problem guppies have is that they don't have the patience to wait. They want a card and they will trade for it. This is fine until you later find out you traded a Fork for a couple of uncommon cards. Secondly, you need to use your knowledge and watch for sharks. Just avoid them until you are more of an experienced trader. Finally, using these hints will help cut down on what you lose when you first begin to trade. You will be on the bad end of a stick a lot of the time, but you don't want to be sharked. This will prevent you from being sharked, but you can't avoid taking some losses when you begin trading. Trade with fish or other guppies.

Value of Cards

The next topic of discussion is the value of cards. This is the single most important aspect of being a good trader. If you don't know what the value of a card is, then you are already lost. There are four different categories when you talk about the value of cards. The first type of value is rarity. Rarity is the number of cards that were printed. In Magic this extends from U1(R) to C4(C). There is also local rarity. Local rarity is determined by how common a certain card is in a given area. Playability is the next type of value for trading cards. Playability is determined by how good the card is in the game. For example, Living Lands and a Fork are both rare, but most people would consider a Fork to be a better playing card. The better the playability of a card, the more trade value it has. The third value of trading cards is price. The price of a card is determined by the majority of the population in

Magic. There are two price systems currently in Magic. One is at the national level and the other is at the local level. Most traders in an area go by the local value unless they have access to the national one. Card dealers price their cards from the demand level of the local area. Do you often wonder why certain cards are more sought after in one place than in another? This is local rarity in action. Local rarity can arise from three different sources. The first is simply that the distribution of a certain card was thin in a certain area. The second is if a card has been horded by sharks trying to increase its value. And lastly, if someone comes up with a good idea for a deck using a certain card, the demand for that card will increase as its potential is realized. The last value to be discussed is personal value. This covers the cards that a person likes and wants to keep or acquire more of. They generally value the card higher than other people do. Also, if a player is trying to build a deck or finish a set, the cards he needs to finish the deck or set become more valuable. A lot of the time they will trade down or be on the wrong end of the stick if they want the card.

The last topic we will discuss is the psychological aspect of trading. At first this may sound a little funny, but this is an important part of trading. When you want a card, what do you normally do? Do you say words like "I want," "I must get" or "have to have" a certain card? These words let other traders know that you want the card, and they may be able to take advantage of this and get a better deal. You should try approaching the situation in a different manner. For example, why don't you first start off by using words like "I am looking for," or just say "does anyone have" this card. These words don't make you sound so desperate. The best approach is to say that you are looking for out of prints or Legends, etc. Then, as you look through the cards, pull out the ones you want and say, "I'm interested in these cards." This approach will help you in you goal of convincing the other person that you are interested but don't have to have the card. In trading, you must be patient. Don't seem rushed and do not rush them. Next, you want to keep an eye out for people who use these "bad words and approaches." Always remember to use the phrase "I do not have to have this card." This will let the other trader know that you are not a guppie and can't be taken advantage of. Trading up refers to upgrading your overall value of cards. Most of the time, you do this by trading low-valued rares for more valuable ones or trading uncommons for rares. Other times it's trading cards that are in print for ones that are out of print, or low-value rares for good uncommons. There are many ways you can go about doing this. Last but not least, you want to hold out for as much as you can get or for as much as you want to get. Finally you need to be in the driver's seat from the beginning. Let the other person make the offer. You want to be able to take advantage of an offer that is better than an even trade. By letting him offer, you are in the "driver's seat." You can accomplish this by saying "I don't know what I really want," or by pulling out a lot more rares than the card is worth. This will allow him to make the mistake of offering too much.

Using these approaches will help keep sharks from bugging you and help you recognize who wants cards. This will result in getting an even or better deal for the cards you want! So, now that you know about the techniques and different values of cards that will lead you to becoming a better trader, le'ts look at some real life examples on how it often works.

The first example will illustrate how to get the best deal from a card shop in Baton Rouge. I was on my way back home when I stopped along the way and went into this store. The clerk tried to put on his pitch and asked what he could do for me. I first said that I was looking for some Legend rares and out of prints. It is usually a good idea not to let them know what you are looking for. I then started to look at his collection. I saw an Abyss for $10 and a Dakkon Blackblade for $15. I then proceeded to ask if he took trade-ins. He said yes and that he would do even trade-ins only on cards that he needed. I then showed him my out of prints. All this time I made sure that he knew I was not some guppie off the street. He soon realized after a couple of futile attempts that I knew what the cards were worth and pulled out some out of prints he wanted. He then asked me what I wanted to offer for these cards, and I played dumb and said "I have no idea, you make the offer." He made an offer that wasn't that great. He wanted my Word of Command, Blaze of Glory, and Raging River for those two cards. I told him what I could get for these cards. I then picked out three cards and wanted $40 in addition to the cards he wanted from me. He stuttered for a while and replied with $25 and three Legends. I said "I can't let these go any cheaper" and started to nudge toward the door. As I started to move, he stopped me and offered $40 plus the cards I wanted; I said that it was a deal. He knew that if I left it would be hard for him to get those cards, which were wanted around there. I was not willing to budge. I made sure he knew that I didn't need the cards he was offering and that I was just remotely interested. I got an Abyss, which sells in Houston for $20, plus a Spirit Link, Serpent Generator, and the $40 in cash.

This situation goes to show you that you can hold out and get what you want as long as you don't show great desire for the card. Let them know that you are interested but don't let them know you need it or collect it. I also used the advantage of being out of town to get him to agree to my rules and prices. When I walked in, I was determined to be in the driver's seat, and when I left I was still in the driver's seat!

The last example I want to show you is an example of a shark at work. This takes place at a small convention in Houston. I walked up to him and asked him, "Hello, do you want to trade or do you need any cards?" He responded by saying that he needed to finish his sets first. There went the red light. So I asked him what he had for trade. He showed me and I took out every good card that he had. At first, I was only getting two rares for one of mine. The cards that I pulled out were ten Moxes, a Timetwister, Time Walk, etc. (These cards were still in print at the time and good rares.) I also did my homework and determined that all the zero casting cost cards were going out of print plus the three blue cards (the spoiler cards). I accomplished a trade by saying this was the last of that card and it was going to be hard for me to part with it. So he offered me two Moxes and the Diamond Valley, which was out of print at the time. As we got closer and closer to finishing his set, I started to slowly ask for three-for-one trades. He said, "Fine, I don't care, I just want to complete this set." That was the worst thing he could have said. By the last two or three cards, I was getting four and five rares apiece. One trade was a Kudzu for four Moxes and a Timetwister. It was the last card he needed for his Unlimited set. To this day, I feel guilty for doing this. I am not a shark anymore, although once in a while, I will do some small sharking for old time's sake. By the end of this trading session, I had quadrupled the rares that I had traded. They were also all good rares in demand.

One does not have to take advantage of others in order to make good trades. You may simply do the service of giving someone the card they want for a card of a slightly higher value. The service you provide them makes up the difference between card values by reducing opportunity cost the person you are trading with must pay to find a better trade. Gradually, through multiple trades, you will significantly increase your card pool without suffering from the bad reputation you usually acquire from sharking.

I hope by reading this chapter you will have discovered a few tricks of trading. The intention was to explain every possible aspect of trading and how to use it to your advantage. In addition, I hope all you guppies out there don't get taken advantage of. In most trades, there are winners and there are losers, and I hope I have shown you how to be on the winning side of a trade more often than not!

— Corey Segall

Section 17

Conclusion

Magic is an elaborate and fascinating game with almost endless possibilities. By now you should have a general idea of what to be prepared for and how to prepare a strong tournament deck. Now that you are ready you should experiment with multiple decks and try out as many variations as you can to improve your playing techniques and become familiar with how to weight your decks. After you prepare a tournament deck you should try your best to refine it by playing with a closed group of strong players whom you trust not to steal your ideas. If you limit the group you play with, you will be able to escape tournament opponents preparing for your deck.

If you are serious about improving your game, move around and play in several different places so you can accumulate different experiences. A good way to do this is to attend as many tournaments as you can, both in and out of town. Tournament players are typically a higher grade of competition compared to those who just dabble, and they will offer a greater quality of play. This quality play will sharpen your skill, drawing you closer to the winning edge.

When I went to Bonn, Germany, for my study-abroad program, I spent a good deal of time in a pub called the Distiller playing with my good friends the two Georges and Reinhart Schunk. In Bonn they play with only one of each card in a deck with the exception of basic land. This new method allowed me to become familiar with a wide variety of cards and ways of playing them. I have played in all of the major cities of Texas and in Colorado Springs, each time picking up more experience and new ideas. If you happen to be out of town, it may be a lot of fun to find a local gaming store and start asking around where people play. This will give you an excellent opportunity to trade cards in situations where you can take advantage of local surpluses and scarcity.

Magic will continue to develop and change as new sets reshape the game. The number of players will continue to increase as Wizards of the Coast begins to enter mainstream markets. You will soon see Magic and games like it internationally distributed in major department stores. The game has not even been out for two years and is already the second most popular strategic game in history, next only to chess. Who knows, perhaps you could be the next Bobby Fischer of Magic.

— George Baxter

Appendix A

Mana Chart and Game Player's Quick Reference

Mana Chart

Magic Type	Draw Power From	Enemies
Black	Swamps	White & Green
Blue	Islands	Red & Green
Green	Forests	Blue & Black
Red	Mountains	Blue & White
White	Plains	Red & Black

Game Phases (sequence of plays)

1. **Untap**:
   A. Untap all of your cards in play unless Effects are preventing you.
   B. Tap card by turning it horizontally.
   C. Card must be tapped if tap symbol (the letter "T" slanted to the right) is present and its power or ability is used.
   D. You cannot play Fast Effects in this phase.

2. **Upkeep**:
   A. Play all effects or damages (actions) as stated on each card.
   B. You can play Fast Effects during this phase.
   C. If no card is in play for upkeep, proceed to Draw phase.

3. **Draw**:
   A. Draw one card from the top of your library and place it in your hand.
   B. If your library is empty, you lose the duel.
   C. You can play Fast Effects during this phase.

4. **Main**:

    A. Play one to three actions:

        1) Cast any type of spell except during attack;

        2) Play one land card only; and

        3) Make one attack with creatures (see below for detailed attack sequences).

    B. You may cast spells or play land card before or after the attack.

    C. During the attack, you can only play Fast Effects.

    D. Can only attack once per turn.

5. **Discard**:

    A. Discard cards until you have seven left.

    B. Fast Effects can be used.

6. **End**:

    A. Inform your opponent that you are done for this turn.

    B. This is the last chance to use Fast Effects.

7. **Heal Creatures**:

    A. Opponent can respond with Fast Effects. You can also respond.

    B. Any creature damage is erased and it is your opponent's turn.

    C. Any Fast Effects expire.

The **Attack** sequence in detail (played in Main phase only):

1. Announce attack to your opponent. This is the last chance for each player to use pre-attack Fast Effects.
2. Declare and tap any attacking creatures.
3. Each player can use Fast Effects.
4. Declare blocking.
5. Each player can use Fast Effects. An attacking creature is still blocked if:

    1) a blocking creature is removed;

    2) a blocking attacking creature is rendered unblockable during this segment.

6. Assign resulting damage.

7. Each player can use damage prevention, damage redirection, and/or regeneration Fast Effects. Can only use Interrupts at this time and any Effects from other spells.

8. Any creature that has lethal damage is automatically sent to the graveyard.

9. Any Effects that were triggered by deaths, such as Vampires gaining counter, Creature Bond damage, etc., take place, and *only* these types of Effects.

Appendix B

Organizations

Magic Players Wanted for a New Gaming Club. Brian Kunkel 2, Kirk Ave., Ronkonkoma, NY, 11779-5014; CompuServe (737)52.160.

Magic League Meets Every Wednesday Night. Mike Fitzgerald, 4 Colonial Place, Norwalk, CT, 06951; (203) 838-0513.

Interested In Forming or Joining New Magic Dueling Groups. Hiep Tran, 16565 Montego Way, Tustin, CA, 92680.

Chico Residents Seeking Opponents. Brad Butts, 1544B Elm St., Chico, CA, 95928; (916) 899-0674.

Looking for Magic Players. Chad Hughes, Lehigh Valley, PA; (610) 767-0891.

Appendix C

Magazines, Catalogs, Publications, Accessories, and Card Collecting

NOTE: All prices shown are subject to change.

Magazines

The DUELIST™, The Official Deckmaster™ Magazine; published quarterly and subscription available for $12 by writing Wizards of the Coast, Inc., P.O. Box 707, Renton, WA 98057-0707; individual issues $3.50; membership to the *Duelist's Convocation*© at $18 includes magazine; advertising available.

SCRYE Magazine, ILM International, Inc., 30617 US Hwy North, Suite 700, Palm Harbor, FL 34684, (813) 785-2113.

Catalogs

Adventures By Mail; cards, display boxes, and Magic flyers; P.O. Box 436, Cohoes, NY 12047; phone 800-2MAGIC6, (518) 237-4870; E-mail bob@abm.com.

The Commissary Games and Hobbies, P.O. Box 1941, Tomball, TX 77377-1941, 1-800-545-4926.

The Complete Strategist, 11 E. 33rd Street, New York, NY 10016, (212) 685-3880.

Comics Plus; Magic: The Gathering™ products; 1926 Superior Avenue, Sheboygan, WI 53081; phone (414) 452-2805.

Crazy Egor's Discount Game Warehouse, NetRep: Eric R. Derby (Scout Troll) derby@spanky.pas.rochester.edu, 1699 Hamlin-Parma Town Line Road, Hilton, NY 14468-9715 USA, 1-800-724-8626 (answering machine only).

Dragonstrike Adventure Shoppes, dstrike@angmar.dataflux.bc.ca.

Forbidden Knowledge Fantasy Shop, 2427 West Clay, St. Charles, MO (314) 940-0702.

Internet Sales, Inc.,7303 Woodhollow #205, Austin, TX 78731, (512) 345-9742, inetsale@netcom.com.

Ivory Tower Trading Card Co., P.O. Box 591653, Houston, TX 77259-1653, email: tower@metronet.com, phone/fax: 1-800-555-1007.

Ludicrous Games, P.O. Box 5965, Bellevue, WA 98006, (206) 643-0539.

Magic by Mail, magic-by-mail@netcom.com.

MULTIVERSAL Trading Company, P.O. Box 4351-779, Hollywood, CA 90028; purchase cards by the case, display, pack or individual card; send $2 for catalog; can be reached by phone 800-900-GAME.

Novastar Games, 3505 Midas Avenue, Rocklin, CA 95677, (916) 624-7113.

The Ship & Soldier, 3431 Woodstock Avenue, Baltimore, MD 21213, (410) 483-9635.

Thee Keep, 2268 Kresge Drive, Amherst, OH 44001; distributor of *Magic: The Gathering™*; *Jyhad™*, and card packs, singles and display boxes; phone 800-771-Keep (5337); Internet Thee Keep@aol.com; AOL: Thee Keep.

Troll Video & Toys, 5009 Nebraska Drive, Huber Heights, OH 45424, (513) 235-0310, Owner: Jon Huston, Mail Order Manager: Alison Walker.

Upsyde Down, upsyde@arcanum.net.

WARGAMES WEST, P.O. Box 9496, Albuquerque, NM 87119-9496, (505) 242-1773; complete sets of 1st edition Magic cards for the Dark™, Legends™, and Jyhad™; foreign catalog available for $4; can be reached by phone 800-SOS-GAME.

Publications

Magic: The Gathering™, A Fantasy Trading Card Game by Richard Garfield, Rule Book; Wizards of the Coast.

The Magic: The Gathering™ Pocket Players' Guide, Wizards of the Coast, Inc., 1994, ISBN 1-880992-29-9.

Accessories

Fantasy & Science Fiction Art Gallery; fantasy/science-fiction paintings and limited editions for Magic: The Gathering™ artists; phone (206) 828-0237; CompuServe 72172,2227.

BQS, Inc., 620 Vista, Suite C, Boise ID 83705; *Deck Deamon* software program available for IBM PC; phone (208) 336-9404, Ext. 715; (208) 336-9315 FAX.

Card Collecting

Magic: The Gathering Collectors' Edition Set Wanted. Adam Dorris, 16219 Shady Elms, Houston, TX 77059; phone (713) 486-1150.

Limited Edition Cards Wanted. Mike Eckrich, 2714 Dover Gardens, Arlington, TX 76017; phone (817) 472-7645.

Magic Antiquities Cards for Trade. Jim Stahlbush, 1706 Hubert Rd., Midland, MI 48640; phone (517) 631-2482.

Limited Edition Magic: The Gathering and Arabian Nights Cards for Sale or Trade. Jon, 5009 Nebraska, Dayton, OH 45424; phone (513) 235-0310.

Magic: The Gathering Cards Wanted. Jim Sekor, 4118 S.W. Thistle St., Seattle, WA 98136; phone (206) 937-1856.

Magic: The Gathering Cards for Trade. Chad Hughes; phone (610) 767-0891.

Magic: The Gathering Cards Wanted. Frank Colevecchia; phone (716) 284-1387.

Magic: The Gathering Cards for Sale. Howard Dawson, 938 Hampton Rd., G.P. Woods, MI 48236; phone nights (313) 885-0705, phone days (810) 772-2020.

Appendix D

Print Run Releases

Randy Asplung-Faith, 2101 S. Circle Dr., Ann Arbor, MI 48103; phone (313) 663-0954.

Edward Beard, Jr.; phone: (401) 739-1511.

Kaja & Phil Foglio, c/o Palliard Press West, 6756 16th Avenue N.W., Seattle, WA 98117-5513.

Randy Gallegos, c/o Green Meese Studio, 6127 Butano Court, San Jose, CA 95123; phone (408) 226-4319.

Heather Hudson, 117 E. Louisa St., #307, Seattle, WA 98102; phone (206) 368-9118.

Scott Kirschner, 2300 Walnut St., Apt. #334, Philadelphia, PA 19103.

Jeff A. Menges, Scarecrow Graphics, P.O. Box 593, Northport, NY 11768.

Margaret Organ-Kean, Moonstone Illustrations, 1916 Pike Place, #12-177, Seattle, WA 98101; M.ORGAN on GENIE.

Mark Poole, 124 Coventry, Lexington, SC 29072; write for free catalog.

Ne Ne Thomas, 2691 E. Blaine Ave., Salt Lake City, UT 84108; phone (801) 581-1715.

Richard Thomas, c/o White Wolf Studios, 4598 Stonegate Indust. Blvd., Stone Mountain, GA 30083.

Byron Wackwitz, 8383 Frankford Ave., Apt. 6, Philadelphia, PA 191361; phone (215) 331-8483.

Wizards F&SF Gallery, Marcus R. Rieck, 117 Main St., Kirkland, WA 98033; phone (206) 828-0237; CompuServe #72172,2227.

Appendix E

On-line Computer Access

questions@wizards.com
E-mail Internet access for general help, commercial services, and additional information.

listserv@wizards.com
Subscribe to the Garfield Games mailing list for the best source of Magic questions. Message entered should be:

subscribe gg-1 *your name*

where your name should be entered as your real name. To trade for cards, enter:

subscribe gg-trading-1 *your name*

@compuserve.com
Information on fantasy and science fiction art gallery called Wizards. Mailing address:

Wizards Gallery
117 Main Street
Kirkland, WA 98033
(206) 828-0237

rec.games.deckmaster.marketplace
Usenet newsgroup subscription.

marvin.macc.wisc.edu
A bunch of interesting files using anonymous FTP in directory "/pub/deckmaster."

http:/www.cis.ufl.edu/~thoth/library/recreation.html
Internet resource for updates on official rule variances, card sets and revisions, tournament information, and the Library of Alexandria.

Appendix F

Deck Construction Worksheet

Deck Name:

Block One	Block Two	Block Three
Pocket 1	**Pocket 1**	**Pocket 1**
Desc:	Desc:	Desc:
Pocket 2	**Pocket 2**	**Pocket 2**
Desc:	Desc:	Desc:
Pocket 3	**Pocket 3**	**Pocket 3**
Desc:	Desc:	Desc:
Pocket 4	**Pocket 4**	**Pocket 4**
Desc:	Desc:	Desc:
Pocket 5	**Pocket 5**	**Pocket 5**
Desc:	Desc:	Desc:

Appendix G

Glossary of *Magic: The Gathering*™ Terms

Artifact Removal Capacity—This category is the ability of a deck to remove artifacts from play.

Block—Refers to one of three groups of twenty cards that make up a 60-card tournament deck. Each block represents 33% of a deck and contains five pockets.

Burn Deck—A deck designed to quickly remove all of opponent's life with direct damage spells.

Card Drawing Capacity—This category pertains to the ability a deck has to draw more cards than those drawn during the draw phase.

Care Bear Magic—A description of a situation in multi-player Magic where everyone refuses to attack one another.

Counter Ability—The "counter ability" of a deck is the most effective measure to stop an opposing player from utilizing his or her deck to the fullest capacity. All counters are played as interrupts, and one must usually stop an action while it is being cast, which is an ineffective counter to special land cards. This also will tie up mana because it is a reaction to the opposing player's spell.

Counter Deck—A deck that is designed mainly around counter cards and their ability to halt your opponent's plans.

Creature Defense Capacity—This is the ability of a card or deck to defend against creatures.

Creature Removal—This is the ability of a card or deck to remove creatures from play. This ability overlaps with damage capacity in the sense that in many cards, such as Lightning Bolts, the ability to do damage to both creatures and the opposing player is present.

Damage Capacity—This factor is a very broad category, as it includes everything in your deck that can inflict damage on your opponent. Most of the time this refers to creatures and direct damage spells. In some deck configurations, it is difficult to discern the damage capacity because only combinations of cards will inflict damage.

Damage Prevention—Refers to the prevention or redirection of damage, the regeneration of a creature that has been assigned damage or a creature that has been sent to the graveyard. Only the fast effects of prevent/redirect damage, regeneration, and interrupts can be used.

Damage Spell Percentage—This category applies strictly to the percentage of damage that instants or sorcery of a deck possess.

Deck—Refers to a deck of cards used to play against an opponent in the game of Magic. Although there is no maximum size, a deck must contain at least 40 cards. Tournament play requires 60 cards.

Dominia—Refers to the place where Magic duels take place.

Duel—Refers to the process of playing an opponent in the game of Magic.

Enchantment Removal Capacity—This category is the ability of a deck to remove enchantments from play.

Environment—The environment is composed of all of the restrictions that certain enchantments and artifacts place upon both players; for example, the Meekstone, Abyss, and Energy Flux.

Evasion Abilities—Refers to a creature's abilities, such as Flying and Landwalking, that prevent it from being blocked during the attack phase.

Fast Deck—A deck designed simply to kill an opponent as quickly as possible, usually sacrificing versatility for speed.

First Strike—Refers to a special ability of some creatures that allows them to inflict damage before an opponent's creature.

Hippy—Jargon for Hypnotic Specter.

Hand Destruction Deck—A deck designed to destroy your opponent's options by removing cards from his or her hand.

Intelligence—This category pertains to a deck's ability to obtain information about an opponent's unseen cards.

Landwalk—Refers to the invasion abilities of cards such as Swampwalk, Mountainwalk, etc.

Land Destruction Capacity—This category pertains to the ability to eliminate the opponent's lands.

Land Destruction Deck—A deck that removes your opponent's ability to cast spells by destroying his or her mana-producing land.

Life Giving Capacity—This category is the ability of a card or deck to add to your total life points.

Mana Capacity—This category is the percentage of mana in a deck.

Offensive Creature Capacity—The ability of a deck to utilize creatures for damaging the opponent.

Pocket—Group of four cards, which is the standard unit of deck construction.

Pulling a Steve—Refers to a player trying to bend the words of a card into the most odd form possible in order to create as many arguments as possible.

Speed Mana—Includes cards that speed up the development of a deck by increasing the amount of mana that a player has early in the game. This is important because you can only play one land per turn. In some cases, it might mean the difference in casting a large creature like a vampire on a second turn instead of a subsequent turn such as the fifth. The classic examples of speed mana are the Moxes, the Lotus, and the Sol Ring. Each of these cards is very powerful, since all except the Sol Ring are out of print.

Tapped Out—When all of a player's mana-producing cards in play are tapped.

Weed—To cut out cards in a deck, thereby fine-tuning the deck.

Appendix H

Complete List of Cards and Our Rating of Them

Legend

Cost: B = Black, G = Green, R = Red, W = White,
                               U = Blue, # = Colorless

Power/Toughness: Power/Toughness rating = value 1-10
Set: AN   = Arabian Nights
                               AQ   = Antiquities
                               DK   = Dark
                               FE   = Fallen Empire
                               LG   = Legends
                               UL   = Unlimited
                               UL/RV   = Unlimited/Revised
                               AN-RV   = Moved from Arabian Nights to Revised
                               AQ-RV   = Moved from Antiquities to Revised

Commonality: R = Rare, C = Common, U = Uncommon
Combo Value [1]:   Value of card in combination with others: A, B, C,
                               D, F

Versatility [1]:   Different uses for card, value 1-10

Standalone Value [1]:   Quality of card isolated from combination relative
                               to cost: A, B, C, D, E, F

1 - This rating is devised by George Baxter and not Wizards of the Coast.

A

Card Name	Type	Cost	Power/ Toughness	Set	Common- ality	Combo Value₁	Versatility₁	Standalone Value	Description
Abomination	Summon Abomination	BB3	2/6	LG	U	C+	4	C	Any green or white creature blocked by, blocking it is destroyed at end of combat.
Abu Ja Far	Summon Leper	W	0/1	AN	U3	B	5	B	If destroyed in combat, all creatures blocked or blocking are destroyed and cannot regenerate.
Acid Rain	Sorcery	U3	...	LG	R	B	3	B	Destroys all forests in play.
Active Volcano	Instant	R	...	LG	R	C	4	C	Destroy blue permanent or send island in play to its owner's hand.
Adun Oakenshield	Summon Legend	BGR	1/2	LG	R	B+	5	B	Bring creature from graveyard to hand (Tap+BGR).
Adventurers' Guildhouse	Land	...	...	LG	U	D	2	F	Your green legends may band with other legends.
Aeolipile	Artifact	2	...	FE	U1	C+	4	C+	1+Tap. Sacrifice Aeolipile to have it deal 2 damage to any target.
Aerathi Berserker	Summon Berserker	RRR2	2/4	LG	U	C+	4	C	Rampage:3.
Air Elemental	Flying	UU3	4/4	UL/RV	U	C	4	B	Flying.
Aisling Leprechaun	Summon Faerie	G	1/1	LG	C1	B	4	C	Turns all creatures blocked by/blocking it to green.
Akron Legionnaire	Summon Legionnaire	WW6	8/4	LG	R	C	2	C-	None of your creatures may attack except Legionnaires.
Al-abara's Carpet	Artifact	...	5	LG	C2	B	3	B+	Prevent all damage done to you by non-flying attacking creatures (Tap+5).
Alabaster Potion	Instant	WWX	...	LG	C2	C+	6	B+	Gain X life or prevent X damage to target.

Card Name	Type	Cost	Power/Toughness	Set	Commonality	Combo Value₁	Versatility₁	Standalone Value	Description
Alchor's Tomb	Artifact	4	...	LG	R	B	3	B	Change the color of one of your permanent to any color (Tap+2).
Ali from Cairo	Summon Ali from Cairo	RR2	0/1	AN	U2	A	4	A	You cannot be reduced below one life due to damage while Ali is in play.
Ali Baba	Summon Ali Baba	R	1/1	AN	U3	C	4	B-	Tap a wall (R).
All Hallow's Eve	Sorcery	B2	...	LG	R	B+	3	C+	Two turns from time of casting all creatures in all graveyards are brought into play.
Aladdin	Summon Aladdin	RR2	1/1	AN	U2	B+	6	A+	Steal artifact (RR1).
Aladdin's Lamp	Mono Artifact	10	...	AN-RV	U2-R	C+	2	D	Instead of drawing in draw phase, draw X cards and keep only one (X,T).
Aladdin's Ring	Mono Artifact	8	...	AN-RV	U2-R	B	3	B-	4 damage to any target (8,T).
Amnesia	Sorcery	3UUU	...	DK	U/R	B	3	B+	Look at target player's hand. Target player discards all non-land cards in hand.
Amrou Kithkin	Summon Kithkin	WW	1/1	LG	C2	B-	4	C+	Cannot be blocked by creatures with power>2.
Amulet of Kroog	Mono Artifact	2	...	AQ	C4	C+	4	C+	Prevent one damage to any target.
Ancestral Recall	Instant	U	...	UL	R	A	5	A+	Draw or force opponent to draw three cards.
Angelic Voices	Enchantment	WW2	...	LG	R	B	3	C+	+1/+1 to all your creatures as long as they are all white or artifact creatures.
Angry Mob	Summon Mob	2WW	2+*/2+*	DK	U/R	B	5	B+	Trample; during your turn, the *'s are both equal to the total number of swamps all opponents control. During any other player's turn, * equals 0.
Angus Mackenzie	Summon Legend	UGW	2/2	LG	R	B	4	B+	No creatures deal damage in combat this turn (Tap+UGW).

Card Name	Type	Cost	Power/ Toughness	Set	Common-ality	Combo Value$_1$	Versatility$_1$	Standalone Value	Description
Animate Artifact	Enchant Artifact	U3	...	UL/RV	U	C+	4	C-	Makes target artifact a '/' creature where * = casting cost; no effect on artifact creatures.
Animate Dead	Enchant Dead Creature	B1	...	UL/RV	U	A-	5	B+	Pull creature from any graveyard at -1 power.
Animate Wall	Enchant Wall	W	...	UL/RV	U	C+	2	D-	Target wall can attack.
Ankh of Mishra	Continuous Artifact	2	...	UL/RV	R	B+	3	C+	2 damage to anyone who plays a land.
Anti-Magic Aura	Enchant Creature	U2	...	LG	C1	B+	4	C+	Destroys enchantments on creature and prevents all further enchantments, instants, and sorceries on it.
Apprentice Wizard	Summon Wizard	BB1	0/1	DK	U	C+	3	C	Tap and pay B to add three colorless mana to your pool.
Arboria	Enchant World	GG2	...	LG	U	B+	3	B-	If a player does not put a card into play or cast a spell they cannot be attacked until their next turn.
Arcades Sabboth	Summon Elder Dragon Legend	UUGG WW2	7/7	LG	R	C+	4	C-	Flying; +0/+1 (W); your untapped and not attacking creatures get +0/+2; pay UGW during upkeep or this card is buried.
Arena of the Ancients	Artifact	3		LG	R	C-	3	C-	Taps all legends as it enters play; legends to not untap as normal.
Argivian Archaeologist	Summon Archaeologist	WW1	1/1	AQ	U1	A+	6	B+	Bring artifact from graveyard to hand (WW+Tap).
Argivian Blacksmith	Summon Smith	WW1	2/2	AQ	C4	C+	4	B-	Tap to prevent 2 damage to any artifact creature.
Argothian Pixies	Summon Faeries	G1	2/1	AQ	C4	C+	4	B+	Cannot be blocked by artifact creatures, ignores damage from artifact sources.

Card Name	Type	Cost	Power/ Toughness	Set	Common- ality	Combo Value₁	Versatility₁	Standalone Value	Description
Argothian Treefolk	Summon Treefolk	GG3	3/5	AQ	C4	C+	4	B+	Ignores damage from artifact sources.
Armageddon	Sorcery	W3	---	UL/RV	R	B+	3	B-	Destroys all lands in play.
Armageddon Clock	Continuous Artifact	6	---	AQ-RV	U2-R	B	3	C	Add one counter each upkeep; does 1 damage to all players for each token at end of upkeep; any player may remove a token for 4 mana.
Armor Thrull	Summon	2B	1/3	FE	C1	C+	4	C+	Tap. Sacrifice to put a +1/+2 counter on a target creature.
Army of Allah	Instant	WW1	---	AN	C3-C1	B+	3	B+	+2/+0 to all attacking creatures until end of turn.
Artifact Blast	Interrupt	R	---	AQ	C4	C	3	B	Counters an artifact being cast.
Artifact Possession	Enchant Artifact	B2	---	AQ	C4	C+	3	C	2 damage when controller taps or powers the target artifact.
Artifact Ward	Enchant Creature	W	---	AQ	C4	B	3	C	Target creature cannot be blocked by artifact creatures, ignores damage from artifact sources, and ignores effects of artifacts that target it.
Ashes to Ashes	Sorcery	BB1	---	DK	C	C+	4	C+	Removes two target non-artifact creatures from the game and does 5 damage to caster.
Ashnod's Altar	Poly Artifact	3	---	AQ	U2	B	3	C	Sacrifice creature to get 2 colorless mana (0).
Ashnod's Battle Gear	Mono Artifact	2	---	AQ	U2	B-	3	C	Give creature +2/-2 (2+Tap); effect remains until untapped, may choose not to untap.
Ashnod's Transmogrant	Mono Artifact	1	---	AQ	U3	B+	3	B-	Give creature a permanent +1/+1 and it becomes an artifact creature; goes to graveyard when used.
Aspect of Wolf	Enchant Creature	G1	---	UL/RV	R	B-	3	B-	Gives +*/+* where *=1/2 number of forests (round down power and up toughness).

147

Card Name	Type	Cost	Power/Toughness	Set	Commonality	Combo Value₁	Versatility₁	Standalone Value	Description
Atog	Summon Atog	R1	1/2	AQ-RV	C4=C	B	4	C+	+2/+0 until end of turn if sacrifice artifact.
Avoid Fate	Interrupt	G	...	LG	C1	C+	3	D-	Counters interrupt or enchantment targeted at one of your permanent.
Axelrod Gummarson	Summon Legend	BBRR4	5/5	LG	R	C	4	C	Trample; gives you one life and does one damage to opponent whenever a creature goes to the graveyard on a turn in which Axelrod damaged it.
Ayesha Tanaka	Summon Legend	UUWW	2/2	LG	R	C+	5	C+	Banding; tap to counter effect of an artifact with an activation cost unless opponent pays W.
Azure Drake	Summon Drake	U3	2/4	LG	U	C+	4	B	Flying.
B									
Backdraft	Instant	R1	...	LG	U	C+	4	B	Does one half of damage done by a sorcery back at the caster.
Backfire	Enchant Creature	U	...	LG	U	B	3	B-	For each one damage done to you by this creature, does one damage to controller of that creature.
Bad Moon	Enchantment	B1	...	UL/RV	R	B+	3	B+	Gives +1/+1 to all black creatures.
Badlands	Land	--	...	UL/RV	R	B+	5	B-	Tap for 1 black or red mana.
Balance	Sorcery	W1	...	UL/RV	R	A-	8	B-	Balance number of creatures, land, and cards in hand.
Ball Lightning	Summon Ball Lightning	RRR	6/1	DK	U/R	B+	3	B+	Trample; May attack on the turn during which it is summoned. Is buried at end of turn.
Balm of Restoration	Artifact	2	...	FE	U1	C	3	C	Tap+1. Sacrifice to gain 2 life or prevent up to 2 damage to any player or creature.

Card Name	Type	Cost	Power/Toughness	Set	Commonality	Combo Value₁	Versatility₁	Standalone Value	Description
Banshee	Summon Banshee	2BB	0/1	DK	U/R	B+	4	B	Banshee does X damage, half (rounded up) to you and half (rounded down) to any one target (Tap+X).
Barbary Apes	Summon Apes	G1	2/2	LG	C1	C+	3	B-	
Barktooth Warbeard	Summon Legend	BRR4	6/5	LG	U	C	3	C+	
Barl's Cage	Artifact	4	...	DK	U/R	B-	3	B-	(3) target creature does not untap as normal during its controller's next untap phase.
Bartel Runeaxe	Summon Legend	BGR3	6/5	LG	R	C+	4	B-	Does not tap when attacking; cannot be targeted by enchant creature spells.
Basal Thrull	Summon	BB	1/2	FE	C1	B	4	B-	Tap. Sacrifice to add BB to your mana pool. Play this ability as an interrupt.
Basalt Monolith	Mono Artifact	3	...	UL/RV	U	B	3	B-	Tap to get 3 mana; untap by spending 3 mana.
Battering Ram	Artifact Creature	2	1/1	AQ	C4	C+	4	C+	Bands only when attacking; destroys defending walls.
Bayou	Land	...	...	UL/RV	R	B+	5	B-	Tap for 1 black or green mana.
Bazaar of Bagdad	Land	...	...	AN	U3	B+	4	C+	
Beasts of Bogardan	Summon Beasts	R4	3/3	LG	U	C	4	C+	Protection from red, +1/+1 if opponent has white cards in play.
Benalish Hero	Summon Hero	W	1/1	UL/RV	C	C+	4	B	Bands.
Berserk	Instant	G	...	UL	U	B-	4	B+	Doubles power of creature and gives Trample until end of turn; creature dies if it attacks.
Bird Maiden	Summon Bird Maiden	R2	1/2	AN	C2/C2	C	4	C+	Flying.

Card Name	Type	Cost	Power/Toughness	Set	Commonality	Combo Value₁	Versatility₁	Standalone Value	Description
Birds of Paradise	Summon Mana Birds	G	0/1	UL/RV	R	A-	6	C+	Flying; tap for one mana or any color.
Black Knight	Summon Knight	BB	2/2	UL/RV	U	B-	4	B	First strike; protection from white.
Black Lotus	Mono Artifact	O	...	UL	R	A+	7	A+	3 mana of one color (one use).
Black Mana Battery	Artifact	4	...	LG	U	B-	3	C+	Add a token to it (Tap+2) or tap for one black mana plus can convert tokens to black mana as well.
Black Vise	Continuous Artifact	1	...	UL/RV	U	A-	3	A+	1 damage during upkeep to opponent for each card over 4 in hand.
Black Ward	Enchant Creature	W	...	UL/RV	U	B	3	C-	Gives protection from black.
Blaze of Glory	Instant	W	...	UL	R	C+	4	B-	Target defending creature can and must block all attackers.
Blazing Effigy	Summon Effigy	R1	0/3	LG	C2	C+	4	C-	When put in graveyard from play, you do 3 damage to any creature. If Effigy was killed by another Effigy, you do damage done by the other Effigy plus 3 to the creature.
Blessing	Enchant Creature	WW	...	UL/RV	R	B	3	B+	+1/+1 (W).
Blight	Enchant Land	BB	...	LG	U	C+	3	C+	If land is tapped, it is destroyed at end of turn.
Blood Lust	Instant	R1	...	LG	U	B+	4	B+	+4/-4 to a creature until end of turn. Does not reduce toughness below 1.
Blood Moon	Enchantment	2R	...	DK	U/R	A	3	A	All non-basic lands are now basic mountains.
Blood of the Martyr	Instant	WWW	...	DK	U/R	C+	3	C	For the remainder of the turn, you may redirect damage done to any number of creatures to yourself instead.
Blue Elemental Blast	Interrupt	U	...	UL/RV	C	B+	2(6)	C+	Destroys red card or counters red spell.

Card Name	Type	Cost	Power/Toughness	Set	Commonality	Combo Value₁	Versatility₁	Standalone Value	Description
Blue Mana Battery	Artifact	4	...	LG	U	C+	3	C+	Add a token to it (Tap+2) or tap for one blue mana plus can convert tokens to blue mana as well.
Blue Ward	Enchant Creature	W	...	UL/RV	U	C+	3	C	Gives protection from blue.
Bog Imp	Summon Imp	1B	1/1	DK	C	C+	4	C+	Flying.
Bog Rats	Summon Rats	B	1/1	DK	C	C	3	C-	Cannot be blocked by walls.
Bog Wraith	Summon Wraith	B3	3/3	UL/RV	U	B	4	B	Swampwalk.
Bone Flute	Artifact	3	...	DK	U/R	C	3	C-	(1) Tap all creatures get -1/-1.
Book of Rass	Artifact	6	...	DK	U	C+	3	C	(2) pay 2 life to draw 1 card. Damage may not be prevented or redirected.
Boomerang	Instant	UU	...	LG	C2	B	7	C+	Send any permanent in play to its owner's hand.
Boris Devilboon	Summon Legend	BR3	2/2	LG	R	C	3	C	
Bottle of Suleiman	Mono Artifact	4	...	AN-RV	U2/R	B+	3	C+	Flip coin and take 5 damage or get 5/5 Flying Djinn token creature (1,T); bottle destroyed when used.
Bottomless Vault	Land	...	...	FE	U1	B	3	B-	Comes into play tapped. You may choose not to untap Bottomless Vault during your untap phase, instead put a storage counter on it. Tap: remove any number of storage counters from Bottomless Vault. For each storage counter removed, add B to your mana pool.
Braingeyser	Sorcery	UUx	...	UL/RV	R	B+	5	A-	Draw (or force opponent to draw) X cards.
Brainwash	Enchant Creature	W	...	DK	C	C+	3	C+	Target creature may not attack unless its controller pays 3 in addition to any other costs required for the creature to attack.

151

Card Name	Type	Cost	Power/Toughness	Set	Commonality	Combo Value₁	Versatility₁	Standalone Value	Description
Brass Man	Artifact Creature	1	1/3	LG	U	C+	3	B	Pay 1 to untap during upkeep.
Brassclaw Ocrs	Summon	2R	3/2	FE	C1	C+	2	C	Cannot be assigned to block any creature of power greater than 1.
Breeding Pit	Enchantment	3B	...	FE	U3	B+	3	B+	During your upkeep, pay BB or bury Breeding Pit. At end of your turn, put a Thrull token into play. Treat this token as a 0/1 black creature.
Brine Hag	Summon Hag	UU2	2/2	LG	U	C+	4	C+	Creatures which damaged the Hag on the turn it goes to the graveyard become 0/2 creatures.
Bronze Horse	Artifact Creature	7	4/4	LG	R	B-	4	B	Trample; not damaged by targeted spells if you have other creatures in play.
Bronze Tablet	Mono Artifact	6	...	AQ	U1	C+	3	C+	Swap Tablet with any card in play (4); Effect is permanent, but can be countered with 10 life lost; Ante games only; Enters play tapped.
Brothers of the Fire	Summon	RR1	2/2	DK	R	C	3	C	RR1: Brothers of Fire does 1 damage to any target and 1 damage to you.
Burrowing	Enchant Creature	R	...	UL/RV	U	C+	3	C	Gives MountainWalk.
C									
Camel	Summon Camel	W	0/1	AN	C5	C	4	D+	Bands; gives immunity to desert damage to all those banded with it.
Camouflage	Instant	G	...	UL	U	C	3	C-	Opponent blocks blindly.
Candelabra of Tawnos	Mono Artifact	1	...	AQ	U1	A-	6	B+	Untap X lands (X).
Carnivorous Plant	Summon Wall	3G	4/5	DK	C	C	2	C+	
Carrion Ants	Summon Ants	BB2	0/1	LG	R	B	4	A	+1/+1 (1).

Card Name	Type	Cost	Power/ Toughness	Set	Common- ality	Combo Value₁	Versatility₁	Standalone Value	Description
Castle	Enchantment	W3	...	UL/RV	U	B	3	B	Untapped (non-attacking) creatures gain +2/+2.
Cat Warriors	Summon Cat Warriors	GG1	2/2	LG	C2	C+	4	B-	ForestWalk.
Cathedral of Serra	Land	...	...	LG	U	C-	1	F	Your white legends may band with other legends.
Cave People	Summon Cave People	1RR	1/4	DK	U/R	C+	4	C+	If declared as an attacker, get +1/-2 until end of turn. Target creature gains MountainWalk until end of turn (Tap+1RR).
Caverns of Despair	Enchant World	RR2	...	LG	R	B+	3	B-	All players may only attack or block with up to 2 creatures each turn.
Celestral Prism	Mono Artifact	3	...	UL/RV	U	C	4	C+	1 mana of any color (2,T).
Chain Lightning	Sorcery	R	...	LG	C2	C+	4	B	3 damage to any target; player or controller of target may spend RR to pick another target; repeat.
Chains of Mephistopheles	Enchantment	B1	...	LG	R	B-	3	C-	For all players, for each card drawn (other than the first one during draw phase) player must discard one card.
Channel	Sorcery	GG	...	UL/RV	U	B+	3	D	Turn life into colorless mana for rest of turn.
Chaos Orb	Mono Artifact	2	...	UL	R	A-	8	B+	Flip into table to destroy cards (1).
Chaoslace	Interrupt	R	...	UL/RV	R	B	3	D	Change one card color to red.
Chromium	Summon Elder Dragon	BBUUWW 2	7/7	LG	R	C	4	D	Flying; Rampage: 2; pay BUW during upkeep or this card is buried.
Circle of Protection: Artifacts	Enchantment	W1	...	AQ	U3	B+	4	C-	Reduce damage from one artifact source to zero (2).

Card Name	Type	Cost	Power/ Toughness	Set	Common- ality	Combo Value	Versatility1	Standalone Value	Description
Circle of Protection: Black	Enchantment	W1	--	UL/RV	C	B+	4	C	Prevent damage from black source (1).
Circle of Protection: Blue	Enchantment	W1	--	UL/RV	C	B+	4	C	Prevent damage from blue source (1).
Circle of Protection: Green	Enchantment	W1	--	UL/RV	C	B+	4	C	Prevent damage from green source (1).
Circle of Protection: Red	Enchantment	W1	--	UL/RV	C	B+	4	C	Prevent damage from red source (1).
Circle of Protection: White	Enchantment	W1	--	UL/RV	C	B+	4	C	Prevent damage from white source (1).
Citanul Druid	Summon Druid	G1	1/1	AQ	U3	C	4	B+	Get a +1/+1 every time opponent casts an artifact.
City in a Bottle	Continuous Artifact	2	--	AN	U2	F	2	D	Removes all Arabian Nights cards from play and prevents any new ones from being put into play.
City of Brass	Land	--	--	AN	U3	B+	6	B	Tap for 1 mana of any color; take 1 damage when City is tapped.
City of Shadows	Land	0	--	DK	UR	B-	3	B-	Sacrifice one of your creatures but remove it from the game instead of placing it in your graveyard. Put a counter on City of Shadows. Add X colorless mana to your mana pool where X is the number of counters on City of Shadows.
Clay Statue	Artifact Creature	4	3/1	AQ	C4	B	4	B+	Regenerates (2).
Cleanse	Sorcery	--	WW2	KG	R	B	3	B	Destroys all black creatures in play.

Card Name	Type	Cost	Power/ Toughness	Set	Common-ality	Combo Value1	Versatility1	Standalone Value	Description
Cleansing	Sorcery	WWW	...	DK	U/R	C+	3	C	All land is destroyed. Players may prevent Cleansing from destroying specific lands by paying 1 life for each land they wish to protect. Effects that prevent or redirect damage may not be used to counter this loss of life.
Clergy of the Holy Nimbus	Summon Priest	W	1/1	LG	C2	C+	3	C	Always regenerates unless opponent pays one colorless mana.
Clockwork Avian	Artifact Creature	5	0/4	AQ	U1	B-	3	B	Flying; starts with four +1/+0 tokens; remove one token after each time it attacks or defends; can replace tokens during upkeep for 1 colorless mana each but this taps the Avian.
Clockwork Beast	Artifact Creature	6	0/4	UL/RV	R	B-	3	B	Starts with 7 +1/+0 tokens; uses token when attacking or defending; do not untap to pay 1 mana per token restored (taps if wasn't already).
Clone	Summon Clone	U3	*/*	UL/RV	U	B+	7	B+	Where * = copies creature and color.
Coal Golem	Artifact	5	3/3	DK	U/R	C-	3	F	(3) sacrifice Coal Golem to add RRR to your mana pool. This ability is played as an interrupt.
Cockatrice	Summon Cockatrice	GG3	2/4	UL/RV	R	C+	5	B	Flying; any non-wall blocked-by/blocking it is destroyed.
Cocoon	Enchant Creature	G	...	LG	U	C	2	D-	Taps creature and holds it tapped for 3 turns, then it gets +1/+1 and flying.
Colossus of Sardia	Artifact Creature	9	9/9	AQ	U1	B+	3	B-	Trample; costs 9 to untap.
Combat Medic	Summon	2W	0/2	FE	C1	C+	3	C+	1W. Prevent 1 damage to any player or creature.
Conch Horn	Artifact	2	...	FE	U1	B-	3	B-	Tap+1. Sacrifice Conch Horn. Draw two cards and put any card from your hand back on top of your library.

Card Name	Type	Cost	Power/Toughness	Set	Commonality	Combo Value	Versatility₁	Standalone Value	Description
Concordant Crossroads	Enchant World	G	...	LG	R	B-	3	B-	Creatures may attack or use abilities which tap them during the turn in which they are brought into play.
Consecrate Land	Enchant Land	W	...	UL	U	B	4	C-	Removes enchantments and protects from further enchantment; prevents destruction of target land.
Conservator	Mono Artifact	4	...	UL/RV	U	C+	3	C+	Prevent loss of up to 2 life (3,T).
Contract from Below	Sorcery	B	...	UL/RV	R	A	3	A	Get new hand but add one card to ante.
Control Magic	Enchant Creature	UU2	...	UL/RV	U	A-	6	A-	Caster takes control of target creature.
Conversion	Enchantment	WW2	...	UL/RV	U	B+	2	C-	All mountains become plains; costs WW during upkeep.
Copper Tablet	Continuous Artifact	2	...	UL	U	C+	3	C-	1 damage to each player in upkeep.
Copy Artifact	Enchantment	U1	...	UL/RV	R	B+	7	A-	Card acts as a copy of an artifact in play.
Coral Helm	Poly Artifact	3	...	AQ	U1	C	2	C+	+2/+2 to creature until end of turn (3 and discard random card from hand).
Cosmic Horror	Summon Horror	BBB3	7/7	LG	R	C	2	B	First Strike; pay BBB3 during upkeep or take 7 damage and destroys this card.
Counterspell	Interrupt	UU	...	UL/RV	U	B	6	A-	Counters spell as being cast.
Craw Giant	Summon Giant	GGGG3	6/4	LG	U	B-	4	B	Trample; Rampage: 2.
Craw Wurm	Summon Wurm	GG4	6/4	UL/RV	C	B-	3	B+	
Creature Bond	Enchant Creature	U1	...	UL/RV	C	B-	3	C-	Creature Bond does damage to controller when creature goes to graveyard.
Crevasse	Enchantment	R2	...	LG	U	C	3	C	Stops use of MountainWalk.
Crimson Kobolds	Summon Kobolds	O	0/1	LG	C2	C+	3	C	

Card Name	Type	Cost	Power/ Toughness	Set	Common- ality	Combo Value₁	Versatility₁	Standalone Value	Description
Crimson Manticore	Summon Manticore	RR2	2/2	LG	R	C	5	C+	Flying; tap to do one damage to attacking or blocking creature.
Crumble	Instant	G	---	AQ-RV	C4>U	C+	3	B-	Buries target artifact and gives controller life equal to its casting cost.
Crusade	Enchantment	WW	---	UL/RV	R	B+	3	B+	+1/+1 to all white creatures.
Crystal Rod	Poly Artifact	1	---	UL/RV	U	C	3	C	+1 life when blue spell cast (1).
Cuombaji Witches	Summon Witches	BB	1/3	AN	C4	C+	4	B+	Tap for each player to do 1 damage to any target, but then allow opponent to do 1 damage to any target.
Curse Artifact	Enchant Artifact	2BB	---	DK	U/R	C	3	C	During upkeep, controller of target artifact may choose to bury target artifact. If controller chooses not to bury target artifact, Curse Artifact does 2 damage.
Cursed Land	Enchant Land	BB2	---	UL/RV	U	B	3	B	1 damage must discard down to 4 cards during discard.
Cursed Rack	Continuous Artifact	4	---	AQ	C1	B	3	B-	Opponent must discard down to 4 cards during discard.
Cyclone	Enchantment	GG2	---	AN	U3	B	3	C+	Gets 1 token each upkeep; must pay G for each token or it is discarded; does 1 damage per token to all players and creatures.
Cyclopean Mummy	Summon Mummy	B1	2/1	LG	C2	C-	2	C-	Leaves game if goes to graveyard from play.
Cyclopean Tomb	Mono Artifact	4	---	UL	R	B+	3	B	Change land to swamp during upkeep (2,T); Land reverts 1 per turn when Tomb is destroyed.

Card Name	Type	Cost	Power/ Toughness	Set	Commonality	Combo Value₁	Versatility₁	Standalone Value	Description
D									
D'Avenant Archer	Summon Archer	W2	1/2	LG	C2	C+	4	B-	Tap for 1 damage to attacking or blocking creature.
Dakkon Blackblade	Summon Legend	BUUW2	*/*	LG	R	B	3	B	Where * is the number of lands you control.
Damping Field	Enchantment	W2	...	AQ	U3	B-	3	B-	Players may untap only one artifact each turn during untap.
Dance of Many	Enchantment	BB	...	DK	R	B+	4	B	Create a token copy of a creature in play with all of its characteristics. The controller must pay BB during their upkeep or Dance of Many is buried. If Dance of Many leaves play, then token creature is destroyed.
Dancing Scimitar	Artifact Creature	4	1/5	AN-RV	U2>R	B	4	B	Flying.
Dandan	Summon Dandan	UU	4/1	AN	C4	C+	2	B-	Cannot attack if opponent does not have islands; destroyed if you have no islands.
Dark Heart of the Wood	Enchantment	BG	...	DK	C	B+	3	B+	You may sacrifice a forest to gain 3 life. Counts as both a black card and a green card.
Dark Ritual	Interrupt	B	...	UL/RV	C	B	3	B+	Add 3 black mana to mana pool.
Dark Sphere	Artifact	0	...	DK	U/R	C	3	C	Sacrifice Dark Sphere to prevent half of the damage done to you by a single source, rounded down.
Darkness	Instant	B	...	LG	C1	C+	3	C+	No creatures deal damage in attack phase this turn.
Darkpact	Sorcery	BBB	...	UL/RV	R	C	3	C	Swap top card of library with either ante.
Deadfall	Enchantment	G2	...	LG	U	C	3	C	Stops all use of ForestWalk in play.
Death Ward	Instant	W	...	UL/RV	C	C	3	C	Regenerates creature.

Card Name	Type	Cost	Power/ Toughness	Set	Common- ality	Combo Value1	Versatility1	Standalone Value	Description
Deathgrip	Enchantment	B	...	UL/RV	R	B+	3	C	Counter green spell as it is cast (BB).
Deathlace	Interrupt	B	...	UL/RV	R	B	3	C	Change one card color to black.
Deep Spawn	Summon	5UUU	6/6	FE	U3	B-	4	B-	Trample. During your upkeep, take two cards from top of your library and put them in your graveyard or destroy Deep Spawn. U: Deep Spawn may not be the target of spells or effects until end of turn and does not untap as normal during your next upkeep phase. If Deep Spawn is untapped, tap it.
Deep Water	Enchantment	BB	...	DK	C	C+	3	C+	If you tap 1 blue, all mana-producing lands produce blue instead of their normal mana until end of turn.
Delif's Cone	Artifact	2	...	FE	U1	C+	3	C	Tap. Sacrifice this card. If target creature you control attacks and is not blocked, you may lose to gain its power in life. If you do so, it deals no damage to opponent this turn.
Delif's Cube	Artifact	1	...	FE	U1	B-	3	C+	Tap+2. If target creature you control attacks and is not blocked, it deals no damage to opponent. Instead, put a cube counter on Delif's Cube. 2: Remove a cube counter to regenerate target creature.
Demonic Attorney	Sorcery	BB1	...	UL/RV	R	C	3	C	All players ante another card or forfeit.
Demonic Hordes	Summon Demons	BBB3	5/5	UL/RV	R	B+	4	B+	Tap to destroy a land; BBB upkeep or lose a land and it becomes tapped.
Demonic Torment	Enchant Creature	B2	...	LG	U	C	3	C+	Creature may not attack and deals no damage during combat.

Card Name	Type	Cost	Power/Toughness	Set	Commonality	Combo Value₁	Versatility₁	Standalone Value	Description
Demonic Tutor	Sorcery	B1	...	UL/RV	U	A-	5	A-	Take any one card from library into hand.
Derelor	Summon	3B	4/4	FE	U1	B-	2	C+	Your black spells cost an additional B to cast.
Desert	Land	...	...	AN	C11	C+	4	B	Tap for 1 colorless mana or to do 1 point of damage to any attacking creature after it deals damage.
Desert Nomads	Summon Nomads	R2	2/2	AN	C4	C	3	C+	DesertWalk; immune to damage from deserts.
Desert Twister	Sorcery	GG4	...	AN	U3	B-	8	B	Destroy any 1 card in play.
Detonate	Sorcery	RX	...	AQ	U3	B-	3	B	Destroys target artifact of casting cost X without regeneration and does X damage to its controller.
Devouring Deep	Summon Devouring Deep	U2	1/2	LG	C2	C	4	C	IslandWalk.
Diabolic Machine	Artifact	7	4/4	DK	U/R	B-	4	B-	(3) regenerates.
Diamond Valley	Land	...	...	AN	U2	B+	4	B	Tap to sacrifice a creature and gain life equal to its toughness.
Dingus Egg	Continuous Artifact	4	...	UL/RV	R	B+	3	C-	2 damage to controller of any land which is destroyed.
Disenchant	Instant	W1	...	UL/RV	C	B-	7	B+	Destroy enchantment or artifact.
Disharmony	Instant	R2	...	LG	R	C	3	C	Take control of an attacking creature until end of turn. It comes across untapped.
Disintegrate	Sorcery	RX	...	UL/RV	C	B	4	B+	X damage to target; cannot regenerate this turn; leaves game if it dies this turn.
Disrupting Scepter	Mono Artifact	3	...	UL/RV	R	B	4	B	Opponent discards one card (3,T).
Divine Intervention	Enchantment	WW6	...	LG	C	C	3	C	Two turns from now game ends as a draw.

Card Name	Type	Cost	Power/ Toughness	Set	Common- ality	Combo Value₁	Versatility₁	Standalone Value	Description
Divine Offering	Instant	W1	---	LG	C2	B	5	B+	Destroy artifact and get life equal to its casting cost.
Divine Transformation	Enchant Creature	WW2	---	LG	R	C	3	C+	+3/+3.
Draconian Cylix	Artifact	3	---	FE	U1	C	3	C	Tap+2. Discard a card at random from your hand to regenerate a target creature.
Drafna's Restoration	Sorcery	U	---	AQ	C4	B-	4	B	Take any number of artifacts from target player's graveyard and place them in any order on top of the library.
Dragon Whelp	Summon Dragon	RR2	2/3	UL/RV	U	B	4	B+	Flying; +1/+0 (R); dies at end of turn if more than RRR spent in one turn.
Dragon Engine	Artifact Creature	3	1/3	AQ-RV	C4>R	B	4	B	+1/+0 (2).
Drain Life	Sorcery	B1	---	UL/RV	R	B	4	B	X damage to target; +X life to caster (X is black).
Drain Power	Sorcery	UU	---	UL/RV	R	B	4	C	Tap all of opponent's land add mana pool into your pool.
Dream Coat	Enchant Creature	U	---	LG	U	B+	3	D-	Creature can change colors once per turn.
Drop of Honey	Enchantment	G	---	AN	U2	B+	3	B+	During upkeep, lowest power creature is destroyed and cannot regenerate; discarded when there are no more creatures.
Drowned	Summon Zombies	B	1/1	DK	R	C+	4	B-	Pay B to regenerate Drowned.
Drudge Skeletons	Summon Skeletons	B3	1/1	UL/RV	C	B-	4	B+	(B) Regenerates.
Durkwood Boars	Summon Boars	G4	4/4	LG	C2	C	3	C+	
Dust to Dust	Sorcery	1WW	---	DK	C	B-	4	B	Removes two target artifacts from the game.

Card Name	Type	Cost	Power/Toughness	Set	Commonality	Combo Value₁	Versatility₁	Standalone Value	Description
Dwarven Armorer	Summon	R	0/2	FE	U1	C	3	C	Tap+R. Discard a card from your hand to put either a +0/+1 or a +1/+0 counter on a target creature.
Dwarven Catapult	Instant	XR	...	FE	U3	B-	3	B-	Dwarven Catapult does X damage divided evenly among all of opponent's creatures (round down).
Dwarven Demolition Team	Summon Dwarves	R2	1/1	UL	U	C	4	C	Tap to destroy wall.
Dwarven Hold	Land	...	...	FE	U1	C+	3	C+	Comes into play tapped. You may choose not to untap Dwarven Hold during your upkeep phase and instead put a storage counter on it. Tap: Remove any number of storage counters from Dwarven Hold. For each storage counter removed, add R to your mana pool.
Dwarven Lieutenant	Summon	RR	2/1	FE	U3	C+	4	C	1R: Target Dwarf gets +1/+0 until end of turn.
Dwarven Ruins	Land	...	...	FE	U2	C	3	C	Comes into play tapped. Tap: Add B to your mana pool, and sacrifice Ebon Stronghold to add BB to your mana pool.
Dwarven Soldier	Summon	1R	2/1	FE	C1	C	3	C	If Dwarven Soldier blocks or is blocked by Orcs, it gets +0/+2 until end of turn.
Dwarven Song	Instant	R	...	LG	U	B	2	C	Change any/all creatures in play to red until end of turn.
Dwarven Warriors	Summon Dwarves	R2	1/1	UL/RV	C	B+	4	B	Tap to make power<3 creature unblockable.
Dwarven Weaponsmith	Summon Dwarves	R1	1/1	AQ/RV	U3/U	C	4	C+	Tap and sacrifice artifact during upkeep to give a permanent +1/+1 to target creature.

E

Card Name	Type	Cost	Power/ Toughness	Set	Common- ality	Combo Value₁	Versatility₁	Standalone Value	Description
Earth Elemental	Summon Elemental	RR3	4/5	UL/RV	U	C+	3	B-	
Earthbind	Enchant Creature	R	---	UL/RV	C	C	3	C	2 damage to creature; loses flying; does not effect non-flying creatures (was not cardable on them).
Earthquake	Sorcery	RX	---	UL/RV	R	B	3	B	All players and non-flying creatures take X damage.
Eater of the Dead	Summon Eater	4B	3/4	DK	U/R	B-	4	B-	Take one creature from any graveyard and remove it from the game. Untap Eater of the Dead.
Ebon Preator	Summon	4BB	5/5	FE	U1	B+	5	B-	Trample, First Strike. During your upkeep, put a -2/-2 counter on Ebon Preator. You may sacrifice a creature during your upkeep to remove a -2/-2 counter from Ebon Preator. If the creature sacrificed was a Thrull, also put a +1/+0 counter on Ebon Preator. Only one creature may be sacrificed in this matter each turn.
Ebon Stronghold	Land	---		FE	U2	C	3	C	Comes into play tapped. Tap: add B to your mana pool, and Sacrifice Ebon Stronghold to add BB to your mana pool.
Ebony Horse	Mono Artifact	3	---	AN-RV	U2>R	C	3	C+	Attacking creatures escape after defense is chosen (2,T).
El-Hajjaj	Summon El-Hajjaj	BB1	1/1	AN-RV	U2>R	B-	5	C-	+1 life for each damage he does to any target.

Card Name	Type	Cost	Power/ Toughness	Set	Common- ality	Combo Value₁	Versatility₁	Standalone Value	Description
Elder Land Wurm	Summon Wurm	WWW4	5/5	LG	R	C	2	D	Trample; cannot attack until after it blocks at least once.
Elder Spawn	Summon Spawn	UUU4	6/6	LG	R	C+	3	D	Cannot be blocked by red creatures; sacrifice an island each upkeep or take 6 damage and bury Spawn.
Electric Eel	Summon Eel	B	1/1	DK	U	D	2	D	Pay RR to give +2/+0 to Electric Eel. Does 1 damage to you and Electric Eel 1 damage to caster when cast.
Elephant Graveyard	Land	---	---	AN	U2	B-	4	C+	Tap for 1 colorless mana or to regenerate an Elephant or Mammoth.
Elven Fortress	Enchantment	1G	---	FE	C1	C+	3	C	1G: Target blocking creature gets +0/+1 until end of turn.
Elven Lyre	Artifact	2	---	FE	U1	C	4	C	Tap+1. Sacrifice Elven Lyre to give a target creature +2/+2 until end of turn.
Elven Riders	Summon Riders	GG3	3/3	LG	R	C+	4	C	Only blockable by walls and flying creatures.
Elves of Deep Shadow	Summon Elves	G	1/1	DK	U/R	C+	4	C+	Add B to your mana pool, and Elves of Deep Shadow does 1 damage to you.
Elvish Archers	Summon Elves	G1	2/1	UL/RV	R	B	4	B	First strike.
Elvish Farmer	Summon	1G	0/2	FE	U1	B+	4	B+	During your upkeep, put a spore counter on Elvish Farmer. O: remove three spore counters from Elvish Farmer to put a Saproling token into play. Treat this token as a 1/1 green creature. O: sacrifice a Saproling to gain 2 life.
Elvish Scout	Summon	G	1/1	FE	C1	C+	3	B-	Tap+G. Untap a target attacking creature you control. That creature neither receives nor deals damage during combat this turn.

Card Name	Type	Cost	Power/Toughness	Set	Commonality	Combo Value₁	Versatility₁	Standalone Value	Description
Emerald Dragonfly	Summon Dragonfly	G1	1/1	LG	C2	C+	4	B-	Flying; first strike (GG).
Enchanted Being	Summon Being	WW1	2/2	LG	C1	B-	4	C-	Takes no damage from creatures with enchantments on them.
Enchantment Alteration	Instant	U	...	LG	C1	B+	5	C	Move one creature or land enchantment to another creature or land without changing its controller.
Energy Flux	Enchantment	U2	...	AQ-RV	U3>U	B+	5	B-	Pay 2 for each artifact during upkeep or it is destroyed.
Energy Tap	Sorcery	U	...	LG	C2	B+	3	C+	Taps a creature for colorless mana equal to its casting cost.
Equinox	Enchant Land	W	...	LG	C1	C	3	C+	Tap this land to counter land destruction spell which affects one or more of your lands.
Erg Raiders	Summon Raiders	B1	2/3	AN-RV	C5>c	C+	2	B-	Take 2 damage if do not attack each turn.
Erhnam Djinn	Summon Djinn	G3	4/5	AN	U2	B-	3	B	Each upkeep gives ForestWalk to one of opponent's creatures until next upkeep.
Erosion	Enchant Land	BBB	...	DK	C	D	2	D	During your opponents upkeep, they must pay one mana or one life, or the land is destroyed. Damage from this may not prevented or redirected.
Eternal Flame	Sorcery	2RR	...	DK	U/R	B-	3	B-	Does an amount of damage to your opponent equal to the number of mountains you control, but it also does half that amount of damage to you, rounding up.
Eternal Warrior	Enchant Creature	R	...	LG	U	B-	3	C+	Creature does not tap when attacking.
Eureka	Sorcery	GG2	...	LG	R	B-	3	B-	Players alternate playing permanent from their hands with no casting cost required.

Card Name	Type	Cost	Power/Toughness	Set	Commonality	Combo Value[1]	Versatility[1]	Standalone Value	Description
Evil Eye of Orms-By-Gore	Summon Evil Eye	B4	3/6	LG	U	B-	3	C+	Blocked only by walls; only your Evil Eyes may attack while they are in play.
Evil Presence	Enchant Land	B	...	UL/RV	U	B-	3	B	Target land is now swamp.
Exorcist	Summon Exorcist	WW	1/1	DK	U/R	B-	4	B+	Target black creature is destroyed (Tap+1W).
Eye for an Eye	Instant	WW	...	AN-RV	U>R	B-	3	B+	Opponent takes damage equal to that inflicted on you by your opponent's spells or creatures.
F									
Fallen Angel	Summon Angel	BB3	3/3	LG	U	B+	5	B	Flying; sacrifice a creature for +2/+1 until end of turn.
Falling Star	Sorcery	R2	...	LG	R	C	3	C	Flip 360 degrees. Does 3 damage to all creatures touched. Taps any creatures it touched but did not kill.
False Orders	Instant	R	...	UL	C	C	3	C	Choose how/if one creature blocks.
Farmstead	Enchant Land	WWW	...	UL/RV	R	D-	2	D-	+1 life during upkeep (WW) once per turn.
Farrelite Priest	Summon	1WW	1/3	FE	U3	B-	4	C	1: Add W to your mana pool. Play this ability as an interrupt. If more than 3 are spent in this way during one turn, bury Farrelite Priest at end of turn.
Farrel's Mantle	Enchant Creature	2W	...	FE	U3	C	3	C	If target creature attacks and is not blocked, it may deal X+2 damage to any other target creature where X is the power of the creature Farrel's Mantle enchants. If it does so, it deals no damage to opponent this turn.

Card Name	Type	Cost	Power/ Toughness	Set	Common-ality	Combo Value1	Versatility1	Standalone Value	Description
Farrel's Zealot	Summon	1WW	2/2	FE	C1	B-	4	B-	If Farrel's Zealot attacks and is not blocked, you may choose to have it deal 3 damage to a target creature. If you do so, it deals no damage to opponent this turn.
Fastbond	Enchantment	G	...	UL/RV	R	B+	3	C+	Can play extra lands for 1 damage each.
Fasting	Enchantment	W	...	DK	U/R	C-	1	D	You may choose to skip your draw phase; if you do so, you gain 2 life. If you draw a card for any reason, Fasting is destroyed. During your upkeep, put a hunger counter on Fasting. When Fasting has five hunger counters on it it is destroyed.
Fear	Enchant Creature	BB	...	UL/RV	C	C+	3	C+	Only blockable by black or artifact creatures.
Feedback	Enchant Enchantment	U2	...	UL/RV	U	C	3	C	1 damage to controller during upkeep.
Feint	Instant	R	...	LG	C1	D+	3	D	Target attacker deals no damage and creatures it blocks deal no damage. Blockers blocking it are tapped.
Feldon's Cane	Mono Artifact	1	...	AQ	C1	B-	3	B	Reshuffle graveyard into library (1); remove Cane from game when it is used.
Fellwar Stone	Artifact	2	...	DK	U/R	B-	4	B	Add 1 mana to your mana pool. This mana may be of any color that any of opponent's lands can produce. This ability is played as an interrupt.
Feral Thallid	Summon	3GGG	6/3	FE	U3	B-	4	B-	During your upkeep, put a spore counter on Feral Thallid. O: Remove three spore counters from Feral Thallid to regenerate it.

Card Name	Type	Cost	Power/ Toughness	Set	Common- ality	Combo Value	Versatility₁	Standalone Value	Description
Festival	Instant	W	...	DK	C	B-	3	C+	Opponent may not declare an attack this turn. Play during opponent's upkeep phase.
Field of Dreams	Enchant World	U	...	LG	R	B+	2	C+	Top card of each player's library is always face-up.
Fire and Brimstone	Instant	3WW	...	DK	U/R	C	3	C-	This card does 4 damage to target player and 4 damage to you. Can only be used during a turn in which target player has declared an attack.
Fire Sprites	Summon Faerie	G1	1/1	LG	C2	C+	4	C+	Flying; (Tap+G) to get one red mana.
Fire Elemental	Summon Elemental	RR3	5/4	UL/RV	U	C+	3	C-	
Fire Drake	Summon Drake	1RR	1/2	DK	U/R	C	4	D-	Flying; +1/+0 until end of turn (R). No more than R may be spent in this way each turn.
Fireball	Sorcery	RX	...	UL/RV	C	B+	5	B+	X damage to target; each extra target (1); split damage evenly.
Firebreathing	Enchant Creature	R	...	UL/RV	C	B	3	C+	Gives +1/+0 (R).
Firestorm Phoenix	Summon Phoenix	RR4	3/2	LG	R	C	5	C	Flying; goes to owner's hand instead of to graveyard when it is destroyed.
Fishliver Oil	Enchant Creature	U1	...	AN	C3/C1	C+	3	C+	Gives IslandWalk.
Fissure	Instant	3RR	...	DK	C	C+	7	B+	Target land or creature is buried.
Flash Flood	Instant	U	...	LG	C2	C+	3	C	Destroys red permanent or sends a mountain in play to its owner's hand.
Flash Counter	Interrupt	U1	...	LG	C2	C+	4	C+	Counters an interrupt or instant.
Flashfires	Sorcery	R3	...	UL/RV	U	B+	3	B	Destroys all plains.
Flight	Enchant Creature	U	...	UL/RV	C	C+	3	C+	Gives flying.

Card Name	Type	Cost	Power/ Toughness	Set	Common- ality	Combo Value₁	Versatility₁	Standalone Value	Description
Flood	Enchantment	B	...	DK	R	B-	3	B-	Pay BB and target non-flying creature may not attack during this turn.
Floral Spuzzem	Summon Spuzzem	G3	2/2	LG	U	B-	4	B-	If not blocked when it attacks, you may destroy an artifact instead of dealing damage.
Flying Carpet	Mono Artifact	4	...	AN-RV	U3>R	B	3	B	Gives flying until end of turn (2,T); destroyed if creature destroyed when using it.
Flying Men	Summon Flying Men	U	1/1	AN	C5	C+	4	B	Flying.
Fog	Instant	G	...	UL/RV	C	B-	3	B-	No damage or other effects from this attack.
Force Spike	Interrupt	U	...	LG	C2	B-	3	B+	Counters spell unless opponent pays 1 colorless mana.
Force of Nature	Summon Force	GGGG2	8/8	UL/RV	R	B	3	B+	Trample; costs GGGG during upkeep or take 8 damage.
Forcefield	Poly Artifact	3	...	UL	R	C+	3	A-	Loose only 1 life to unblocked creature (1).
Forest-Big Tree	Land	...	...	UL/RV	C	C	3	C	Tap for 1 green mana.
Forest-Path	Land	...	...	UL/RV	C	C	3	C	Tap for 1 green mana.
Forest-Shadows	Land	...	...	UL/RV	C	C	3	C	Tap for 1 green mana.
Forethought Amulet	Artifact	5	...	LG	R	B	4	B-	Reduces damage done by sorceries and instants to 2; pay 3 mana during upkeep or Amulet is destroyed.
Fork	Interrupt	RR	...	UL/RV	R	B+	9	B-	Copy Sorcery or Instant and control the duplicate.
Fortified Area	Enchantment	WW1	...	LG	U	C	3	C	All your walls get +1/+0 and banding.
Fountain of Youth	Artifact	0	...	DK	U/R	B	3	B	(Tap+2) gain 1 life.

Card Name	Type	Cost	Power/ Toughness	Set	Common- ality	Combo Value₁	Versatility₁	Standalone Value	Description
Frankenstein's Monster	Summon Monster	XBB	0/1	DK	U/R	C+	3	B	When Frankenstein's Monster is brought into play, if you do not take X creatures from your graveyard and remove them from the game, Frankenstein's Monster is countered. For each creature removed from your graveyard, you may choose to give Frankenstein's Monster a permanent +2/+0, +1/+1, or +0/+2.
Frost Giant	Summon Giant	RRR3	4/4	LG	U	C+	3	C+	Rampage: 2.
Frozen Shade	Summon Shade	B2	2/2	UL/RV	R	B-	3	B-	+1/+1 (B).
Fungal Bloom	Enchantment	GG	...	FE	U1	B+	3	B	GG: Put a spore counter on a target Fungus.
Fungusaur	Summon Fungusaur	G3	2/2	UL/RV	R	B+	3	B	Gets +1/+1 token when damaged and not killed.
G									
Gabriel Angelfire	Summon Legend	GGWW3	4/4	LG	R	C	5	C	Each upkeep can get flying; first strike; trample or rampage:3 until beginning of next upkeep.
Gaea's Avenger	Summon Gaea's Avenger	GG1	*+1/*+1	AQ	U1	C+	3	B+	Where * = number of artifacts opponent has in play.
Gaea's Liege	Summon Gaea's Liege	GGG3	*/*	UL/RV	R	B+	3	B+	Where * = number of forests of opponent when attacking.
Gaea's Touch	Enchantment	GG	...	DK	C	C+	3	C+	You may put one additional land in play during each of your turns, but that land must be a basic forest. You may sacrifice Gaea's Touch to add GG to your mana pool. This ability is played as an interrupt.
Gaseous Form	Enchant Creature	U2	...	LG	C1	C+	3	C+	Creature takes and deals no damage in combat.

Card Name	Type	Cost	Power/ Toughness	Set	Common- ality	Combo Value₁	Versatility₁	Standalone Value	Description
Gate to Phyrexia	Enchantment	BB	---	AQ	U3	B+	3	B+	Sacrifice a creature during upkeep to destroy any one artifact in play.
Gauntlet of Might	Continuous Artifact	4	---	UL	R	A+	4	B+	+1/+1 to all red creatures; mountains produce 1 extra red mana.
Gauntlets of Chaos	Artifact	5	---	LG	R	B-	7	B+	Sacrifice this card and pay 5 mana to swap control of land, creature, or artifact until end of game. Destroys enchantments on the cards swapped.
Ghazban Ogre	Summon Ogre	G	2/2	AN	C4	C+	2	B-	During upkeep moves to player with most life.
Ghost Ship	Summon	BB2	2/4	DK	C	C+	5	B-	Flying; pay BBB to regenerate Ghost Ship.
Ghosts of the Damned	Summon Ghosts	BB1	0/2	LG	C2	C	2	D	Tap to give -1/-0 to a creature until end of turn.
Giant Growth	Instant	G	---	UL/RV	C	C+	4	B+	+3/+3 to creature until end of turn.
Giant Shark	Summon Shark	B5	4/4	DK	C	C+	3	C+	If Shark blocks or is blocked by a creature that is damaged this turn, Shark gains +2/+0 and trample until end of turn. Shark can only attack if opponent controls at least one island. Shark is buried immediately at any time if controller owns no islands.
Giant Slug	Summon Slug	B1	1/1	LG	C2	C+	4	B-	Gains basic LandWalk ability of choice starting next upkeep and going until end of turn (5).
Giant Spider	Summon Spider	G3	2/4	UL/RV	C	C+	4	B-	Can block flying creatures.
Giant Strength	Enchant Creature	RR	---	LG	C2	C	3	B	+2/+2.
Giant Tortoise	Summon Tortoise	U1	1/1	AN	C3/C1	C	3	B	+0/+3 while untapped.
Giant Turtle	Summon Turtle	GG1	2/4	LG	C2	C	2	C+	Cannot attack if it did so last turn.

171

Card Name	Type	Cost	Power/Toughness	Set	Commonality	Combo Value₁	Versatility₁	Standalone Value	Description
Glasses of Urza	Mono Artifact	1	---	UL/RV	U	B	4	A-	Tap to look at one opponent's hand.
Gloom	Enchantment	B2	---	UL/RV	U	B-	3	C	White spells and white enchantments cost 3 more (was white spells and circles of protection).
Glyph of Delusion	Instant	U	---	LG	C1	C	3	C	One creature blocked by target wall becomes tapped for N turns where N is the casting cost of the creature.
Glyph of Destruction	Instant	R	---	LG	C2	C	3	C	Wall gains +10/+0 and takes no damage while blocking, but it is destroyed at end of turn.
Glyph of Doom	Instant	B	---	LG	C2	C	3	C	Destroys all creatures blocked by target wall at end of combat.
Glyph of Life	Instant	W	---	LG	C2	C	3	C	All damage done to target wall so far this turn is added to your life.
Glyph of Reincarnation	Instant	G	---	LG	C1	C	3	C	All creatures which survive being blocked by target wall are buried, and then pull one creature of choice out of attacker's graveyard and into play for each one that was buried.
Goblin Artisans	Summon Goblins	R	1/1	AQ	U3	B-	4	C+	Tap when you cast an artifact then flip a coin with opponent calling heads or tails; opponent's favor=counters artifact; your favor=draw one card.
Goblin Balloon Brigade	Summon Goblins	R	1/1	UL/RV	U	B-	4	B	Flying (R).
Goblin Caves	Enchant Land	1RR	---	DK	C	B-	3	C	If target land is a basic mountain, all Goblins gain +0/+2.
Goblin Chirurgeon	Summon	R	0/2	FE	C1	B-	3	C	O: Sacrifice a Goblin to regenerate a target creature.

Card Name	Type	Cost	Power/ Toughness	Set	Common-ality	Combo Value₁	Versatility₁	Standalone Value	Description
Goblin Digging Team	Summon Goblins	R	1/1	DK	C	B-	4	C+	Sacrifice this card to destroy target wall.
Goblin Flotilla	Summon	2R	2/2	FE	C1	B-	4	B	IslandWalk. At the beginning of the attack, pay R or any creatures blocking or blocked by Goblin Flotilla gain first strike until end of turn.
Goblin Grenade	Sorcery	R	...	FE	C1	B-	3	B+	Sacrifice a Goblin to have Goblin Grenade deal 5 damage to one target.
Goblin Hero	Summon Goblin	2R	2/2	DK	C	C+	3	C	
Goblin King	Summon Goblin King	RR1	2/2	UL/RV	R	A-	3	C+	All goblins get +1/+1 and MountainWalk.
Goblin Kites	Enchantment	1R	...	FE	U3	C+	3	C+	R: A target creature you control, which cannot have a toughness greater than 2, gains flying until end of turn. Other effects may later be used to increase the creature's toughness. At end of turn, flip a coin; opponent calls heads or tails while coin is in the air. If the flip ends up in the opponent's favor, bury that creature.
Goblin Rock Sled	Summon Rock Sled	1R	3/1	DK	C	C	2	C	Trample; may not attack unless opponent controls at least one mountain. Does not untap as normal during your untap phase if it attacked during your last turn.
Goblin Shrine	Enchant Land	1RR	...	DK	C	C+	3	C	If target land is a basic mountain, all Goblins gain +1/+0; does 1 damage to all Goblins if it leaves play.
Goblin War Drums	Enchantment	2R	...	FE	C1	B	3	B-	Each attacking creature you control that opponent chooses to block may not be blocked with fewer than two creature.

Card Name	Type	Cost	Power/Toughness	Set	Commonality	Combo Value	Versatility	Standalone Value	Description
Goblin Warrens	Enchantment	2R	...	FE	U1	B+	3	B	2R: Sacrifice two Goblins to put three Goblin tokens into play. Treat these tokens as 1/1 red creatures.
Golbin Wizard	Summon Goblin	2RR	1/1	DK	U/R	B+	4	C+	Take a Goblin from your hand and put it directly into play. Treat this goblin as if it were just summoned. Target Goblin gains protection from white until end of turn.
Goblins of the Flarg	Summon Goblins	R	1/1	DK	C	B-	4	B+	MountainWalk; this card is buried if controller controls any Dwarves.
Golgothian Sylex	Mono Artifact	4	...	AQ	U1	C-	2	B-	Destroys all antiquities cards in play including itself (1).
Gosta Dirk	Summon Legend	UUWW3	4/4	LG	R	C	3	C	First strike; stops all use of IslandWalk in play.
Granite Gargoyle	Summon Gargoyle	R2	2/2	UL/RV	R	C	3	C	Flying, +0/+1 (R).
Grapeshot Catapult	Artifact Creature	4	2/3	AQ	C4	B+	3	B	Tap for 1 damage to any flying creature.
Grave Robbers	Summon Robbers	1BB	1/1	DK	U/R	C	3	B-	Take one artifact from any graveyard and remove it from the game (Tap+B). Gain 2 life.
Gravity Sphere	Enchant World	B2	...	LG	R	B+	3	C+	All creatures lose flying ability.
Gray Ogre	Summon Ogre		2/2	UL/RV	C	C	3	C	
Great Defender	Instant	W	...	LG	U	C	3	C	+0/+N to a creature where N is its casting cost.
Greater Realm of Preservation	Enchantment	W1	...	LG	U	B+	4	B+	Reduces damage from red or black source to zero (W1).
Great Wall	Enchantment	W2	...	LG	U	C	3	C	Stops all use of PlainsWalk in play.
Greed	Enchantment	B3	...	LG	R	B	3	B+	Draw a card and lose two life points (B).
Green Ward	Enchant Creature	W	...	UL/RV	U	C+	3	C	Gives protection from green.

Card Name	Type	Cost	Power/Toughness	Set	Commonality	Combo Value₁	Versatility₁	Standalone Value	Description
Green Mana Battery	Artifact	4	--	LG	U	C	3	C	Add a token to it (Tap+2) or tap for one green mana plus can convert tokens to green mana as well.
Grizzly Bears	Summon Bears	G1	2/2	UL/RV	C	C	3	C+	
Guardian Angel	Instant	WX	--	UL/RV	C	C	4	C	Prevents X damage to target; can pay to prevent further damage to the target this turn.
Guardian Beast	Summon Guardian	B3	2/4	AN	U2	B+	4	B+	If untapped prevents stealing.
Gwendlyn Di Corci	Summon Legend	BBUR	3/5	LG	R	B	4	B+	Tap to make opponent discard a card. Can only be used on your turn.
H									
Halfdane	Summon Legend	BUW1	*/*	LG	R	C	4	B	Where * is 3 at casting time and changes each upkeep to be equal to power of a creature in play. If there are no creatures, * = 0.
Hammerheim	Legendary Land	--	--	LG	U	C	4	B-	Tap for one red mana or tap to remove LandWalk ability from a creature until end of turn.
Hand of Justice	Summon	5W	2/6	FE	U1	B-	4	B+	Tap three target white creatures you control to destroy any target creature.
Hasran Ogress	Summon Ogre	BB	3/2	AN	C3/C2	C	2	C	Pay 2 when attacking or take 3 damage.
Haunting Wind	Enchantment	B3	--	AQ	U3	B	3	B-	1 damage to anyone who taps or powers an artifact.
Havenwood Battleground	Land	--	--	FE	U2	C	3	C	Comes into play tapped. Add G to your mana pool, and sacrifice Havenwood Battleground to add GG to your mana pool.

Card Name	Type	Cost	Power/ Toughness	Set	Common- ality	Combo Value	Versatility	Standalone Value	Description
Hazezon Tamar	Summon Legend	GRW4	2/4	LG	R	A-	4	B+	On the upkeep after Hazezon enters play, you get a 1/1 green, white, and red Sand Warrior token creature for each land you control. The tokens leave play if Hazezon does.
Headless Horseman	Summon Horseman	B2	2/2	LG	C1	C	3	C	
Healing Salve	Instant	W	...	UL/RV	C	C+	4	C+	+3 life or prevent 3 damage.
Heaven's Gate	Instant	W	...	LG	U	A-	3	C	Change any/all creatures in play to white until end of turn.
Hell Swarm	Instant	B	...	LG	C1	C-	2	C-	-1/-0 to all creatures until end of turn.
Hellfire	Sorcery	BBB2	...	LG	R	A-	3	B-	Destroys all non-black creatures and does 3 damage plus one damage to you for each creature that goes to the graveyard.
Hell's Caretaker	Summon Hell's Caretaker	B3	1/1	LG	R	A-	4	B+	Tap and sacrifice a creature during upkeep to bring a creature from your graveyard directly into play.
Helm of Chatzuk	Mono Artifact	1	...	UL/RV	R	B-	3	B	Give creature banding until end of turn (1,T).
Heroism	Enchantment	2W	...	FE	U3	C+	3	C	O: sacrifice a white creature to have attacking red creatures deal no damage during combat this turn. The attacking player may pay 2 R for an attacking creature to have it deal damage as normal.
Hidden Path	Enchantment	2GGGG	...	DK	U/R	C	3	C	All green creatures gain ForestWalk.
High Tide	Instant	U	...	FE	C1	B	3	C-	Until end of turn, all islands produce an additional U when tapped for mana.
Hill Giant	Summon Giant	R3	3/3	UL/RV	C	C	3	C	

Card Name	Type	Cost	Power/ Toughness	Set	Common- ality	Combo Value₁	Versatility₁	Standalone Value	Description
Hollow Trees	Land	---	---	FE	U1	C	3	B	Comes into play tapped. You may choose not to untap Hollow Trees during your untap phase and instead put a storage counter on it. Tap: remove any number of storage counters from Hollow Trees. For each storage counter removed, add G to your mana pool.
Holy Armor	Enchant Creature	W	---	UL/RV	C	C+	3	C	+0/+2; +0/+1 (W).
Holy Day	Instant	W	---	LG	C1	C+	3	C+	No creatures deal or take damage from combat this turn.
Holy Light	Instant	2W	---	DK	C	B-	3	C+	All non-white creatures get -1/-1 until end of turn.
Holy Strength	Enchant Creature	W	---	UL/RV	C	C	3	C	Gives +1/+2.
Homarid	Summon	2U	2/2	FE	C1	C+	3	C+	Put a tide counter on Homarid when it is brought into play and during your upkeep. If there is one tide counter on Homarid, it gets -1/-1. If there are three tide counters on Homarid, it gets +1/+1. When there are four tide counters on Homarid, remove them all.
Homarid Shaman	Summon	2UU	2/1	FE	U1	B-	3	C+	U: Tap a target green creature.
Homarid Spanning Bed	Enchantment	UU	---	FE	U3	B	3	B	1UU: Sacrifice a blue creature to put X Camarid tokens into play where X is the casting cost of the sacrificed creature. Treat these tokens as 1/1 blue creature.
Homarid Warrior	Summon	4U	3/3	FE	C1	C	3	C	U: Homarid Warrior may not be the target of spells or effects until end of turn and does not untap as normal during your next untap phase. If Homarid Warrior is untapped, tap it.

Card Name	Type	Cost	Power/ Toughness	Set	Common- ality	Combo Value₁	Versatility₁	Standalone Value	Description
Horn of Deafening	Artifact	4	...	LG	R	C	3	B-	Make a creature deal no damage this turn (Tap+2).
Hornet Cobra	Summon Cobra	GG1	2/1	LG	C2	C+	4	B-	First strike.
Horror of Horrors	Enchantment	BB3	...	LG	U	C+	3	B+	Can sacrifice a swamp to regenerate a black creature.
Howl from Beyond	Instant	BX	...	UL/RV	C	C+	3	B-	+X/+0 until end of turn.
Howling Mine	Continuous Artifact	2	...	UL/RV	R	B-	3	B	All players draw 1 extra card during draw phase.
Hunding Gjornersen	Summon Legend	UUW3	5/4	LG	U	C	3	C	Rampage: 1.
Hurkyl's Recall	Instant	U1	...	AQ-RV	U1>R	B+	4	B-	Sends all of target player's artifacts from play into hand.
Hurloon Minotaur	Summon Minotaur	RR1	2/3	UL/RV	C	C	3	C	
Hurr Jackal	Summon Jackal	R	1/1	AN	C4	B-	4	B-	Tap to prevent creature from regenerating this turn.
Hurricane	Sorcery	GX	...	UL/RV	U	B-	4	B-	All players and flying creatures take X damage.
Hymn to Tourach	Sorcery	BB	...	FE	C1	B+	3	B	Target player discards two cards at random from his or her hand. If target player does not have enough cards, his or her entire hand is discarded.
Hyperion Blacksmith	Summon Smith	RR1	2/2	LH	U	B-	4	B	Tap to tap or untap an opponent's artifact.
Hypnotic Specter	Summon Specter	BB1	2/2	UL/RV	U	B-	4	B+	Flying; player discards if damaged by specter.
Icatian Infantry	Summon	W	1/1	FE	C1	B-	5	B-	1: Bands until end of turn. 1: First strike until end of turn.

Card Name	Type	Cost	Power/Toughness	Set	Commonality	Combo Value₁	Versatility₁	Standalone Value	Description
Icatian Javelineers	Summon	W	1/1	FE	C1	B+	4	B+	When Icatian Javelineers is brought into play, put a javelin counter on it. Tap: Remove the javelin counter to have Icatian Javelineers deal 1 damage to any target.
Icatian Moneychanger	Summon	W	0/2	FE	C1	C	3	C	Moneychanger deals 3 damage to you when summoned; put three credit counters on Moneychanger at that time. During your upkeep, put one credit counter on Moneychanger. O: Sacrifice Moneychanger to gain 1 life for each credit counter on it. Use this ability only during your upkeep.
Icatian Lieutenant	Summon	WW	1/2	FE	U1	B	4	B	1W: Target Soldier gets +1/+0 until end of turn.
Icatian Phalanx	Summon	4W	2/4	FE	U3	B	3	C+	Bands.
Icatian Priest	Summon	W	1/1	FE	U3	B-	4	B-	1WW: Target creature gets +1/+1 until end of turn.
Icatian Scout	Summon	W	1/1	FE	C1	B+	4	B	Tap+1. Target creature gains first strike until end of turn.
Icatian Skirmishers	Summon	3W	1/1	FE	U1	B+	3	B-	Bands, First Strike. All creatures that band with Skirmishers to attack, gain first strike until end of turn.
Icatian Store	Land	...	...	FE	U1	C	3	C+	Tap. Add 1 mana of any color to your mana pool. Control of Rainbow Vale passed to opponent at end of turn.
Icatian Town	Sorcery	5W	...	FE	U1	C+	3	B	Put 4 Citizen tokens into play. Treat these tokens as 1/1 white creature.

Card Name	Type	Cost	Power/ Toughness	Set	Common-ality	Combo Value₁	Versatility₁	Standalone Value	Description
Ice Storm	Sorcery	G2	...	UL	U	B-	3	B-	Destroy one land.
Ichneumon Druid	Summon Druid	GG1	1/1	LG	U	C	3	C	Opponent takes 4 damage for each instant past the first one cast each turn.
Icy Manipulator	Mono Artifact	4	...	UL	U	A-	7	A-	Tap one creature, artifact or land (1,T).
Ifh-Biff Efreet	Summon Efreet	GG2	3/3	AN	U2	B+	5	B+	Flying; any player can pay G for 1 damage to all players and flying creatures.
Illusionary Mask	Poly Artifact	2	...	UL	R	B-	4	C+	Can summon creatures face down (X); creature becomes face up once used or damaged.
Immolation	Enchant Creature	R	...	LG	C1	C+	4	C	+2/-1.
Implements of Sacrifice	Artifact	2	...	FE	U1	C	4	C	Tap+1. Sacrifice Implements of Sacrifice to add 2 mana of any one color to your mana pool. Play this ability as an interrupt.
Imprison	Enchant Creature	B	...	LG	R	C+	3	B+	Pay 1 mana each time creature attacks, blocks, or is tapped in order to prevent that action; enchantment is destroyed if you do not pay.
In the Eye of Chaos	Enchant World	U2	...	LG	R	B+	3	B	All instants and interrupts are countered unless the spell cost is paid a second time with any color mana.
Indestructible Aura	Instant	W	...	LG	C2	B-	3	B	Creature takes no damage for rest of turn.
Infernal Medusa	Summon Medusa	BB3	2/4	LG	U	B-	3	B+	All creatures blocked by/blocking it are destroyed at end of combat.
Inferno	Instant	5RR	...	DK	U/R	B	4	B	Inferno does 6 damage to all players and all creatures.

Card Name	Type	Cost	Power/ Toughness	Set	Common- ality	Combo Value1	Versatility1	Standalone Value	Description
Infinite Authority	Enchant Creature	WWW	---	LG	R	B-	4	B-	Destroys all creatures of toughness < 4 that block it; gets +1/+1 at end of turn for each creature that it sends to the graveyard.
Initiates of the Ebon Hand	Summon	B	1/1	FE	C1	B+	4	B	1: Add B to your mana pool. Play this ability as an interrupt. If more than 3 is spent in this way during one turn, bury Initiates of the Ebon Hand at end of turn.
Inquisition	Sorcery	2B	---	DK	C	C+	3	C	Look at target player's hand. Does 1 damage to target player for each white card in hand.
Instill Energy	Enchant Creature	G	---	UL/RV	U	B	3	C	May untap once during your turn in addition to the untap phase; may attack on turn it enters play.
Invisibility	Enchant Creature	UU	---	UL	C	B	3	B	Target blocked only by walls.
Invoke Prejudice	Enchantment	UUUU	---	UL	C	B	3	B	Opponent must pay N additional mana to cast summon spells that are not the same color as one of your creatures; N is the cost of the summon spell.
Iron Star	Poly Artifact	1	---	UL/RV	U	C	3	C	+1 life when red spell cast (1).
Ironclaw Orcs	Summon Orcs	R1	2/2	UL	C	C	2	C	Cannot block creatures with power greater than 1.
Ironroot Treefolk	Summon Treefolk	G4	3/5	UL/RV	C	C	3	C	
Island Fish Jasconius	Summon Island Fish	UUU4	6/8	AN-RV	U2>R	C	2	B	Pay UUU to untap during upkeep; cannot attack if opponent does not have islands; destroyed if you have no islands.
Island-Greenish	Land	---	---	UL/RV	C	C	3	C	Tap for 1 blue mana.
Island-Purplish	Land	---	---	UL/RV	C	C	3	C	Tap for 1 blue mana.

Card Name	Type	Cost	Power/Toughness	Set	Commonality	Combo Value₁	Versatility₁	Standalone Value	Description
Island-Red Sky ✗	Land	---	---	UL/RV	C	C	3	C	Tap for 1 blue mana.
Island of Wak-Wak	Land	---	---	AN	U2	B	3	B	Tap to change power of one flying creature to 0.
Ivory Cup	Poly Artifact	1	---	UL/RV	U	C	3	C	+1 life when white spell cast (1).
Ivory Guardians	Summon Guardians	WW4	3/3	LG	U	C	4	C	Protection from red; gets +1/+1 if opponent has red cards in play.
Ivory Tower	Continuous Artifact	1	---	AQ-RV	U3>R	B-	4	A	+1 life for each card over 4 in hand at beginning of turn.
J									
Jacques le Vert	Summon Legend	GRW1	3/2	LG	R	C	4	C	All your green creatures get +0/+2.
Jade Monolith	Poly Artifact	4	---	UL/RV	R	B	3	C	Transfer damage to self from creature (1).
Jade Statue	Artifact	4	---	UL	U	B-	4	B-	3/6 creature for attack or block (2).
Jalum Tome	Mono Artifact	3	---	AQ	U2	B-	3	B+	Draw a card.
Jandor's Ring	Mono Artifact	6	---	AN-RV	U2>R	B-	3	C	Discard the card just drawn and replace it (2,T).
Jandor's Saddlebags	Mono Artifact	2	---	AN-RV	U2>R	C	3	C	Untap a creature (3,T).
Jasmine Boreal	Summon Legend	GW3	4/5	LG	U	C	3	C	
Jayemdae Tome	Mono Artifact	4	---	UL/RV	R	B-	3	A-	Draw a card (4,T).
Jedit Ojanen	Summon Legend	UWW4	5/5	LG	U	C	3	C	
Jerrard of the Closed Fist	Summon Legend	GGR3	6/5	LG	U	C	2	C+	
Jeweled Bird	Mono Artifact	1	---	AN	U3	C	3	C	Exchange for your ante and draw a new card.
Jihad	Enchantment	WWW	---	AN	U2	B+	3	B+	+2/+1 to white creatures while chosen color of opponent's is in play; discarded if no cards of that color.

Card Name	Type	Cost	Power/Toughness	Set	Commonality	Combo Value₁	Versatility₁	Standalone Value	Description
Johan	Summon Legend	GRW3	5/4	LG	R	B-	4	B	If does not attack and is not tapped then none of your creatures tap when attacking.
Jovial Evil	Sorcery	B2	...	LG	R	B+	3	C-	Opponent takes 2 damage for each white creature controlled.
Juggernaut	Artifact Creature	4	5/3	UL/RV	U	B+	3	A-	Must attack; cannot be blocked by walls.
Jump	Instant	U	...	UL/RV	C	C-	3	C-	Creature is flying until end of turn.
Junun Efreet	Summon Efreet	BB1	3/3	AN	U2	C+	3	C+	Flying; pay BB during upkeep or destroyed.
Juxtapose	Sorcery	U3	...	LG	R	B-	5	C-	You and your opponent each trade control of your highest cost creature and highest cost artifact.
Juzam Djinn	Summon Djinn	BB2	5/5	AN	U2	A-	3	A-	Take 1 damage during upkeep.
K									
Karakas	Legendary Land	...	...	LG	U	B+	4	C+	Tap for one white mana or tap to send a legend from play into its owner's hand.
Karma	Enchantment	WW2	...	UL/RV	U	B	3	C	1 damage during upkeep for each swamp.
Kasmir the Lone Wolf	Summon Legend	UW4	5/3	LG	U	D	1	D	
Keepers of the Faith	Summon Keepers	WW1	2/3	LG	C2	C	3	C	
Kei Takahashi	Summon Legend	GW2	2/2	LG	R	C	4	C+	Tap to prevent up to 2 damage to a creature.
Keldon Warlord	Summon Lord	RR2	*/*	UL/RV	U	B+	3	B	Where * = number of non-wall creatures you have.
Khabal Ghoul	Summon Ghoul	B2	1/1	AN	U3	B-	4	B	+1/+1 token at end of turn for each creature that was destroyed.
Killer Bees	Summon Bees	GG1	0/1	LG	R	B	4	A	Flying; +1/+1 (G).

Card Name	Type	Cost	Power/Toughness	Set	Commonality	Combo Value₁	Versatility₁	Standalone Value	Description
King Suleiman	Summon King	W1	1/1	AN	U2	C-	2	C-	Tap to destroy Efreet or Djinn.
Kird Ape	Summon Ape	R	1/1	AN	C5	B	3	A	+1/+2 if you have forests.
Kismet	Enchantment	W3	---	LG	U	B+	7	B	All opponent's creatures, land, and artifacts enter play tapped.
Knights of Thorn	Summon Knights	3W	2/2	DK	U/R	B	4	B-	Protection from red, banding.
Knowledge Vault	Artifact	4	---	LG	R	B	3	B	Put a card from your library under Vault (2,T); sacrifice Vault and your entire hand to use cards under Vault as your hand.
Kobold Drill Sergeant	Summon Drill Sergeant	R1	1/2	LG	U	C+	3	C	Gives all your Kobolds +0/+1 and Trample.
Kobold Overlord	Summon Lord	R1	1/2	LG	R	C+	3	C	First Strike; gives all your Kobolds First Strike.
Kobolds of Kher Keep	Summon Kobolds	0	0/1	LG	C2	C+	3	C+	
Kormus Bell	Continuous Artifact	4	---	UL/RV	R	B	3	C	All swamps become 1/1 creatures.
Kry Shield	Artifact	2	---	LG	U	C	3	B	Give +0/+N to a creature where N is its casting cost (2,T).
Kudzu	Enchant Land	GG1	---	UL/RV	R	C+	3	C-	Destroys land when land is tapped then moves to another land.
L									
Lady Caleria	Summon Legend	GGWW3	3/6	LG	R	C	4	C+	Tap to do 3 damage to attacker or blocker.
Lady Evangela	Summon Legend	BUW	1/2	LG	R	C	4	C	Cause a creature not to deal damage during combat (BW,T).
Lady of the Mountain	Summon Legend	GR4	5/5	LG	U	C	3	C	
Lady Orca	Summon Legend	BR5	7/4	LG	U	C	3	C	

Card Name	Type	Cost	Power/Toughness	Set	Common-ality	Combo Value₁	Versatility₁	Standalone Value	Description
Lance	Enchant Creature	W	...	UL/RV	U	C	3	C	Gives First Strike.
Land Equilibrium	Enchantment	UU2	...	LG	R	B+	3	C+	If opponent has at least as many land as you do, then opponent must sacrifice a land when playing a new one.
Land Leeches	Summon Leeches	1GG	2/2	DK	C	C	3	B	First Strike.
Land Tax	Enchantment	W	...	LG	U	A	4	B+	If opponent has more land than you, during upkeep you may pull up to 3 basic land from your library to your hand.
Land's Edge	Enchant World	RR1	...	LG	R	A	3	B	Any player may discard at any time. If discard a land, can do 2 damage to any player.
Lesser Werewolf	Summon Lycanthrope	B3	2/4	LG	U	B-	4	B-	When blocked by/blocking creatures, may take -1/-0 until end of turn to give a permanent -1/-0 token to creature (B).
Leviathan	Summon Leviathan	BBBB5	10/10	DK	R	B-	2	C+	Trample. When Leviathon comes into play, you must sacrifice two islands. In order to attack with Leviathon, you must sacrifice two islands. To untap, you must also sacrifice two islands.
Ley Druid	Summon Cleric	G2	1/1	UL/RV	U	B	4	C	Tap to untap land of choice.
Library of Alexandria	Land	...	...	AN	U3	B+	3	B	Tap for 1 colorless mana or draw one card from library, must already have exactly 7 cards.
Library of Leng	Continuous Artifact	1	...	UL/RV	U	B+	3	C+	Skip discard phase; can discard to top of library; (was no limit to hand size).
Lich	Enchantment	BBBB	...	UL	R	B+	3	C-	Lose cards in play instead of life lost; gain cards in hand instead of life gain; die if cannot sacrifice card or Lich destroyed.

Card Name	Type	Cost	Power/ Toughness	Set	Common- ality	Combo Value	Versatility1	Standalone Value	Description
Life Chisel	Artifact	4	---	LG	U	B-	3	C+	Sacrifice a creature during upkeep to gain life equal to its toughness.
Life Matrix	Artifact	4	---	LG	R	B-	3	B-	Add regeneration token to a creature (4,T); can only be used during your upkeep.
Lifeblood	Enchantment	WW2	---	LG	R	B-	3	C+	+1 life each time opponent taps a mountain.
Lifeforce	Enchantment	GG	---	UL/RV	U	B-	3	C	Counter black spell as cast (GG).
Lifelace	Interrupt	G	---	UL/RV	R	C+	3	C	Changes card color to green.
Lifetap	Enchantment	UU	---	UL/RV	U	B+	3	C+	+1 life when opponents tap forests.
Lightning Bolt	Instant	R	---	UL/RV	C	C+	5	A	3 damage to one target.
Living Armor	Artifact	4	---	DK	U/R	C	3	C	Sacrifice Living Armor to put +0/+X counter on target creature, where X is the target creature's casting cost.
Living Artifact	Enchant Artifact	G	---	UL/RV	R	B	3	B	Put one token on artifact for each life lost; can convert one token to +1 life each upkeep.
Living Lands	Enchantment	G3	---	UL/RV	R	B	3	B-	Treat all forests in play as 1/1 creatures.
Living Plane	Enchant World	GG2	---	LG	R	A-	3	B+	All lands in play are 1/1 creatures as well as lands.
Living Wall	Artifact Creature	4	0/6	UL/RV	U	B	3	B	Wall; regenerates (1).
Livonya Silone	Summon Legend	GGRR2	4/4	LG	R	C	3	C	First Strike; Legendary LandWalk.
Llanowar Elves	Summon Elves	G	1/1	UL/RV	C	B	5	B	Tap for 1 green mana.
Lord Magnus	Summon Legend	GWW3	4/3	LG	U	C	4	C-	First Strike; stops all use of PlainsWalk and ForestWalk in play.
Lord of Atlantis	Summon Lord	UU	2/2	UL/RV	R	B-	4	C+	All Merfolk get +1/+1 and IslandWalk.

Card Name	Type	Cost	Power/Toughness	Set	Commonality	Combo Value₁	Versatility₁	Standalone Value	Description
Lord of the Pit	Summon Demon	BBB4	7/7	UL/RV	R	B-	4	B	Trample; Flying, sacrifice one creature during upkeep or take 7 damage.
Lost Soul	Summon Lost Soul	BB1	2/1	LG	C2	C	4	B-	SwampWalk.
Lure	Enchant Creature	GG1	---	UL/RV	U	B+	3	C+	All creatures able to block target creature must do so.
Lurker	Summon Lurker	2G	2/3	DK	U/R	C+	4	C+	Lurker may not be the target of any spell unless Lurker was declared as an attacker or blocker this turn.
M									
Magical Hack	Interrupt	U	---	UL/RV	R	A	4	C	Change land type references on one card.
Magnetic Mountain	Enchantment	RR1	---	AN-RV	U3>R	C+	3	C	Blue creatures cost 4 to untap during upkeep.
Mahamoti Djinn	Summon Djinn	UU4	5/6	UL/RV	R	C+	3	B+	Flying.
Mana Clash	Sorcery	R	---	DK	U/R	C	2	D	You and target player each flip a coin. Mana Clash does 1 damage to any player whose coin comes up tails. Repeat this process until both players' coins come up heads at the same time.
Mana Drain	Interrupt	UU	---	LG	U	A	8	A	Counters target spell and gives N colorless mana to you next turn. N is the cost of the spell countered.
Mana Flare	Enchantment	R2	---	UL/RV	R	B	3	C	All mana producing lands produce one extra mana.
Mana Matrix	Artifact	6	---	LG	R	C	3	C	You pay up to two less on the colorless mana part of instant, interrupt, or enchantment spells.
Mana Short	Instant	U2	---	UL/RV	R	B-	4	B	All opponent's land is tapped and pool emptied.

Card Name	Type	Cost	Power/ Toughness	Set	Common- ality	Combo Value₁	Versatility₁	Standalone Value	Description
Mana Vault	Mono Artifact	1	---	UL/RV	R	B-	3	C+	Tap for 3 colorless mana; untap for 4 mana during upkeep or take 1 damage.
Mana Vortex	Enchantment	BB1	---	DK	R	B	3	C-	Each player sacrifices one land during their upkeep. If there are no lands in play, Mana Vortex is destroyed. If you do not sacrifice a land when Mana Vortex is cast, Mana Vortex is countered.
Manabarbs	Enchantment	R3	---	UL/RV	R	B+	3	C	1 damage to anyone who taps a land.
Marble Priest	Artifact Creature	5	3/3	LG	U	C	4	C-	All walls able to block Priest must do so; does not take damage from walls.
Marhault Elsdragon	Summon Legend	GRR3	4/6	LG	U	C	4	C	Rampage: 1.
Marsh Gas	Instant	B	---	DK	C	C+	3	C	All creatures get -2/-0 until end of turn.
Marsh Golbins	Summon Goblins	BR	1/1	DK	C	C+	4	C	SwampWalk; counts as both a black card and a red card.
Marsh Viper	Summon Viper	3G	1/2	DK	C	B-	4	C+	If Marsh Viper damages opponent, opponent gets two poison counters. If opponent ever has ten or more poison counters, opponent loses game.
Martyr's Cry	Sorcery	WW	---	DK	U/R	B+	4	C+	All white creatures are removed from the game. Players must draw one card for each white creature they control that is lost in this manner.
Martyrs of Korlis	Summon Bodyguard	WW3	1/6	AQ	U3	B-	5	B	If untapped, all artifact damage is taken from you to one of your Bodyguards.
Master of the Hunt	Summon Master	GG2	2/2	LG	R	B	4	B+	Creates 1/1 green Wolves of the Hunt token creature which has Bands with other (GG2).

Card Name	Type	Cost	Power/ Toughness	Set	Common- ality	Combo Value$_1$	Versatility$_1$	Standalone Value	Description
Maze of Ith	Land	0	---	DK	C	B-	4	A-	Target attacking creature becomes untapped. This creature neither deals nor receives damage as a result of combat.
Meekstone	Continuous Artifact	1	---	UL/RV	R	B+	3	B+	Creatures with power>2 do not untap.
Merchant Ship	Summon Ship	U	0/2	AN	U3	C+	3	B+	+2 life if attacks and is not blocked; cannot attack if opponent does not have islands; destroyed if you have no islands.
Merfolk Assassin	Summon Merfolk	BB	1/2	DK	R	D-	4	C+	Tap Merfolk Assassin to destroy target creature that has IslandWalk.
Merfolk of the Pearl Trident	Summon Merfolk	U	1/1	UL/RV	C	C+	3	C	
Merseine	Enchant Creature	2UU	---	FE	C1	C	3	C	Put three net counters on Merseine when it is brought into play. Target creature Merseine enchants does not untap as normal during it's controller's untap phase as long as any net counters remain. As a fast effect, target creature's controller may pay creature's casting cost to remove a net counter.
Mesa Pegasus	Summon Pegasus	W1	1/1	UL/RV	C	B	4	C+	Flying; bands.
Metamorphosis	Sorcery	G	---	AN	C4	C+	3	C+	Sacrifice creature for casting cost+1 mana of any color which can only be used for summonings.
Mightstone	Continuous Artifact	4	---	AQ	U2	C	3	C	+1/+0 to all attacking creatures.
Mijae Djinn	Summon Djinn	RRR	6/3	AN-RV	U2>R	C+	2	B	Flip coin when attacking.
Millstone	Mono Artifact	2	---	AQ-RV	U3>R	B+	4	B	Opponent discards 2 cards from top of library (2,T).

Card Name	Type	Cost	Power/Toughness	Set	Common-ality	Combo Value₁	Versatility₁	Standalone Value	Description
Mine Bomb	Sorcery	B	---	DK	R	D	2	D	All players must discard three cards from their hand or else suffer 1 damage for each card they keep.
Mind Twist	Sorcery	BX	---	UL/RV	R	B	6	A	Opponent discards X cards at random.
Mindstab Thrull	Summon	1BB	2/2	FE	C1	B	4	C+	If Mindstab Thrull attacks and is not blocked, you may sacrifice it to force the player it attacked to discard three cards. If you do so, it deals no damage during combat this turn. If that player does not have enough cards, his or her entire hand is discarded.
Miracle Worker	Summon Miracle Worker	W	1/1	DK	C	C	3	C	Destroy target enchantment card on a creature you control.
Mirror Universe	Artifact	6	---	LG	R	A-	3	B+	Tap and sacrifice this card during upkeep to switch life totals with your opponent.
Mishra's Factory-Red Balloon/Spring/Dark Green	Land	---	---	AQ	U1	A	9	A	Tap for 1 colorless mana or tap to give +1/+1 to any Assembly Worker or spend 1 colorless mana to turn land into a 2/2 Assembly Worker artifact-land creature until end of turn.
Mishra's Factory-No Balloon/Winter/White	Land	---	---	AQ	U1	A	9	A	Tap for 1 colorless mana or tap to give +1/+1 to any Assembly Worker or spend 1 colorless mana to turn land into a 2/2 Assembly Worker artifact-land creature until end of turn.
Mishra's Factory-Blue Balloon/Summer/Pale Green	Land	---	---	AQ	C1	A	1	A	Tap for 1 colorless mana or tap to give +1/+1 to any Assembly Worker or spend 1 colorless mana to turn land into a 2/2 Assembly Worker artifact-land creature until end of turn.

Card Name	Type	Cost	Power/ Toughness	Set	Common- ality	Combo Value₁	Versatility₁	Standalone Value	Description
Mishra's Factory-Two Balloons/Fall/Red	Land	...	...	AQ	U1	A	9	A	Tap for 1 colorless mana or tap to give +1/+1 to any Assembly Worker or spend 1 colorless mana to turn land into a 2/2 Assembly Worker artifact-land creature until end of turn.
Mishra's War Machine	Artifact Creature	7	5/5	AQ-RV	U1>R	C-	1	D	Bands; discard 1 card from hand each upkeep or take 3 damage and becomes tapped.
Mishra's Workshop	...	...	...	AQ	U1	A	3	A	Tap for 3 colorless mana which can only be used to cast artifacts.
Moat	Enchantment	WW2	...	LG	R	B	3	B+	All players' non-flying creatures cannot attack.
Mold Demon	Summon Mold Demon	BB5	6/6	LG	R	C	2	C	Must sacrifice two swamps when it comes into play.
Mons's Goblin Raiders	Summon Goblins	R	1/1	UL/RV	C	C+	3	C-	
Moorish Cavalry	Summon Cavalry	WW2	3/3	AN	C4/C1	C+	4	B	Trample.
Morale	Instant	1WW	...	DK	C	B-	3	B-	All attacking creatures gain +1/+1 until end of turn.
Moss Monster	Summon Monster	GG3	3/6	LG	C2	C	3	B	
Mountain	Land	...	...	AN	C1	C	3	C	Tap for 1 red mana.
Mountain-Blue Sky	Land	...	...	UL/RV	C	C	3	C+	Tap for 1 red mana.
Mountain-Green Sky	Land	...	...	UL/RV	C	C	3	C	Tap for 1 red mana.
Mountain-Red Sky	Land	...	...	UL/RV	C	C	3	C	Tap for 1 red mana.
Mountain Stronghold	Land	...	...	LG	U	D	1	F	Your red legends may band with other legends.
Mountain Yeti	Summon Yeti	RR2	3/3	LG	U	C	4	C+	MountainWalk; protection from white.
Mox Emerald	Mono Artifact	0	...	UL	R	A	4	A	Tap for 1 green mana.

Card Name	Type	Cost	Power/Toughness	Set	Common-ality	Combo Value₁	Versatility₁	Standalone Value	Description
Mox Jet	Mono Artifact	0	---	UL	R	A	4	A	Tap for 1 black mana.
Mox Pearl	Mono Artifact	0	---	UL	R	A	4	A	Tap for 1 white mana.
Mox Ruby	Mono Artifact	0	---	UL	R	A	4	A	Tap for 1 red mana.
Mox Sapphire	Mono Artifact	0	---	UL	R	A	4	A	Tap for 1 blue mana.
Murk Dwellers	Summon Murk Dwellers	3B	2/2	DK	C	C+	3	C	When attacking, Murk Dwellers gain +2/+0 if not blocked.
N									
Nafs Asp	Summon Asp	G	1/1	AN	C3/C2	C	4	C+	1 damage during opponent's upkeep if Asp inflicts damage.
Nameless Race	Summon Nameless Race	3B	*/*	DK	U/R	C+	3	C+	Pay * life when bringing Nameless Race into play. Effects that prevent or redirect damage may not be used to counter this loss of life. When Nameless Race is brought into play, * may not be greater than the total number of white cards all opponents have in play and in their graveyards.
Natural Selection	Instant	G	---	UL	R	B+	7	C	Look at top 3 cards of any library then rearrange them or shuffle the library.
Nebuchadnezzar	Summon Legend	BU3	3/3	LG	R	B	5	B-	(X,T) to see X random cards in opponent's hand. Name a card before looking and if it is there it is discarded. Can only be used on your turn.

Card Name	Type	Cost	Power/ Toughness	Set	Common- ality	Combo Value₁	Versatility₁	Standalone Value	Description
Necrite	Summon	1BB	2/2	FE	C1	C+	4	B	If Necrite attacks and is not blocked, you may sacrifice it to bury a target creature controlled by the player Necrite attacked this turn. If you do, Necrite deals no damage during combat this turn.
Necropolis	Artifact	5	0/1	DK	U/R	C	2	D	Counts as a wall. Take a creature in your graveyard and remove it from the game. Put X +0/+1 counters on Necropolis, where X is the removed creature's casting cost.
Nether Shadow	Summon Spell	2B	1/1	UL/RV	R	B-	4	C+	If Nether Shadow is in the graveyard and 3 creatures are above it, then it comes into play during the upkeep phase.
Nether Void	Enchant World	B3	---	LG	R	B+	3	B	All spells require 3 more mana or else they are countered.
Nettling Imp	Summon Imp	B2	1/1	UL/RV	U	B	4	C+	Tap to force a non-wall to attack or die.
Nevinyrral's Disk	Mono Artifact	4	---	UL/RV	R	B+	5	B-	Destroy all creatures, enchantments and artifacts (1,T); begins tapped.
Niall Silvain	Summon Niall Silvain	GGG	2/2	DK	U/R	C	4	C	Target creature is regenerated (GGGG,T).
Nicol Bolas	Summon Elder Dragon Legend	BBUURR2	7/7	LG	R	C-	5	C-	Flying; if opponent is damaged by Nicol, he must discard his entire hand; pay BUR during upkeep or Nicol is buried.
Night Soil	Enchantment	GG	---	FE	C1	B	3	B	1: Remove two creatures in any graveyard from the game to put a Saproling token into play. Treat this token as a 1/1 green creature.

Card Name	Type	Cost	Power/Toughness	Set	Commonality	Combo Value₁	Versatility₁	Standalone Value	Description
Nightmare	Summon Nightmare	B5	*/*	UL/RV	R	C	4	C+	Where * = number of swamps, Flying.
North Star	Artifact	4	---	LG	R+	C+	3	C+	Cast a spell with any color mana (4,T).
Northern Paladin	Summon Paladin	WW2	3/3	UL/RV	R	B+	4	B+	Destroy black card (WW,T).
Nova Pentacle	Artifact	4	---	LG	R	B+	4	B	Redirect damage done by one source from yourself to a creature of opponent's choice (3,T).
O									
Oasis	Land	---	---	AN	U4	C	3	B-	Tap to prevent one damage to any creature.
Obelisk of Undoing	Mono Artifact	1	---	AQ	U1	C+	5	B	Return one of your cards in play to hand (6).
Obsianus Golem	Artifact Creature	4	6/6	UL/RV	U	B	3	B	
Old Man of the Sea	Summon Marid	UU1	2/3	AN	U2	A-	5	B+	Tap to control creature of power less than or equal to the Old Man's; may choose not to untap; lose control if it becomes untapped or power becomes greater than Old Man's.
Onulet	Artifact Creature	3	2/2	AQ-RV	U3>R	B+	4	C+	Controller gets +2 life when destroyed.
Orc General	Summon General	2R	2/2	DK	U/R	C+	4	C	Sacrifice one Orc or Goblin to give all Orcs +1/+1 until end of turn.
Orcish Artillery	Summon Orcs	RR1	1/3	UL/RV	U	B+	4	C+	Tap for 2 damage to target; 3 damage to controller.
Orcish Captain	Summon	R	1/1	FE	U3	C	3	C	1: Choose a target Orc. Flip a coin; opponent calls heads or tails while coin is in the air. If the flip ends up in your favor, that Orc gets +2/+0 until end of turn. Otherwise, that Orc gets -0/-2 until end of turn.

Card Name	Type	Cost	Power/ Toughness	Set	Common- ality	Combo Value1	Versatility1	Standalone Value	Description
Orcish Mechanics	Summon Orcs	R2	1/1	AQ	C4	C+	4	C	Tap and sacrifice one or your artifacts to do 2 damage to any target.
Orcish Oriflamme	Enchantment	R3	---	UL/RV	U	B-	3	B-	
Orcish Spy	Summon	R	1/1	FE	C1	B+	4	B-	Tap. Look at the top three cards of target player's library and return them in the same order.
Orcish Veteran	Summon	2R	2/2	FE	C1	B	3	B	Cannot be assigned to block any white creature of power greater than 1. R: First strike until end of turn.
Order of Leitbur	Summon	WW	1/0	FE	C1	B	5	B	Protection from black. WW: +1/+0 until end of turn. W: First strike until end of turn.
Order of the Ebon Hand	Summon	BB	2/1	FE	C1	B	5	B	Protection from white. BB: +1/+0 until end of turn. B: First strike until end of turn.
Orgg	Summon	3RR	6/6	FE	U1	C+	2	C	Trample. Orgg may not attack if opponent controls an untapped creature of power greater than 2. Orgg cannot be assigned to block any creature of power greater than 2.
Ornithopter	Artifact Creature	0	0/2	AQ-RV	C4>U	B-	3	B-	Flying.
Osai Vultures	Summon Vultures	W1	1/1	LG	C1	C	4	B-	Flying; gains a counter at end of turn if a creature went to the graveyard that turn. May turn in 2 counters for +1/+1 until end of turn.
Oubliette	Enchantment	BB1	---	AN	C2/C2	C+	3	C+	Holds creature out of play.

P

Card Name	Type	Cost	Power/Toughness	Set	Commonality	Combo Value[1]	Versatility[1]	Standalone Value	Description
Palladia-Mors	Summon Elder Dragon Legend	GGRRWW2	7/7	LG	R	C-	4	C+	Flying; trample; pay GRW during upkeep or buried.
Paralyze	Enchant Creature	B	...	UL/RV	C	B-	3	C+	Taps creature; requires 4 to untap creature during upkeep.
Part Water	Sorcery	UXX	...	LG	U	C+	3	C	Gives X creatures IslandWalk.
Pavel Maliki	Summon Legend	BR4	5/3	LG	U	D	3	D	+1/+0 (BR).
Pearled Unicorn	Summon Unicorn	W2	2/2	UL/RV	C	C+	3	C	
Pendelhaven	Legendary Land	...	...	LG	U	B	4	B	Tap for one green mana or tap to give +1/+2 to a 1/1 creature until end of turn.
People of the Woods	Summon People of the Woods	GG	1/*	DK	U/R	B-	3	B	* = number of forests controlled by People of the Wood's controller.
Personal Incarnation	Summon Avatar	WWW3	6/6	UL/RV	R	C+	4	B+	Can redirect damage from it to controller; lose 1/2 of life if it dies (rounding loss up).
Pestilence	Enchantment	BB2	...	UL/RV	C	B	5	B+	1 damage to creatures and players (B); discard if no creatures in play at end of turn.
Petra Sphinx	Summon Sphinx	WWW2	3/4	LG	R	B+	4	B	Tap to have a player guess the top card of their library. If right, they get the card. If wrong, it goes to the graveyard.
Phantasmal Forces	Summon Phantasm	U3	4/1	UL/RV	U	C	2	C+	Flying; costs U during upkeep or dies.
Phantasmal Terrain	Enchant Land	UU	...	UL/RV	C	B	4	C+	Changes land to a basic type of choice.
Phantom Monster	Summon Phantasm	U3	3/3	UL/RV	U	C	4	B-	Flying.

Card Name	Type	Cost	Power/ Toughness	Set	Commonality	Combo Value₁	Versatility₁	Standalone Value	Description
Phyrexian Gremlins	Summon Gremlins	B2	1/1	AQ	C4	B-	4	B	Tap to tap an artifact; artifact stays tapped until Gremlins are untapped; may choose not to untap Gremlins.
Piety	Instant	W2	...	AN	C3/C1	D-	2	D-	+0/+3 to all defending creature until end of turn.
Pikemen	Summon Pikemen	1W	1/1	DK	C	B-	5	B+	Banding; first strike.
Pirate Ship	Summon Ship	U4	4/3	UL/RV	R	B-	4	B-	Tap to do 1 damage to target; opponent must have islands to attack with this card; destroyed if you have no islands.
Pit Scorpion	Summon Scorpion	B2	1/1	LG	C2	C+	4	C	Gives poison token each time hits opponent. Player loses if he ever has 10 poison tokens.
Pixie Queen	Summon Pixies	GG2	1/1	LG	R	C+	4	B-	Flying; give other creature flying (GGG,T).
Plague Rats	Summon Rats	B2	*/*	UL/RV	C	C	3	C	Where * = number of rats in play.
Plains-Dark	Land	...	...	UL/RV	C	C	3	C	Tap for 1 white mana.
Plains-Dots	Land	...	...	UL/RV	C	C	3	C	Tap for 1 white mana.
Plains-Trees	Land	...	...	UL/RV	C	C	3	C	Tap for 1 white mana.
Planar Gate	Artifact	6	...	LG	R	C+	3	C+	You pay up to 2 less on the colorless mana part of summon spells.
Plateau	Land	...	...	UL/RV	R	B+	5	B-	Tap for 1 red or white mana.
Power Artifact	Enchant Artifact	UU	...	AQ	U3	B+	3	C	Reduce artifact use cost by 2 (minimum of 1); does not affect artifacts with no use cost.
Power Leak	Enchant Enchantment	U1	...	UL/RV	C	B+	3	C	Enchantment costs 2 during upkeep or take 1 damage for each unpaid mana.
Power Sink	Interrupt	UX	...	UL/RV	C	B+	5	B	Opponent spends X mana or spell fails, if cannot all lands tapped.

Card Name	Type	Cost	Power/Toughness	Set	Commonality	Combo Value₁	Versatility₁	Standalone Value	Description
Power Surge	Enchantment	RR	...	UL/RV	R	B+	3	B-	During upkeep phase, all players take 1 damage per land which was untapped at beginning of turn.
Powerleech	Enchantment	GG	...	AQ	U3	C	3	B	+1 life whenever opponent taps or powers an artifact.
Pradesh Gypsies	Summon Gypsies	G2	1/1	LG	U	C	3	C	Give a creature -2/-0 until end of turn (G1,T).
Preacher	Summon Preacher	1WW	1/1	DK	U/R	B+	5	B-	Gain control of one of opponent's creatures. Opponent chooses which target creature you control. If Preacher becomes untapped, you lose control of this creature; you may choose not to untap Preacher as normal during your untap phase. You also lose control of the creature if Preacher leaves play or at end of game.
Presence of the Master	Enchantment	W3	...	LG	U	B	3	B	Counters all enchantment spells while this is in play.
Priest of Yawgmoth	Summon Cleric	B1	1/2	AQ	C4	C+	4	C	Tap to sacrifice one of your artifacts for black mana equal to artifact casting cost.
Primal Clay	Artifact Creature	4	...	AQ-RV	U3>R	B-	5	C+	At casting choose to make it a 3/3 creature, a 1/6, Wall, or a 2/2 flying creature.
Primordial Ooze	Summon Ooze	R	1/1	LG	U	C+	2	C	Must attack if possible; gets +1/+1 token each upkeep. Must pay one mana per token or it taps and you take damage equal to number of tokens.
Princess Lucrezia	Summon Legend	BUU3	5/4	LG	U	C	3	C	Tap for one blue mana.
Prodigal Sorcerer	Summon Wizard	U2	1/1	UL/RV	C	B+	4	B	Tap for 1 damage to target.

Card Name	Type	Cost	Power/ Toughness	Set	Common- ality	Combo Value₁	Versatility₁	Standalone Value	Description
Psionic Entity	Summon Entity	U4	2/2	LG	R	B-	3	C-	Tap for 2 damage to any target but takes 3 damage to itself.
Psionic Blast	Instant	U2	---	UL	U	C	3	B	4 damage to target, 2 damage to self.
Psychic Allergy	Enchantment	BB3	---	DK	R	C+	2	C	When you cast Psychic Allergy, choose a color. During your opponent's upkeep, Psychic Allergy deals 1 damage to your opponent for each card he controls of that color.
Psychic Purge	Sorcery	U	---	LG	C1	C+	4	C	Does 1 damage to any target. If this card is discarded by your opponent's action, opponent loses 5 life.
Psychic Venom	Enchant Land	U1	---	UL/RV	C	B-	3	C+	2 damage when target land is tapped.
Puppet Master	Enchant Creature	UUU	---	LG	U	B-	3	C	If creature goes to graveyard, you may instead put it in your hand. If you pay UUU when this happens, you may also reclaim this card.
Purelace	Interrupt	W	---	UL/RV	R	C+	3	C	Change one card to white.
Pyramids	Poly Artifact	6	---	AN	U2	B-	3	C	Prevent a land from being destroyed or remove an enchantment from a land (2).
Pyrotechnics	Sorcery	R4	---	LG	C2	B+	4	B-	Distribute 4 damage any way you want to.
Q									
Quagmire	Enchantment	B2	---	LG	U	C	3	C	Stops all use of SwampWalk in play.
Quarum Trench Gnomes	Summon Gnomes	R3	1/1	LG	R	C+	4	C	Tap to make one plains generate colorless mana instead of white mana for rest of game.

Card Name	Type	Cost	Power/ Toughness	Set	Common- ality	Combo Value₁	Versatility₁	Standalone Value	Description
R									
Rabid Wombat	Summon Wombat	GG2	0/1	LG	U	B+	5	B	Does not tap when attacking; gets +2/+2 for each enchantment on it.
Radjan Spirit	Summon Spirit	G3	3/2	LG	U	B-	4	C+	Tap to remove flying from a creature until end of turn.
Rag Man	Summon Rag Man	2BB	2/1	DK	U/R	B	4	B	If opponent has any creature cards in hand, he or she discards one of them at random. This ability can only be used during controller's turn (BBB,T).
Raging Bull	Summon Bull	R2	2/2	LG	C1	C	3	C	
Raging River	Enchantment	RR	...	UL	R	B-	3	C+	Opponents must split ground defenses.
Ragnar	Summon Legend	UGW	2/2	LG	R	C	4	C+	Regenerate a creature (UGW,T).
Raiding Party	Enchantment	2R	...	FE	U3	B-	4	C+	Raiding Party may not be the target of white spells or effects. O: Sacrifice an Orc to destroy all plains. A player may tap a white creature to prevent up to two plains from being destroyed. Any number of creatures may be tapped in this manner.
Rainbow Vale	Land	...	...	FE	U1	C	3	C	Tap. Add 1 mana of any color to your mana pool. Control of Rainbow Vale passes to opponent at end of turn.
Raise Dead	Sorcery	B	...	UL/RV	C	C+	3	C+	Return creature from graveyard to hand.
Rakalite	Poly Artifact	6	...	AQ	U3	C	4	C	Prevent 1 damage to any target (2); return to hand at end of turn in which it is used.
Ramirez DePietro	Summon Legend	BBU3	4/3	LG	U	D-	4	D	First Strike.

Card Name	Type	Cost	Power/Toughness	Set	Common-ality	Combo Value₁	Versatility₁	Standalone Value	Description
Ramses Overdark	Summon Legend	BBUU2	4/3	LG	R	B-	4	B-	Tap to destroy a creature with an enchantment on it.
Rapid Fire	Instant	W3	---	LG	R	C-	2	D	Give a creature First Strike and Rampage:2 (if it does not already Rampage) until end of turn. Played before defense is chosen.
Rasputin Dreamweaver	Summon Legend	UW4	4/1	LG	R	B	4	B+	Has 7 counters which can be used to either prevent one damage to him or get one colorless mana. Add a counter during upkeep if untapped at beginning of turn and less than 7 counters.
Rebirth	Sorcery	GGG3	---	LG	R	C	3	C+	Each player may add a card to their ante and be returned to 20 life points. Only used in ante games.
Recall	Sorcery	UXX	---	LG	R	A	7	A	Sacrifice X cards from hand and bring X cards of choice from your graveyard to your hand.
Reconstruction	Sorcery	U	---	AQ-RV	C4>C	B	4	C	Take artifact from your graveyard to your hand.
Red Elemental Blast	Interrupt	R	---	UL/RV	C	B-	2(6)	C	Counters blue spell or destroys blue card.
Red Mana Battery	Artifact	4	---	LG	U	C	3	C	Add a token to it (2,T) or tap for one red mana plus can convert tokens to red mana as well.
Red Ward	Enchant Creature	W	---	UL/RV	U	B	3	C-	Gives protection from red.
Reflecting Mirror	Artifact	4	---	DK	U/R	C	3	C-	Tap+X where X is twice the casting cost of target spell. Target spell, which targets you, targets the player of your choice instead. This ability is played as an interrupt.
Regeneration	Enchant Creature	GG1	---	UL/RV	C	C+	3	B+	Gives Regenerates (G).
Regrowth	Sorcery	G1	---	UL/RV	U	A	7	A-	Return any card from graveyard to hand.

Card Name	Type	Cost	Power/ Toughness	Set	Common- ality	Combo Value₁	Versatility₁	Standalone Value	Description
Reincarnation	Instant	GG1	...	LG	U	B+	3	B	If target creature goes to graveyard this turn, may pull any creature of choice into play from graveyard.
Relic Barrier	Artifact	2	...	LG	U	B+	5	B-	Tap an artifact (T).
Relic Bind	Enchant Artifact	U2	...	LG	U	C+	4	C	Give one life or one damage to a player whenever artifact is tapped.
Remove Enchantments	Instant	W	...	LG	C1	B+	4	B	Bring enchantments you own to your hand and destroy opponent's. Affects all enchantments you control plus all of opponent's enchantments that are in your territory. Attacking creatures are in your territory.
Remove Soul	Interrupt	U1	...	LG	U2	C	3	B	Counters a summon spell.
Repentant Blacksmith	Summon Smith	W1	1/2	AN	U2	C	4	C+	Protection from red.
Reset	Interrupt	UU	...	LG	U	B	3	C+	Untaps all your lands. Played on opponent's turn after upkeep.
Resurrection	Sorcery	WW2	...	UL/RV	U	B	4	B-	Take creature from graveyard into play.
Revelation	Enchant World	G	...	LG	R	C	3	C+	All players play with hand face up on the table.
Reverberation	Instant	UU2	...	LG	R	C	3	B	Redirects damage done by one sorcery back at its caster.
Reverse Damage	Instant	WW1	...	UL/RV	R	B+	3	B	All damage from one source is instead added to life.
Reverse Polarity	Instant	WW	...	AQ-RV	C4>U	B+	4	C+	All damage done by artifacts to you so far this turn is instead added to life.
Righteous Avengers	Summon Avengers	W4	3/1	LG	U	C+	3	B+	PlainsWalk.

Card Name	Type	Cost	Power/ Toughness	Set	Common- ality	Combo Value₁	Versatility₁	Standalone Value	Description
Righteousness	Instant	W	...	UL/RV	R	C+	3	B-	+7/+7 to defending creature.
Ring of Immortals	Artifact	5	...	LG	R	C+	3	B-	Counter interrupt or enchantment which targets one of your permanents (3,T).
Ring of Ma'ruf	Mono Artifact	5	...	AN	U2	C+	5	B-	Select one card from outside the game instead of drawing (5).
Ring of Renewal	Artifact	5	...	FE	U1	C+	3	C+	Tap+5. Discard a card at random from your hand and draw two cards.
Riptide	Instant	B	...	DK	C	B	3	C	Causes all blue creatures to tap.
Riven Turnbull	Summon Legend	BU5	5/7	LG	U	C	4	C	Tap for one black mana.
River Merfolk	Summon	UU	2/1	FE	U1	B-	4	B-	U: MountainWalk until end of turn.
Roc of Kher Ridges	Summon Roc	R3	3/3	UL/RV	R	C	4	B	Flying.
Rock Hydra	Summon Hydra	RRX	0/0	UL/RV	R	B-	3	B+	Starts with X +1/+1 tokens; loses 1 token for each point of damage unless R spent; pay RRR during upkeep to get new token.
Rocket Launcher	Poly Artifact	4	...	AQ-RV	U3>R	B	3	C+	1 damage to any target (2); goes to graveyard at end of turn in which it is used; cannot be used until begins your turn in play.
Rod of Ruin	Mono Artifact	4	...	UL/RV	U	B-	3	C+	1 damage to any target (3,T).
Rohgahh of Kher Keep	Summon Legend	BBRR2	5/5	LG	R	B-	3	C+	Your Kobolds of Kher Keep get +2/+2; pay RRR during upkeep or taps and takes Kobolds with him to opponent's control.
Royal Assassin	Summon Assassin	BB1	1/1	UL/RV	R	B	4	B+	Tap to destroy one tapped creature.
Rubina Soulsinger	Summon Legend	UGW2	2/3	LG	R	B+	5	B+	Tap to control a creature; may choose not to untap; lose control of creature if Rubina becomes untapped or leaves play.

Card Name	Type	Cost	Power/Toughness	Set	Commonality	Combo Value₁	Versatility₁	Standalone Value	Description
Ruins of Trokair	Land	---	---	FE	U2	C	3	C	Comes into play tapped. Tap. Add W to your mana pool and sacrifice Ruins of Trokair to add WW to your mana pool.
Rukh Egg	Summon Egg	R3	0/3	AN	C3/C1	B+	4	B	If destroyed, a 4/4 Flying creature is put into play at end of turn.
Runesword	Artifact	4	---	DK	U/R	C	3	C	Target attacking creature gains +2/+0 until end of turn. Any creature damaged by target creature may not be regenerated this turn; if such a creature is placed in graveyard this turn, remove it from the game. If target creature leaves play before end of turn, Runesword is buried (3,T).
Rust	Interrupt	G	---	LG	C2	C	3	C	Counters effect of an artifact with an activation cost.
S									
Sacrifice	Interrupt	B	---	UL/RV	U	C+	3	C	Sacrifice creature and add casting cost as black mana to pool.
Safe Haven	Land	0	---	DK	U/R	A-	4	B+	Remove target creature you control from game (2,T). This ability is played as an interrupt. During upkeep, sacrifice Safe Haven to return all creatures it has removed from game directly into play. Treat this as if they were just summoned.
Sage of Lat-Nam	Summon Sage	U1	1/2	AQ	C4	C	4	C	Tap and sacrifice one of your artifacts to draw a card.
Samite Healer	Summon Cleric	W	1/1	UL/RV	C	C+	4	C+	Tap to prevent 1 damage to any target.

Card Name	Type	Cost	Power/ Toughness	Set	Common- ality	Combo Value₁	Versatility₁	Standalone Value	Description
Sand Silos	Land	---	---	FE	U1	C	3	C+	Comes into play tapped. You may choose not to untap Sand Silos during your untap phase and instead put a storage counter on it. Tap. Remove any number of storage counters from Sand Silos. For each storage counter removed, add U to your mana pool.
Sandals of Abdallah	Mono Artifact	4	---	AN	U3	C+	3	C	Gives IslandWalk for one turn (2); discard if creature destroyed when using it.
Sandstorm	Instant	G	---	AN	U3	C	3	C+	All attacking creatures take 1 damage.
Savaen Elves	Summon Elves	G	1/1	DK	C	C	4	C	Target enchant land is destroyed (GG,T).
Savannah	Land	---	---	UL/RV	R	C	3	C+	Tap for 1 green or white mana.
Savannah Lions	Summon Lions	W	2/1	UL/RV	R	C	3	C+	
Scarecrow	Artifact Creature	5	2/2	DK	U/R	B-	4	B	Until end of turn, all damage done to you by flying creatures is reduced to 0 (Tap+6).
Scarwood Bandits	Summon Bandits	2GG	2/2	DK	U/R	B-	3	B	Take control of target artifact. Opponent may counter this action by paying 2. You lose control of target artifact if Scarwood Bandits leaves play or at end of game (2G,T).
Scarwood Goblins	Summon Goblins	GR	2/2	DK	C	C	3	C	Counts as both a green card and a red card.
Scarwood Hag	Summon Hag	1G	1/1	DK	U/R	C	3	C	Target creature gains ForestWalk until end of turn (GGGG,T). Target creature loses ForestWalk until end of turn.
Scathe Zombies	Summon Zombies	B2	2/2	UL/RV	C	B+	7	B-	
Scavenger Folk	Summon Scavenger	G	1/1	DK	C	C+	4	B-	Sacrifice this card to destroy target artifact (G,T).

Card Name	Type	Cost	Power/ Toughness	Set	Common- ality	Combo Value₁	Versatility₁	Standalone Value	Description
Scavenging Ghoul	Summon Ghoul	B3	2/2	UL/RV	U	C+	3	C	+1 token of regeneration at end of turn for each creature that dies.
Scrubland	Land	...	...	UL/RV	R	B+	5	B-	Tap for 1 black or white mana.
Scryb Sprites	Summon Faeries	G	1/1	UL/RV	C	B	4	B	Flying.
Sea King's Blessing	Instant	U	...	LG	U	C+	3	C	Changes any/all creatures in play to blue until end of turn.
Sea Serpent	Summon Serpent	U5	5/5	UL/RV	C	C	2	C-	Opponent must have islands to attack with this card; buried if you have no Islands.
Seafarer's Quay	Land	...	...	LG	U	C-	1	F	Your blue legends may band with other legends.
Seasinger	Summon	1UU	0/1	FE	U3	B+	4	B+	Bury Seasinger if you control no islands. Tap. Gain control of target creature if its controller controls at least one island. You lose control of target creature if Seasinger leaves play, if you lose control of Seasinger, or if Seasinger becomes untapped. You may choose not to untap Seasinger as normal during your untap phase.
Season of the Witch	Enchantment	BBB	...	DK	U/R	B+	2	C+	At end of each player's turn, all untapped creatures that could have attacked but did not are destroyed. If you do not pay 2 life during your upkeep, Season of the Witch is destroyed. Effects that prevent or redirect damage may not be used to counter this loss of life.
Sedge Troll	Summon Troll	R2	2/2	UL/RV	R	B-	4	B+	+1/+1 if have swamps, Regenerate (B).
Seeker	Enchant Creature	WW2	...	LG	U	C	3	C	Creature can only be blocked by white and artifact creatures.

Card Name	Type	Cost	Power/ Toughness	Set	Common- ality	Combo Value₁	Versatility₁	Standalone Value	Description
Segovian Leviathan	Summon Leviathan	U4	3/3	LG	U	B	4	B	IslandWalk.
Sengir Vampire	Summon Vampire	BB3	4/4	UL/RV	U	B-	3	B+	Flying; gets +1/+1 token when creature dies which was damaged by the vampire.
Sentinel	Artifact Creature	4	1/*	LG	R	C	3	C+	Where *=1 at time of casting but can be changed to N+1 during combat where N is the power of a creature blocked by/blocking the Sentinel.
Serendib Djinn	Summon Djinn	UU2	5/6	AN	U2	B-	2	B	Flying; destroys a land during upkeep; take 3 damage if the destroyed land is an Island.
Serendib Efreet	Summon Efreet	U2	3/4	AN-RV	U2>R	C+	3	B+	Flying; take 1 damage during upkeep.
Serpent Generator	Artifact	6	---	LG	R	B-	3	B	Create 1/1 Poison Snake token creature (4,T); if Snake damages opponent, give opponent a poison token. If opponent has 10 or more poison tokens, he or she loses.
Serra Angel	Summon Angel	WW3	4/4	UL/RV	U	B	4	A-	Flying; does not tap when attacking.
Shahrazad	Sorcery	WW	---	AN	U2	C	3	C	Forces sub-game of magic...loser of that game loses 1/2 of life in this game.
Shanodin Dryads	Summon Nymphs	G	1/1	UL/RV	C	C+	4	C	ForestWalk.
Shapeshifter	Artifact Creature	6	*/7-*	AQ	U1	B-	4	B	Where * is chosen on casting and each upkeep.
Shatter	Instant	R1	---	UL/RV	C	C	3	C	Destroy one artifact.
Shatterstorm	Sorcery	RR2	---	AQ-RV	U11>U	C	3	B	All artifacts in play are buried.
Shelkin Brownie	Summon Faerie	G1	1/1	LG	C1	D	3	D	Tap to remove Bands with Other ability from creature until end of turn.
Shield Wall	Instant	W1	---	LG	U	D+	3	D	+0/+2 to all your creatures until end of turn.

Card Name	Type	Cost	Power/ Toughness	Set	Common- ality	Combo Value₁	Versatility₁	Standalone Value	Description
Shimian Night Stalker	Summon Night Stalker	BB3	4/4	LG	U	C+	4	C+	Redirect damage done to you by one creature from you to Stalker (B,T).
Shivan Dragon	Summon Dragon	RR4	5/5	UL/RV	R	B	4	A-	Flying; +1/+0 (R).
Silhouette	Instant	U1	---	LG	U	C+	3	B-	Creature is not damaged by spells or effects that target it until end of turn.
Simulacrum	Instant	B1	---	UL/RV	U	B	3	B	Transfer all damage so far this turn from self to a creature.
Sindbad	Summon Sindbad	U1	1/1	AN	U3	B	4	C	Tap to draw a new card but can only keep it if it is a land.
Singing Tree	Summon Singing Tree	G3	0/3	AN	U2	B	4	B	Tap to reduce attacking creature's power to 0.
Sinkhole	Sorcery	BB	---	UL	C	B	3	B+	Destroy land.
Sir Shandlar of Eberyn	Summon Legend	GW4	4/7	LG	U	D	3	D+	
Siren's Call	Instant	U	---	UL/RV	U	C+	3	C	All non-walls of opponent attack or die.
Sisters of the Flame	Summon Sisters	1RR	2/2	DK	U/R	C+	4	C+	Add R to your mana pool. This ability is played as an interrupt.
Sivitri Scarzam	Summon Legend	BU5	6/4	LG	U	D	3	D	
Skull of Orm	Artifact	3	---	DK	U/R	B	3	B	Bring one enchantment card from your graveyard to your hand (5,T).
Sleight of Mind	Interrupt	U	---	UL/RV	R	A-	5	C+	Change color type references on one card.
Smoke	Enchantment	RR	---	UL/RV	R	B-	3	C+	Players may only untap one creature during untap.

Card Name	Type	Cost	Power/ Toughness	Set	Common-ality	Combo Value₁	Versatility₁	Standalone Value	Description
Sol 'kanar the Swamp King	Summon Legend	BUR2	5/5	LG	R	B-	3	A-	SwampWalk; gain one life each time a black spell is cast.
Sol Ring	Mono Artifact	1	...	UL/RV	U	B	3	A-	Tap for 2 colorless mana.
Sorceress Queen	Summon Sorceress	BB1	1/1	AN-RV	U3>R	A-	4	B+	Tap to make a creature 0/2 until end of turn.
Sorrow's Path	Land	0	...	DK	U/R	F	0	F	Exchange two of opponent's blocking creatures. This exchange may not cause an illegal block. Sorrow's Path does 2 damage to you and 2 damage to each creature you control whenever it is tapped.
Soul Exchange	Sorcery	BB	...	FE	U3	B	4	B	Sacrifice a creature but remove it from the game instead of putting it in your graveyard. Take a creature from your graveyard and put it directly into play as though it were just summoned. Put a +2/+2 counter on this creature if the creature sacrificed was a Thrull.
Soul Net	Poly Artifact	1	...	UL/RV	U	B-	3	C+	+1 life when creature goes to graveyard (1).
Spectral Cloak	Enchant Creature	UU	...	LG	U	B+	3	B	Creature cannot be target of instants, sorceries, fast effects or enchantments unless it is tapped.
Spell Blast	Interrupt	UX	...	UL/RV	C	C	5	C+	Counters target spell of cost X.
Spinal Villain	Summon Villain	R2	1/2	LG	R	B	3	C+	Tap to destroy a blue creature.
Spirit Link	Enchant Creature	W	...	LG	U	B+	4	B+	Each point of damage done by creature gives you one life.
Spirit Shackle	Enchant Creature	BB	...	LG	C1	C+	3	C+	Creature gets a -0/-2 token each time it is tapped.

Card Name	Type	Cost	Power/Toughness	Set	Commonality	Combo Value₁	Versatility₁	Standalone Value	Description
Spirit Shield	Artifact	3	...	FE	U1	C	3	C	Tap+2. Target creature gets +0/+2 as long as Spirit Shield remains tapped. You may choose not to untap Spirit Shield as normal during your untap phase.
Spiritual Sanctuary	Enchantment	WW2	...	LG	R	C	3	C	+1 life during upkeep of any player that has plains.
Spitting Slug	Summon Slug	1GG	2/4	DK	U/R	C	4	C	Spitting Slug gains first strike until end of turn. If this ability is not activated, all creatures blocking or blocked by Spitting Slug gain first strike until end of turn.
Spore Cloud	Instant	1GG	...	FE	C1	C+	3	C+	Tap all blocking creatures. No creatures deal damage in combat this turn. Neither attacking nor blocking creatures untap as normal during their controller's next untap phase.
Spore Flower	Summon	GG	0/1	FE	U3	B-	4	B	During your upkeep, put a spore counter on Spore Flower. O: Remove three spore counters from Spore Flower. No creatures deal damage in combat this turn.
Squire	Summon Squire	1W	1/2	DK	C	C	3	C	
Staff of Zegon	Mono Artifact	4	...	AQ	C4	C-	3	C-	-2/-0 to target until end of turn (3,T).
Standing Stones	Artifact	3	...	DK	U/R	C	3	C	Pay 1 life and add 1 mana of any color to your mana pool. This ability is played as an interrupt. Effects that prevent or redirect damage may not be used to counter this loss of life (1,T).

Card Name	Type	Cost	Power/Toughness	Set	Commonality	Combo Value₁	Versatility₁	Standalone Value	Description
Stangg	Summon Legend	GR4	3/4	LG	R	C+	3	B	When comes into play also place a 3/4 green and red Stangg Twin token creature into play. If either Stangg or the Twin leaves play, the other does as well.
Stasis	Enchantment	U1	---	UL/RV	R	B+	3	C	No untap phase; costs U in upkeep.
Steal Artifact	Enchant Artifact	UU2	---	UL/RV	U	B	4	B	Takes control of artifact.
Stone Calendar	Artifact	5	---	DK	U/R	C	3	C	Your spells cost up to 1 less to cast; casting cost of spells cannot go below 0.
Stone Giant	Summon Giant	RR2	3/4	UL/RV	U	B	4	C	Tap to fly other creature of toughness less than Giant's power (kills it).
Stone Rain	Sorcery	R2	---	UL/RV	C	C+	3	B-	Destroy one land.
Stone-Throwing Devils	Summon Devils	B	1/1	AN	C3/C1	C+	4	B	First Strike.
Storm Seeker	Instant	G3	---	LG	U	C+	3	B-	Opponent takes one damage for each card in their hand.
Stream of Life	Sorcery	GX	---	UL/RV	C	C+	3	B	+X life to target player.
Strip Mine-Even steps/Sky	Land	---	---	AQ	U1	B-	5	B	Tap for 1 colorless mana or tap and destroy Strip Mine to destroy any one land.
Strip Mine-No tower/No sky/Wide steps	Land	---	---	AQ	C1	B-	5	B	Tap for 1 colorless mana or tap and destroy Strip Mine to destroy any one land.
Strip Mine-Small tower in lower left.No sky	Land	---	---	AQ	U1	B-	5	B	Tap for 1 colorless mana or tap and destroy Strip Mine to destroy any one land.

Card Name	Type	Cost	Power/ Toughness	Set	Common-ality	Combo Value₁	Versatility₁	Standalone Value	Description
Strip Mine-Uneven steps/Sky	Land	...	...	AQ	U1	B-	5	B	Tap for 1 colorless mana or tap and destroy Strip Mine to destroy any one land.
Subdue	Instant	G	...	LG	C1	C+	3	C+	Gives a creature +0/+N until end of turn but is deals no damage in combat. N is the casting cost of the creature.
Su-Chi	Artifact Creature	4	4/4	AQ	U3	B+	4	B	Controller gets 4 colorless mana when destroyed.
Sunastain Falconer	Summon Legend	GR3	4/4	LG	U	C+	3	B	Tap for two colorless mana.
Sunglasses of Urza	Continuous Artifact	3	...	UL/RV	R	B-	3	C+	Can use white mana as red mana.
Sunken City	Enchantment	BB	...	DK	C	C	3	C	Adds +1/+1 to all blue creatures. Controller must pay BB during upkeep or Sunken City is buried.
Svyelunite Priest	Summon	1U	1/1	FE	U3	C+	3	C	Tap+UU. Target creature may not be the target of spells or effects until end of turn. Use this ability only during your upkeep.
Svyelunite Temple	Land	...	...	FE	U2	C	3	C	Comes into play tapped. Tap. Add U to your mana pool, and sacrifice Svyelunite Temple to add UU to your mana pool.
Swamp-Brownish	Land	...	...	UL/RV	C	C	3	C	Tap for 1 black mana.
Swamp-Greenish	Land	...	...	UL/RV	C	C	3	C	Tap for 1 black mana.
Swamp-Whitish	Land	...	...	UL/RV	C	C	3	C	Tap for 1 black mana.
Swamp-Yellowish	Land	...	...	UL/RV	C	C	3	C	Tap for 1 black mana.

Card Name	Type	Cost	Power/ Toughness	Set	Common- ality	Combo Value₁	Versatility₁	Standalone Value	Description
Sword of the Ages	Artifact	6	...	LG	R	B+	3	B+	Tap and sacrafice this card and as many of your creatures as you want to do damage to one target equal to the sum of the power of all creatures sacraficed.
Swords to Plowshares	Instant	W	...	UL/RV	U	B-	4	B-	Target creature is removed from game and controller gains life = power of creature.
Sylvan Library	Enchantment	G1	...	LG	U	B+	5	B	May draw 2 extra cards during draw then put two back on the library in any order; lose 4 life for each card not put back.
Sylvan Paradise	Instant	G	...	LG	U	C+	3	C	Change any/all creatures in play to green until end of turn.
Syphon Soul	Sorcery	B2	...	LG	C2	C	3	B-	2 damage to all players except caster. Caster gets one life for each unprevented point of damage.
T									
Tablet of Epityr	Poly Artifact	1	...	AQ	C4	C+	3	C	+1 life when an artifact goes to graveyard (1).
Taiga	Land	...	...	UL/RV	R	B+	5	B-	Tap for 1 green or red mana.
Takklemaggot	Enchant Creature	BB2	...	LG	U	B+	4	B-	Creature gets a -0/-1 token each upkeep; when creature goes to graveyard, creature's controller places this on another creature; if no creatures, then it becomes an enchantment and does 1 damage each upkeep to the controller of the last creature that was killed.
Tangle Kelp	Enchant Creature	B	...	DK	U	C	3	C	Tangle Kelp forces creature to remain tapped during the untap phase if it attacked last turn.

213

Card Name	Type	Cost	Power/Toughness	Set	Common-ality	Combo Value₁	Versatility₁	Standalone Value	Description
Tawnos's Coffin	Mono Artifact	2	...	AQ	U1	A-	4	B+	Remove creature from game (3); effect remains until untapped; may choose not to untap.
Tawnos's Wand	Mono Artifact	4	...	AQ	U3	B-	3	C-	Makes creature of power <= 2 blockable only by artifact creatures until end of turn (2,T).
Tawnos's Weaponry	Mono Artifact	2	...	AQ	U3	B-	3	C+	+1/+1 to target creature (2); effect remains until untapped; may choose not to untap.
Telekinesis	Instant	UU	...	LG	R	C+	3	C	Makes a creature not deal damage this turn. Also taps it and keeps it tapped for two turns.
Teleport	Instant	UUU	...	LG	R	B-	3	C+	Makes creature unblockable until end of turn; played after attackers chosen but before blockers chosen.
Tempest Efreet	Summon Efreet	RRR1	3/3	LG	R	C+	4	C+	Tap and bury Efreet in opponent's graveyard to take a random card from their hand into yours. Swap is permanent. Can be countered by losing 10 life. Play only in ante games.
Terror	Instant	B1	...	UL/RV	C	C+	3	C+	Buries non-black/Artifact creature.
Tetravus	Artifact Creature	6	1/1	AQ	U1	B-	5	B	Flying; starts with three +1/+1 tokens; during upkeep, can convert tokens to or from 1/1, flying artifact creatures which cannot be enchanted.
Tetsuo Umezawa	Summon Legend	BUR	3/3	LG	R	B-	4	B+	Destroy a tapped or blocking creature (BBUR,T); cannot be targeted by enchant creature spells.

Card Name	Type	Cost	Power/ Toughness	Set	Common-ality	Combo Value₁	Versatility₁	Standalone Value	Description
Thallid	Summon	G	1/1	FE	C1	B	4	B-	During your upkeep, put a spore counter on Thallid. O: Remove three spore counters from Thallid to put a Saproling token into play. Treat this token as a 1/1 green creature.
Thallid Devourer	Summon	1GG	2/2	FE	U3	B+	4	B	During your upkeep, put a spore counter on Thallid Devourer. O: Remove three spore counters from Thallid Devourer to put a Saproling token into play. Treat this token as a 1/1 green creature. O: Sacrifice a Saproling to give Thallid Devourer +1/+2 until end of turn.
The Abyss	Enchant World	B3	...	KG	R	A	3	B	All players bury one non-artifact creature each upkeep.
The Brute	Enchant Creature	R1	...	LG	C1	C-	3	C-	+1/+0; regenerates (RRR).
The Fallen	Summon Fallen	1BBB	2/3	DK	U/R	B	4	B	During its controller's upkeep, The Fallen does 1 damage to each opponent it has previously damaged.
The Hive	Mono Artifact	5	...	UL/RV	R	C+	3	C+	Make 1/1 flying wasp (5,T).
The Rack	Continuous Artifact	1	...	AQ-RV	U3>U	C+	3	C	Opponent takes 1 damage for each card less than 3 in hand at beginning of turn.
The Tabernacle at Pendrell Vale	Legendary Land	...	...	LG	R	B+	4	B-	Gives all creatures an upkeep cost of 1 colorless mana in addition to other costs. If not paid, creature is destroyed.
The Wretched	Summon Wretched	BB3	2/5	LG	R	B	4	B-	At end of combat, take control of all creatures which block this card; lose control of them if this card leaves play.

Card Name	Type	Cost	Power/Toughness	Set	Commonality	Combo Value₁	Versatility₁	Standalone Value	Description
Thelonite Druid	Summon	2G	1/1	FE	U3	B	4	B	Tap+1G. Sacrifice a creature to turn all your forests into 2/3 creatures until end of turn. The forests still count as lands but may not be tapped for mana if they were brought into play this turn.
Thelonite Monk	Summon	2GG	1/2	FE	U1	C	3	C	Tap. Sacrifice a green creature to turn a target land into a basic forest. Mark changed land with a counter.
Thelon's Chant	Enchantment	1GG	---	FE	U3	C+	3	C+	During your upkeep, pay G or bury Thelon's Chant. Whenever a player puts a swamp into play, Thelon's Chant deals 3 damage to him or her unless that player puts a -1/-1 counter on a target creature he or she controls.
Thelon's Curse	Enchantment	GG	---	FE	U1	C+	3	C	Blue creatures do not untap as normal during their controller's untap phase. During his or her upkeep, a blue creature's controller may pay an additional U to untap it. Each creature may be untapped in this way only once per turn.
Thicket Basilisk	Summon Basilisk	GG3	2/4	UL/RV	U	B	4	B	Any non-wall blocked-by/blocking it is destroyed.
Thorn Thallid	Summon	1GG	2/2	FE	C1	C+	4	C	During your upkeep, put a spore counter on Thorn Thallid. O: Remove three spore counters from Thorn Thallid to have it deal 1 damage to any target.
Thoughtlace	Interrupt	U	---	UL/RV	R	B+	3	C-	Change card color to blue.
Throne of Bone	Poly Artifact	1	---	UL/RV	U	C	3	C	+1 life when black spell cast (1).

Card Name	Type	Cost	Power/Toughness	Set	Commonality	Combo Value₁	Versatility₁	Standalone Value	Description
Thrull Champion	Summon	4B	2/2	FE	U1	B+	4	B+	All Thrulls get +1/+1. Tap. Take control of a target Thrull. You loose control of target Thrull if Thrull Champion leaves play or you lose control of Thrull champion.
Thrull Retainer	Enchant Creature	B	---	FE	U3	B+	4	B	Target creature gets +1/+1. Sacrifice Thrull Retainer to regenerate the creature it enchants.
Thrull Wizard	Summon	2B	1/1	FE	U3	B	4	B	1B: Counters a target black spell if caster of target spell does not pay an additional B or 3. Play this ability as an interrupt.
Thunder Spirit	Summon Spirit	WW1	2/2	LG	R	C+	5	B+	Flying; first strike.
Tidal Flats	Enchantment	U	---	FE	C1	C+	3	C+	UU: All your creatures that are blocking any non-flying creatures gain first strike until end of turn. The attacking player may pay 1 for each attacking creature to prevent Tidal Flats from giving that creature's blockers first strike.
Tidal Influence	Enchantment	2U	---	FE	U3	C+	3	C	Put a tide counter on Tidal Influence when it is brought into play and during your upkeep. If there is one tide counter on Tidal Influence, all blue creatures get -2/-0. If there are three tide counters on Tidal Influence, all blue creatures get +2/+0. When there are four tide counters on Tidal Influence, remove them all. You may not cast Tidal Influence if there is another Tidal Influence in play.
Timber Wolves	Summon Wolves	G	1/1	UL/RV	R	C+	4	C+	Bands.

Card Name	Type	Cost	Power/ Toughness	Set	Commonality	Combo Value₁	Versatility₁	Standalone Value	Description
Time Elemental	Summon Elemental	U2	0/2	LG	R	A	10	A-	Send permanent to owner's hand (UU2,T); take 5 damage and destroy elemental if it is used to attack or block.
Time Vault	Mono Artifact	2	...	UL	R	A+	4	B	Skip turn to untap; tap for extra turn.
Time Walk	Sorcery	U1	...	UL	R	B+	5	A+	Take an extra turn after the current one.
Timetwister	Sorcery	U2	...	UL	R	A	4	A	Everyone shuffles decks, graveyards, and hands and draws 7 cards.
Titania's Song	Enchantment	G3	...	AQ-RV	U3>R	C+	4	B-	All artifacts lose their abilities and become artifact creatures with power/toughness = casting cost.
Tivadar's Cursade	Sorcery	1WW	...	DK	U/R	C	3	B	All Goblins are destroyed.
Tobias Andrion	Summon Legend	UW3	4/4	LG	U	C	3	C	
Tolaria	Legendary Land	...	...	LG	U	C+	4	C	Tap for one blue mana or tap to remove banding or bands with other ability from creature until end of turn.
Tor Wauki	Summon Legend	BBR2	3/3	LG	U	C+	4	B+	Tap to do 2 damage to an attacking or blocking creature.
Tormod's Crypt	Artifact	0	...	DK	U/R	B-	3	B-	Sacrifice Tormod's Crypt to remove all cards in target player's graveyard from the game.
Torsten Von Ursus	Summon Legend	GGW3	3/3	LG	U	C	3	B	
Touch of Darkness	Instant	B	...	LG	U	B+	3	C	Changes color of any/all creatures to black until end of turn.

Card Name	Type	Cost	Power/Toughness	Set	Commonality	Combo Value₁	Versatility₁	Standalone Value	Description
Tourach's Chant	Enchantment	1BB	---	FE	U3	C	3	C	During your upkeep, pay B or bury Tourach's Chant. Whenever a player puts a forest into play, Tourach's Chant deals 3 damage to him or her unless that player puts a -1/-1 counter on a target creature he or she controls.
Tourach's Gate	Enchant Land	1BB	---	FE	U1	B	3	C+	Can only be played on a target land you control. Sacrifice a Thrull to put three time counters on Tourach's Gate. During your upkeep, remove a time counter form Tourach's Gate. If there are no time counters on Tourach's Gate, bury it. O: Tap land Tourach's Gate enchants. All attacking creatures you control get +2/-1 until end of turn.
Tower of Coireall	Artifact	4	---	DK	U/R	C+	2	C	Target creature cannot be blocked by walls until end of turn.
Tracker	Summon Tracker	2G	2/2	DK	U/R	B+	4	B+	Tracker does an amount of damage equal to its power to target creature. Target creature does an amount of damage equal to its power to Tracker (GG,T).
Tranquility	Sorcery	G2	---	UL/RV	C	C+	3	C+	Destroys all enchantments.
Transmutation	Instant	B1	---	LG	C1	B-	5	C+	Switch power and toughness of a creature until end of turn; effects of altering effects are also switched.
Transmute Artifact	Sorcery	UU	---	AQ	U3	B	5	C	Send one of your artifacts in play to the graveyard and place any artifact from your library into play; you must pay difference in casting cost.

Card Name	Type	Cost	Power/Toughness	Set	Common-ality	Combo Value₁	Versatility₁	Standalone Value	Description
Triassic Egg	Artifact	4	...	LG	R	C+	3	C-	Put one counter Egg (3,T); sacrifice Egg with two or more counters to bring any creature from your hand or graveyard directly into play.
Triskelion	Artifact Creature	6	1/1	AQ	U1	C+	3	C+	Starts with three +1/+1 tokens; can discard a token to do 1 damage to any target.
Tropical Island	Land	...	...	UL/RV	R	B+	5	B-	Tap for 1 blue or green mana.
Tsunami	Sorcery	G3	...	UL/RV	U	B-	3	C	Destroys all Islands.
Tuknir Deathlock	Summon Legend	GGRR	2/2	LG	R	C+	4	C	Flying; give a creature +2/+2 until end of turn (GR,T).
Tundra	Land	...	...	UL/RV	R	B+	4	B-	Tap for 1 blue or white mana.
Tundra Wolves	Summon Wolves	W	1/1	LG	C2	C+	4	B-	First strike.
Tunnel	Instant	R	...	UL/RV	U	C	3	C	Buries one Wall.
Twiddle	Instant	U	...	UL	C	B+	5	B-	Tap or untap one creature, land or artifact.
Two-Headed Giant of Foriys	Summon Giant	R4	4/4	UL	R	B	5	B+	Trample; may block 2 attackers.
Typhoon	Sorcery	G2	...	LG	R	C+	3	C	Opponent takes 1 damage for each Island she has.
U									
Uncle Istvan	Summon Uncle Istvan	1BBB	1/3	DK	U/R	B-	4	B-	All damage done to Uncle Istvan by creatures is reduced to 0.
Underground Sea	Land	...	...	UL/RV	R	B+	5	B-	Tap for 1 black or blue mana.
Undertow	Enchantment	U2	...	LG	U	C+	3	C-	Stops all use of IslandWalk in play.
Underworld Dreams	Enchantment	BBB	...	LG	U	B+	3	B+	Opponent takes one damage for each card drawn.

Card Name	Type	Cost	Power/Toughness	Set	Commonality	Combo Value₁	Versatility₁	Standalone Value	Description
Unholy Citadel	Land	...	...	LG	U	D	1	D	Your black Legends may Band with other Legends.
Unholy Strength	Enchant Creature	B	...	UL/RV	C	C+	3	C	Gives +2/+1.
Unstable Mutation	Enchant Creature	U	...	AN-RV	C5>C	C+	4	B	Gives +3/+3; gets -1/-1 token each upkeep; tokens remain even if enchantment is removed.
Unsummon	Instant	U	...	UL/RV	C	B-	4	B-	Return creature to owner's hand.
Untamed Wilds	Sorcery	G2	...	LG	U	C	3	C	Bring one basic land from library into play.
Ur-Drago	Summon Legend	BBUU3	4/4	LG	R	C	4	C+	First strike; stops all use of SwampWalk in play.
Urborg	Legendary Land	...	...	LG	U	C-	4	C-	Tap for one black mana or tap to remove First Strike or SwampWalk ability from creature until end of turn.
Urza's Avenger	Artifact Creature	6	4/4	AQ	U1	B	5	C+	Each upkeep can give Bands, Flying, Trample, and/or First Strike at -1/-1 for each.
Urza's Chalice	Poly Artifact	1	...	AQ	C4	C+	3	C	+1 life when artifact is cast (1).
Urza's Mine-Bathyscape/Sphere	Land	...	...	AQ	C2	B-	3	C-	Tap for 1 colorless mana; if Urza's Power Plant and Urza's Tower are also in play, you get 2 colorless mana.
Urza's Mine-Pulley	Land	...	...	AQ	C1	B-	3	C-	Tap for 1 colorless mana; if Urza's Power Plant and Urza's Tower are also in play, you get 2 colorless mana.
Urza's Mine-Tower	Land	...	...	AQ	C2	B-	3	C-	Tap for 1 colorless mana; if Urza's Power Plant and Urza's Tower are also in play, you get 2 colorless mana.

Card Name	Type	Cost	Power/Toughness	Set	Commonality	Combo Value₁	Versatility₁	Standalone Value	Description
Urza's Mine-Tunnel Mouth	Land	---	---	AQ	C1	B-	3	C-	Tap for 1 colorless mana; if Urza's Power Plant and Urza's Tower are also in play, you get 2 colorless mana.
Urza's Miter	Poly Artifact	3	---	AQ	U1	C+	3	C+	Draw one card when one of your artifacts goes to the graveyard (3); does not work when you gain other benefits for sending the artifact there.
Urza's Power Plant-Columns	Land	---	---	AQ	C1	B-	3	C-	Tap for 1 colorless mana; if Urza's Mine and Urza's Tower are also in play, you get 2 colorless mana.
Urza's Power Plant-Sphere	Land	---	---	AQ	C2	B-	3	C-	Tap for 1 colorless mana; if Urza's Mine and Urza's Tower are also in play, you get 2 colorless mana.
Urza's Power Plant-Vat	Land	---	---	AQ	C1	B-	3	C-	Tap for 1 colorless mana; if Urza's Mine and Urza's Tower are also in play, you get 2 colorless mana.
Urza's Tower-Fall/Forest	Land	---	---	AQ	C2	B-	3	C-	Tap for 1 colorless mana; if Urza's Mine and Urza's Power Plant are also in play, you get 3 colorless mana.
Urza's Tower-Spring/Seashore	Land	---	---	AQ	C1	B-	3	C-	Tap for 1 colorless mana; if Urza's Mine and Urza's Power Plant are also in play, you get 3 colorless mana.
Urza's Tower-Summer/Plains	Land	---	---	AQ	C1	B-	3	C-	Tap for 1 colorless mana; if Urza's Mine and Urza's Power Plant are also in play, you get 3 colorless mana.
Urza's Tower-Winter/Mountains	Land	---	---	AQ	C1	B-	3	C-	Tap for 1 colorless mana; if Urza's Mine and Urza's Power Plant are also in play, you get 3 colorless mana.

Card Name	Type	Cost	Power/ Toughness	Set	Common- ality	Combo Value₁	Versatility₁	Standalone Value	Description
Uthden Troll	Summon Troll	R2	2/2	UL/RV	U	C+	4	B+	Regenerates (1).
V									
Vaevictis Asmadi	Summon Elder Dragon Legend	BBGGRR2	7/7	LG	R	C	4	C+	Flying; +1/+0 (B or G or R); pay BGR during upkeep or this card is buried.
Vampire Bats	Summon Bats	B	0/1	LG	C2	C	4	C+	Flying; +1/+0 (B) with maximum of two B each turn.
Venarian Gold	Enchant Creature	UUX	---	LG	C1	C	3	C	Taps creature and keeps it tapped for X turns.
Venduran Enchantress	Summon Enchantress	GG1	0/2	UL/RV	R	B-	3	B+	Can draw a card whenever you cast an enchantment.
Venom	Enchant Creature	1GG	---	DK	C	B-	3	C+	All non-wall creatures target creature blocks or is blocked by are destroyed at end of combat.
Vesuvan Doppelganger	Summon Doppelganger	UU3	*/*	UL/RV	R	B+	6	B+	Where *=copies creature but not color; can change creature imitated during upkeep.
Veteran Bodyguard	Summon Bodyguard	WW3	2/5	UL/RV	R	B-	4	B+	When not tapped it takes all damage done to you.
Visions	Sorcery	W	---	LG	U	C+	3	C-	Look at top 5 cards of any library, then may choose to scuffle it.
Vodalian Knights	Enchantment	2U	2/2	FE	U1	B	4	B+	First Strike. U: Flying until end of turn. Vodalian Knights may not attack unless opponent controls at least one island. Bury Vodalian Knights if you control no islands.
Vodalian Mage	Summon	2U	1/1	FE	C1	B-	4	C+	Tap+U. Counters a target spell if caster of target spell does not pay an additional 1. Play this ability as an interrupt.

Card Name	Type	Cost	Power/Toughness	Set	Commonality	Combo Value₁	Versatility₁	Standalone Value	Description
Vodalian Soldiers	Summon	1U	1/2	FE	C1	C+	3	C,	
Vodalian War Machine	Summon	1UU	0/4	FE	U1	C+	3	C+	O: Tap target Merfold you control to allow Vodalian War Machine to attack this turn or give a +2/+1 until end of turn. If Vodalian War Machine is put in the graveyard, all Merfolk tapped in this manner this turn are destroyed.
Volcanic Eruption	Land	UUUX	---	UL/RV	R	C+	4	C-	Destroys X Mountains in play doing 1 damage to all players and creatures for each destroyed (was X damage).
Volcanic Island	Land	---	---	UL/RV	R	B+	5	B-	Tap for 1 blue or red mana.
Voodoo Doll	Artifact	6	---	LG	R	C+	3	B-	Do N damage to any target (N+N,T); N is the number of tokens on this card; add one token each upkeep; if untapped at end of your turn, take N damage and destroy Doll.
W									
Walking Dead	Summon Walking Dead	B1	1/1	LG	C1	B	4	B+	Regenerates (B).
Wall of Air	Summon Wall	UU1	1/5	UL/RV	U	C	2	C	Flying; Wall.
Wall of Bone	Summon Wall	B2	1/4	UL/RV	U	C	2	C	Wall; regenerates (B).
Wall of Brambles	Summon Wall	G2	2/3	UL/RV	U	C	3	C	Wall; regenerates (G).
Wall of Caltrops	Summon Wall	W1	2/1	LG	C1	C	2	C	Wall; bands only with other Walls in defense.
Wall of Dust	Summon Wall	R2	1/4	LG	U	C	2	C	Wall; creatures blocked by wall cannot attack next turn.
Wall of Earth	Summon Wall	R1	0/6	LG	C2	C	2	C	Wall.
Wall of Fire	Summon Wall	RR1	0/5	UL/RV	U	C	2	C	Wall; +1/+0 (R).

Card Name	Type	Cost	Power/Toughness	Set	Commonality	Combo Value	Versatility	Standalone Value	Description
Wall of Heat	Summon Wall	R2	2/6	LG	C1	C	2	C	Wall.
Wall of Ice	Summon Wall	G2	0/7	UL/RV	U	C	2	C	Wall.
Wall of Light	Summon Wall	W2	1/5	LG	U	C	2	C	Wall; protection from black.
Wall of Putrid Flesh	Summon Wall	B2	2/4	LG	U	C	2	C	Wall; protection from white; not damaged by creatures with enchantments on them.
Wall of Shadows	Summon Wall	BB1	0/1	LG	C2	C	3	B+	Wall; takes no damage when blocking creatures and cannot be targeted by spells that target only walls.
Wall of Spears	Artifact Creature	3	2/3	AQ	U3	C	2	C-	First Strike; Wall.
Wall of Stone	Summon Wall	RR1	0/8	UL/RV	U	C+	2	C	Wall.
Wall of Swords	Summon Wall	W3	3/5	UL/RV	U	C	2	B-	Flying; Wall.
Wall of Tombstones	Summon Wall	B1	0/1+*	LG	U	C	3	C	Where * is the number of creatures in your graveyard at the end of upkeep.
Wall of Vapor	Summon Wall	U3	0/1	LG	C2	C	2	B+	Takes no damage when blocking creatures.
Wall of Water	Summon Wall	UU1	0/5	UL/RV	U	C	2	B-	Wall; +1/+0 (U).
Wall of Wonder	Summon Wall	UU2	1/5	LG	U	B+	4	B+	Wall; +4/-4 and can attack (UU2).
Wall of Wood	Summon Wall	G	0/3	UL/RV	C	C-	2	C-	Wall.
Wand of Ith	Artifact	4	---	DK	U/R	B-	3	B-	Look at one card at random from target player's hand. If card is not a land, target player must choose either to discard it or pay amount of life equal to its casting cost. If card is a land, target player must choose either to discard it or pay 1 life. Effects that prevent or redirect damage may not be used to counter this loss of life. Can only be used during controller's turn (3,T).

225

Card Name	Type	Cost	Power/Toughness	Set	Commonality	Combo Value₁	Versatility₁	Standalone Value	Description
Wanderlust	Enchant Creature	G2	...	UL/RV	U	C	3	C	1 damage to creature's controller during upkeep.
War Barge	Artifact	4	...	DK	U/R	B+	3	C	Target creature gains IslandWalk until end of turn. If War Barge leaves play this turn, target creature is buried.
War Elephant	Summon Elephant	W3	2/2	AN	C3/C1	B-	5	C+	Trample; bands.
War Mammoth	Summon Mammoth	G3	3/3	UL/RV	C	C	4	C	Trample.
Warp Artifact	Enchant Artifact	BB	...	UL/RV	R	B+	3	B	1 damage during upkeep to artifact's controller.
Water Elemental	Summon Elemental	UU3	5/4	UL/RV	U	C	3	B	
Water Wurm	Summon Wurm	B	1/1	DK	C	C	3	C	Water Wurm gains +0/+1 if opponent controls at least one island.
Weakness	Enchant Creature	B	...	UL/RV	C	C	3	C	Gives -2/-1.
Weakstone	Continuous Artifact	4	...	AQ	U3	B-	3	C	-1/-0 to all attacking creatures.
Web	Enchant Creature	G	...	UL/RV	R	C	3	C+	Gives +0/+2; allows creature to block flying creatures.
Wheel of Fortune	Sorcery	R2	...	UL/RV	R	B+	4	B+	All discard and draw a new hand.
Whippoorwill	Summon Whippoorwill	G	1/1	DK	U/R	C+	4	C	Until end of turn, target creature may not regenerate and damage done to target creature may not be prevented or redirected. If target creature goes to the graveyard, remove it from the game (GG,T).
Whirling Dervish	Summon Dervish	GG	1/1	LG	U	B-	5	B+	Protection from black; gets a +1/+1 token each time it damages opponent.
White Knight	Summon Knight	EE	2/2	UL/RV	U	B-	5	B-	First strike; protection from black.

Card Name	Type	Cost	Power/ Toughness	Set	Common-ality	Combo Value₁	Versatility₁	Standalone Value	Description
White Mana Battery	Artifact	4	...	LG	U	C	3	C	Add a token to it (2,T) or tap for one white mana plus can convert tokens to white mana as well.
White Ward	Enchant Creature	W	...	UL/RV	U	C	3	C	Gives protection from white.
Wild Growth	Enchant Land	G	...	UL/RV	C	C+	3	C	+1 green mana to any land when tapped for mana (was whenever tapped).
Will-O-The-Wisp	Summon Wisp	B	0/1	UL/RV	R	C+	4	A-	Flying; regenerates (B).
Willow Satyr	Summon Satyr	GG2	1/1	LG	R	C	2	C	Tap to take control of a Legend; may choose not to untap; lose control of Legend if Satyr becomes untapped or leaves play.
Winds of Change	Sorcery	R	...	LG	U	B-	5	B-	All players shuffle hands into library and draw up to same number of cards in hand as before.
Winter Blast	Sorcery	GX	...	LG	R	B-	4	B	Taps X creatures and does 2 damage to each of them that has Flying.
Winter Orb	Continuous Artifact	2	...	UL/RV	R	B+	4	B	All players untap only one land per turn.
Witch Hunter	Summon Hunter	2WW	1/1	DK	U/R	B+	5	B-	Does 1 damage to target player. Return target creature opponent controls from play to owner's hand. Enchantments on target creature are destroyed (1WW,T).
Wolverine Pack	Summon Wolverine Pack	GG2	2/4	LG	C2	B+	4	B	Rampage: 2.
Wood Elemental	Summon Elemental	G3	*/*	LG	R	C-	2	C-	Where *=number of untapped Forests sacrificed when it is brought into play.
Wooden Sphere	Poly Artifact	1	...	UL/RV	U	C	3	C	+1 life when green spell cast (1).
Word of Binding	Sorcery	XBB	...	DK	C	C+	3	C+	X target creatures become tapped.
Word of Command	Instant	BB	...	UL	R	B-	4	B-	Cast one of opponent's spells using their mana.

227

Card Name	Type	Cost	Power/Toughness	Set	Commonality	Combo Value1	Versatility1	Standalone Value	Description
Worms of the Earth	Enchantment	2BBB	---	DK	U/R	B	3	C	No new land may be brought into play. During any player's upkeep, any player may destroy Worms of the Earth by sacrificing two lands or taking 5 damage.
Wormwood Treefolk	Summon Treefolk	3GG	4/4	DK	U/R	C	4	C	Wormwood Treefolk gains ForestWalk until end of turn and does 2 damage to you (GG). WormwoodTreefolk gains SwampWalk until end of turn and does 2 damage to you (BB).
Wrath of God	Sorcery	WW2	---	UL/RV	R	B-	3	A-	All creatures in play are destroyed and cannot regenerate.
Wyluli Wolf	Summon Wolf	G1	1/1	AN	C4/C1	B-	4	B	Tap to give +1/+1 for one turn to any creature.
X									
Xenic Poltergeist	Summon Poltergeist	BB1	1/1	AQ	U3	B+	4	C+	Tap to turn target artifact into a creature of power/toughness equal to its casting cost until beginning of your next turn.
Xira Arien	Summon Legend	BGR	1/2	LG	R	B-	4	B+	Flying; player draws one card (BGR,T).
Y									
Yawgmoth Demon	Summon Demon	BB4	6/6	AQ	U1	B-	4	B-	Flying; First strike; sacrifice artifact during upkeep or take 2 damage and Demon taps.
Ydwen Efreet	Summon Efreet	RRR	3/6	AN	U2	C	2	C	Flip coin when defending if in opponent's favor.
Yotian Soldier	Artifact Creature	3	1/4	AQ	C4	B-	4	B	Does not tap when attacking.

Z

Card Name	Type	Cost	Power/ Toughness	Set	Common- ality	Combo Value₁	Versatility₁	Standalone Value	Description
Zelyon Sword	Artifact	3	----	FE	U1	C	3	C	Tap+3. Target creature gets +2/+0 as long as Zelyon Sword remains tapped. You may choose not to untap Zelyon Sword as normal during your untap phase.
Zephyr Falcon	Summon Falcon	U1	1/1	LG	C2	C+	4	B	Flying; does not tap when attacking.
Zombie Master	Summon Lord	BB1	2/3	UL/RV	R	B-	3	B-	All Zombies get SwampWalk and regeneration.

Errata to Cards, All Editions/Expansions

General Rules

- Any card which reads as "discarding" permanents should be read as "destroying" them.
- Any card which reads as destroying or discarding itself when used should be read as sacrificing itself when used.
- Any card which talks about paying mana during the untap phase or otherwise requires a fast effect to be used during the untap phase, should be read as applying during upkeep, as fast effects are illegal during untap. These are not cases of cards overriding the rules.

Card Specific Rules

All Hallow's Eve (Legends)	"Sorcery" should be "Enchantment."
Ashnod's Transmogrant (Antiquities)	Add "The +1/+1 and artifact status are represented by a counter." Thus the effect is permanent.
Basalt Monolith (Gathering)	Insert after first: "This mana may not be used to untap any Basalt Monolith or Mana Vault."
Blood Lust (Legends)	Should say "Target creature gains..."
Clockwork Avian (Antiquities)	The counter is not lost until end of combat.
Clockwork Beast (Gathering)	The counter is not lost until end of combat.
Cocoon (Legends)	Should say "Tap target creature you control and put three counters on Cocoon."
Conservator (Gathering)	Read as "3, tap: Prevent up to 2 damage to any player."

Card Specific Rules (Continued)

Cyclopean Tomb (alpha)	Casting cost is 4.
Distintegrate (Revised)	Add "Target creature may not be regenerated this turn."
Firestorm Phoenix (Legends)	Ignore the "instead."
Forcefield (alpha/beta/Unlimited)	Read as "1: Prevent all but 1 damage from an unblocked attacker."
Fork (Gathering)	Read "just cast" as "being cast."
Gaea's Liege (alpha/beta/Unlimited)	The Liege's power and toughness are equal to the number of forest you control at all times, except when attacking, at which time they are dependent on the defending player's forests. This is just like the Revised text.
Knowledge Vault (Legends)	Last sentence should read "If Knowledge Vault leaves play or your control, put all cards under it in your graveyard."
Kudzu (Gathering)	Should be played as: "If target land becomes tapped, target land's controller moves Kudzu to another land in play, and the original target is destroyed. If Kudzu has no other valid target, Kudzu is destroyed."
Living Artifact (Gathering)	Should be read as "Put a counter on Living Artifact for each damage done to you."
Mana Vault (Gathering)	Insert after first sentence: "This mana may not be used to untap any Basalt Monolith or Mana Vault."
Nettling Imp (Gathering)	Last sentence should say "May not be used on creatures which entered their controller's territory this turn."
Onulet (AQ, Revised)	Should say "If Onulet goes to the graveyard *from play* ..."
Personal Incarnation (Revised)	Should say "If Personal Incarnation goes to the graveyard *from play* ..."
Power Surge (alpha/beta/Unlimited)	Text is broken and contradictory. Should be played with the Revised text: "At the beginning of a player's turn, before the untap phase, the player must take a counter for each of his lands that is not tapped. During the player's upkeep, Power Surge does 1 damage to that player for each counter; the counters are then discarded."
Relic Bind (Legends)	Should be read as "When target artifact that opponent controls is tapped..."
Rukh Egg (AN)	Should say "If Rukh Egg goes to the graveyard *from play* ..."
Siren's Call (Gathering)	Last sentence should say "Creatures which entered their controller's territory this turn are unaffected by Siren's Call."
Spectral Cloak (Legends)	Append "Does not destroy itself, any enchantments already on target creature, or any enchantments placed on target creature while it is tapped."
Su-Chi (AQ)	Should say "If Su-Chi goes to the graveyard *from play* ..."
Venarian Gold (Legends)	Should say "Put X counters on Venarian Gold..."
White Ward (Gathering)	Should say "The protection granted by White Ward will not cause itself to be destroyed." The same fix to all other Wards.

Index